"Steven Félix-Jäg............ .... those who think worship is just about moving through ritual or getting their spiritual tank refilled! Deploying a generous view of worship and Pentecostalism that makes room for Christians who harken from all theological traditions to find themselves in his writing, Félix-Jäger reminds us that it is uniquely in worship that we most immediately experience God's overflowing salvation. Through music, testimonies, and other acts of worship, we discern the power of the Spirit, are formed into the likeness of Christ, and are reconciled to the Father as one holy people. We are then sent forth as prophetic messengers to carry this message of hope to others and plant new worshiping communities throughout the world. Biblically grounded, doxologically shaped, carefully argued in conversation with a wide range of scholars, and thoughtfully engaged with the lived experience of Christians, *Renewal Worship* situates the practice of renewal worship at the heart of the Christian life."

Mark R. Teasdale, E. Stanley Jones Professor of Evangelism at Garrett-Evangelical Theological Seminary

"It is rare that Pentecostal/charismatic worship is put under the liturgical theology microscope. If you are keen to understand the theological nuts and bolts of the fastest-growing global Christian movement in the twenty-first century, this book by Félix-Jäger is indispensable. Be prepared to have your eyes opened."

Lim Swee Hong, Deer Park Associate Professor of Sacred Music and director of the Master of Sacred Music program at Emmanuel College of Victoria University in the University of Toronto, Canada

"Studies on Pentecostal worship have been mostly descriptive, from a social science perspective, or critical. Steven Félix-Jäger's is a rare exception by offering a constructive theology of Pentecostal worship. It argues that Pentecostal worship is the response to the distinctive way in which God reveals himself in Pentecostal experience. For anyone seeking to understand why Pentecostals worship the way they do, I cannot think of a better book to recommend."

Simon Chan, formerly professor of systematic theology at Trinity Theological College, Singapore, and currently editor of the *Asia Journal of Theology*

"Steven Félix-Jäger is the right person to provide a Pentecostal perspective to this important Dynamics of Christian Worship series at this time. He masterfully brings the nascent scholarship in Pentecostal worship into dialogue with the main lines of worship studies and theologies of worship, while bridging these theoretical frames with contemporary praise culture and practices. This book is the perfect springboard not only for next steps in Pentecostal theologies of worship for the diversity of world Christian movements, but also for all who seek to worship God in spirit and in truth."

Amos Yong, professor of theology and mission at Fuller Seminary

"*Renewal Worship* claims that worship is the measure of all things in the church. And renewal worship is the revolutionary power of Spirit-empowered Christianity. Steven Félix-Jäger in this book crafts an innovative hermeneutics of worship that brilliantly theologizes both the abstract, universal dimension of worship and its concrete, particular nature as a contextualized social activity. The result is an original, incisive, and concise theology of worship constructed not only for Pentecostals but also for the whole body of Christ."

Nimi Wariboko, author of *The Pentecostal Hypothesis: Christ Talks, They Decide*

"*Renewal Worship* is a welcome addition to renewal studies by providing language categories—in short, a theology—for what people of the Spirit come to do so intuitively. At the same time, intuition can be shaped in different directions; therefore, this book can serve a larger purpose of providing not only a theology of renewal worship but also a logic that can keep it attuned to its character and aims. Pastors and worship leaders can especially benefit from its proposals."

Daniel Castelo, William Kellon Quick Professor of Theology and Methodist Studies at Duke Divinity School

"There is a need for good, scholarly work that assesses both the theological foundations and the Pentecostal character of contemporary worship. *Renewal Worship* meets this need. Through his study of the Pentecostal movement and its impact on the contemporary worship culture, Steven Félix-Jäger sets forth a charismatic vision for the contemporary church and gives scholars a multitude of research trails to follow."

Jonathan Powers, assistant professor of worship studies at Asbury Theological Seminary

"Astutely descriptive and helpfully prescriptive, Steven Félix-Jäger creatively weaves a theologically rich tapestry enabling the reader to hear and understand the distinct dynamic of renewal worship. This is a significant contribution to Pentecostal-charismatic worship and theological studies, for it reveals the very heart of the existence of renewal traditions— worship. Highly Recommended!"

Kenneth J. Archer, author of *The Gospel Revisited: Towards a Pentecostal Theology of Worship and Witness*

"I've often advised my tribes with these words: 'Every great worship leader needs at least one Pentecostal friend.' Why? Because without the Pentecostal witness, the rest of us would flame out. Make no mistake, though. This is a work of liturgical theology—a discerning of biblical truth from (rather than merely onto) the worship experience. We were due for a fresh, accessible theology of worship, and here we have it—clear, humble, passionate, generous, informed, up to date, and yes, full of the Spirit."

Zac Hicks, author of *The Worship Pastor*

"In this innovative study, Steven Félix-Jäger explores global Pentecostal and renewalist aesthetics in accessible, insightful ways. With an artist's attention to detail and beauty, Félix-Jäger analyzes a movement on the rise for the benefit of those inside and outside its porous boundaries."

Leah Payne, associate professor of American religious history at George Fox University

"Steven Félix-Jäger's book is a penetratingly insightful theology of Pentecostal worship that focuses on Christ's abundant outpouring of the Holy Spirit at Pentecost and the human participation in the divine life that it invites and enables. His insights and theological method have broad ecumenical relevance. This was a truly delightful read for me."

Frank D. Macchia, professor of systematic theology at Vanguard University and associate director of the Centre for Pentecostal and Charismatic Studies at Bangor University, Wales

"Finally, a textbook for teaching worship from a Pentecostal/charismatic perspective! Steven Félix-Jäger delivers a robust overture of renewal worship that provides a theoretical framework for understanding its biblical and theological contours while also engaging its dynamic flow in the power of the Spirit. A must-read for anyone seeking to unpack what it means to worship God in Spirit and in truth."

Sammy Alfaro, professor of theology at Grand Canyon Theological Seminary

DYNAMICS OF CHRISTIAN WORSHIP

RENEWAL WORSHIP

A THEOLOGY OF PENTECOSTAL DOXOLOGY

STEVEN FÉLIX-JÄGER

Academic
An imprint of InterVarsity Press
Downers Grove, Illinois

InterVarsity Press
P.O. Box 1400 | Downers Grove, IL 60515-1426
ivpress.com | email@ivpress.com

InterVarsity Press® is the publishing division of InterVarsity Christian Fellowship/USA®.
For more information, visit intervarsity.org.

Scripture quotations, unless otherwise noted, are from the New Revised Standard Version Bible, copyright
© 1989 National Council of the Churches of Christ in the United States of America. Used by permission.
All rights reserved worldwide.

The publisher cannot verify the accuracy or functionality of website URLs used in this book beyond the date of publication.

Cover design and image composite: Kate Irwin
Interior design: Jeanna Wiggins

ISBN 978-1-5140-0014-4 (print) | ISBN 978-1-5140-0015-1 (digital)

Printed in the United States of America ♾

Library of Congress Cataloging-in-Publication Data
A catalog record for this book is available from the Library of Congress.

29 28 27 26 25 24 23 22 | 9 8 7 6 5 4 3 2 1

CONTENTS

ACKNOWLEDGMENTS

AS CHAIR OF a worship arts program at a Pentecostal university, I have focused a lot of my thought and study around renewal worship. After recognizing the lack of academic resources for renewal worship, I felt inspired—even called—to write on the subject. As I embarked on this mission, I knew God would supply many voices to encourage, challenge, and even correct my thinking along the way. God did, and this book wouldn't be possible without their insight.

I'd first like to thank my colleagues and students at Life Pacific University, my primary dialogue partners who helped me work out these ideas. I would particularly like to thank Luci Sanders, Eric Lopez, Ryan Lytton, Josh Ortega, and Marlene Muñoz for reading through parts of the manuscript and offering feedback. While their insights undoubtedly made the book better, any mistakes found throughout these pages should in no way reflect on them. I would also like to thank the good folks at the Society for Pentecostal Studies for giving me a platform to test out these ideas.

I'd like to extend my gratitude to Amos Yong for his encouragement and for connecting me with the folks at IVP, and to the Dynamics of Christian Worship advisory board members for choosing this book to be a part of the series. What an incredible honor! I would like to thank the incredible staff at IVP, and especially my outstanding editor, David McNutt. His steady hand and brilliant guidance made this process extremely rewarding.

Finally, I'd like to thank my personal support system, which includes my wife, Connie; daughter, Mila; and all my friends and family who encouraged me along the way. It is my hope and prayer that professors, students, and worship pastors will find this book illuminating, with both theological and practical insight.

INTRODUCTION

WHY RENEWAL WORSHIP?

Ascribe to the LORD, O families of the peoples,
ascribe to the LORD glory and strength.
Ascribe to the LORD the glory due his name;
bring an offering, and come before him.
Worship the LORD in holy splendor;
tremble before him, all the earth.
The world is firmly established; it shall never be moved.
Let the heavens be glad, and let the earth rejoice,
and let them say among the nations,
"The LORD is king!"

1 CHRONICLES 16:28-31

THE PASSAGE ABOVE is part of King David's famous psalm of praise recorded in 1 Chronicles 16. After bringing the ark of God to Jerusalem from Obed-Edom, David quickly commenced with a ceremony commemorating the installation of the ark in a temporary tent he made. The ceremony included burnt offerings, a feast distributed to every adult in Israel, benedictions, a call to remember God's covenant with the Israelites, and of course, a psalm of thanksgiving. David's psalm indicates broadly what worship is all about—ascribing worth to the worthy God. For David, worship is our universal response of adoration to God. This response is eternal, stretching across the entire earth, engaging every nation, and even reaching to the heavens.

Worship connects people with God and others in the worshiping community. It animates the relational vitality of the people of God.

Worship is, before all else, the most appropriate response we can give to God who has been revealed to us by the Son and through the Holy Spirit. But while we can easily understand that Christians *should* worship, we might find ourselves asking how worship corresponds with our understanding of God and the Christian faith, and what God's self-revelation really means. Because these questions are theological by nature, the best way to fully answer them would be to heed a theology of worship. But what exactly is a theology of worship? If Christian *theology* concerns the study of God in relation to humanity and the nature of Christian faith, then a theology *of worship* studies how religious devotion to God (worship) bears upon Christian faith and doctrine (theology). To be sure, worship and theology are necessarily bound together. They affect each other in a person's holistic expression of faith, so a "theology of worship" naturally encloses the full expression of Christian spirituality. Furthermore, theologies of worship reflect the theological commitments of worshiping communities, so as worshiping communities differ in their spirituality and ecclesial traditions, so do their theological understandings of worship. Hence, a distinct theology of worship could be written for any Christian tradition that forms and sustains a worshiping community. This book looks at how renewal worship—which particularly emphasizes the renewing presence of the Holy Spirit in its reading of Scripture, its theology, and its practice—works in Pentecostal and charismatic traditions. While we could certainly zero in on specific denominations within the renewal tradition, we will look at the movement of Pentecostalism broadly, endeavoring to uncover the common language voiced by renewal worship.

This chapter is our prelude—the short opening section of music that establishes the key, tempo, and feel for our principal composition. It serves as the introduction to our study on renewal worship. The first section looks at the hermeneutical approach this study takes. Not only does it explain the method used in this book, but it also makes an argument for developing hermeneutical approaches whenever studying cultural customs or practices. The next section profiles the global Pentecostal movement in its varied, multifaceted context. It makes an argument for studying renewal worship while also defining and situating pertinent terms and concepts used throughout the book. Finally, the last section briefly outlines the structure of the book's content. Because of renewal worship's pervasive influence on contemporary worship around the globe, crafting a theology of renewal worship is both needed and consequential. When we better understand renewal worship, we can better understand what God is doing globally through contemporary worship.[1]

A HERMENEUTICAL APPROACH FOR UNDERSTANDING WORSHIP

Christian worship has two principal aims: to glorify God and to help people enter into God's presence. It accomplishes these aims by continually reinforcing the gospel narrative both privately to the individual worshiper, and communally to the gathered worshiping community. There is a single story that unites every Christian throughout history, and Christian worship sustains that gospel message as its guiding narrative. As author and worship pastor Zac Hicks states, "The vast witness of the history of Christian worship across traditions agrees that the gospel is the story we should tell. And a truly Christian worship service should tell this story."[2] So, while Christian worship unilaterally proclaims and reinforces the gospel narrative, Christian traditions differ, and particular worshiping communities emphasize different aspects of the same Christian narrative. Here we can be encouraged by Paul's teaching of the one body and many members (1 Cor 12:12-27). Each Christian community can be viewed as a different member of the same body, but they are all ultimately unified by the same Spirit of God. Paul emphasizes both the unity of the church as every member of the body has a function and mutually contributes to the body, and the diversity of the church as each member has

---

[1] Although there is debate about the definitions, the term *renewal* was introduced by the Pew Foundation as an umbrella term referring collectively to classical Pentecostal, charismatic, and neo-Pentecostal expressions of the Christian faith. See "Pew Forum on Religion & Public Life Releases Results from a 10-Country Public Opinion Survey of Pentecostals," Pew Research Center, October 5, 2006, www .pewforum.org/2006/10/05/pew-forum-on-religion-amp-public-life-releases-results-from-a-10 -country-public-opinion-survey-of-pentecostals/ (accessed November 20, 2021). Throughout this book, I refer to "renewal worship" in a related way—as worship from those Christian traditions that accentuate the Spirit's renewing presence and work in the lives of believers. This usage of renewal worship may include traditions that are not typically deemed to be "Pentecostal" but still practice a form of spirituality congruent with Pentecostal and charismatic expressions of worship.

[2] Zac Hicks, *The Worship Pastor: A Call to Ministry for Worship Leaders and Teams* (Grand Rapids, MI: Zondervan, 2016), 158.

a different function. One of the main points of the body metaphor, which Paul uses in several areas (Rom 12:3-9, 1 Cor 6:9-20, Col 1:15-20, and Eph 4:11-16), is that every member of the body is equally valuable. The church is intimately united with Christ, and even in its diversity Christ is the head of the universal church. Before anything else, Christian worship is a devotional practice that unites the church toward intimacy with God. This does not disregard the various expressions of worship found throughout different Christian traditions, but it does indicate they are all united by the same Spirit even in their differences.

Almost every Christian tradition utilizes Scripture reading, praying, preaching, music, offering, and the observance of Communion and baptism in their worship. Some traditions, however, observe additional sacraments, and formally incorporate other rites like processionals, the reading of creeds, responsive prayers, and benedictions in worship. Furthermore, some traditions informally integrate other practices such as testimony, dance, drama, prophetic art, and footwashing as acts of worship. Every tradition utilizes many of these elements but de-emphasizes or discards others. Rather than looking at "the right way to do" worship, it is more helpful to simply examine how different traditions contribute to the body of Christ in their own ways. Here one can take an inclusive, interdenominational approach that simultaneously focuses on the unity of the global church while underscoring the worship practices of a particular worshiping community. This sort of approach can be accomplished by utilizing hermeneutical tools to both understand and situate a particular worshiping community in the broader global milieu. Before we discuss different approaches to understand and evaluate Christian worship, however, let's take a moment to define worship as a unified concept.

Worship is constantly talked about in the Bible but is never actually defined. In fact, the Bible has more than six hundred references to worship, with at least eighty-seven different Hebrew and Greek words used to describe it.[3] But in its multiplicity, something that is consistent is that God is the one glorified, and worship begins with God.[4] Some scholars use these

---

[3]Steven Brooks, *Worship Quest: An Exploration of Worship Leadership* (Eugene, OR: Wipf & Stock, 2015), 20.

[4]It should be noted that sometimes scholars distinguish the terms *praise* and *worship*, seeing praise as celebrating the deeds of God, and worship as centering around the character of God. For

distinctions to define worship as reflecting back God's self-revealed worth.[5] What's good about this definition is that it recognizes the fact that worship begins with and returns back to God. The problem with this definition, however, is that it implies passivity in the human response. With this definition the worshiper is like a mirror, merely reflecting something back to God. Humans become purely passive vessels, and worse, God emerges as a vain self-aggrandizer. But if we adopt a definition that focuses on an *active* response, we'll accentuate God's relational character and avoid human passivity. I suggest that we define worship as turning our hearts toward God as a response to God's self-revelation. Here worshipers are relational, responding to a relational God. This definition sees worship as active and participatory, and recognizes both the human and divine elements involved in worship, while firmly establishing its beginning and end with God. As worship scholar Constance Cherry writes, "True worship is the experience of encountering God *through the means that God usually employs*, a conversation built on revelation/response. Viewing worship as a conversation implies a relationship."[6] Emphasizing relationality indicates that worship is not something worshipers make, but is a response to who God is. It implies that worship necessitates the church's response to God's self-revelation. To this point liturgical theologian Ruth Duck adds, "A relational theology of worship holds together the conviction that God truly is present, revealing Godself in worship, and the conviction that worship is not complete without the church's response in faith and love."[7] Worship is a two-way street that requires reciprocal action, and the human response to God happens both individually and communally.

---

instance, Ps 105:2 is a great example of David praising the good deeds of God when he states, "Sing to him, sing praises to him; tell of all his wondrous works!" Conversely, in Ps 99:9 David honors God's holiness, stating, "Extol the Lord our God, and worship at his holy mountain; for the Lord our God is holy." In these cases, both praise and worship are biblical and neither is better than the other. It all just depends on which form is more appropriate for the given context. In this book, I will be using the term *worship* as a blanket term, covering both the concepts of praise and worship unless otherwise noted.

[5]Brooks, *Worship Quest*, 23; Jim Altizer, *The Making of a Worship Leader* (Thousand Oaks, CA: Sound & Light Publishing, 2013), 14.

[6]Constance Cherry, *The Worship Architect: A Blueprint for Designing Culturally Relevant and Biblically Faithful Services* (Grand Rapids, MI: Baker Academic, 2010), 9.

[7]Ruth Duck, *Worship for the Whole People of God: Vital Worship for the 21st Century* (Louisville, KY: Westminster John Knox, 2013), 13.

The Bible uses several words in both Hebrew and Greek to form a broad understanding of worship,[8] but there are two primary groupings of words in the Old and New Testaments that describe worship exclusively.[9] Worship is known as "reverence" with the Hebrew word *shakhah*, which means to depress, to bow down, or to prostrate oneself, and with the Greek word *proskyneo*, which means to bow down and kiss, as in to kiss the hand of a superior. These words convey that worship is an expression of active reverence as a person literally bows down and reveres a subject. Worship is also known as a work of "service" with the Hebrew word *'abad*, which means to work for another or to serve another by labor, and with the Greek word *leitourgia*, which means the service or work of the people. Both of these words are commonly attributed to priests and clergy, and convey worship as an act of service. Using these groupings as a guide, this book will look at worship as both an *expression* of reverence and as a *work* conducted by the people. In so doing, this book looks at worship both abstractly as a concept and concretely as a social activity.

Having defined worship we can determine what approach we'll use to study renewal worship. Prescriptive nonfiction books are like how-to books that teach and guide readers to learn about or improve skills. Many books about worship are prescriptive, explaining how to lead a congregation in worship, or how to enter into God's presence, or how to foster spiritual formation through worship. While these books are practical and helpful in their own ways, the more foundational books about worship are not prescriptive, but hermeneutical, discussing what worship is (abstractly) and how worship works (concretely). This approach helps us understand some of the underlying mechanisms behind worship practices before their proper administration is ever prescribed. I have chosen to use a hermeneutical approach because prescriptive approaches are often too exclusive and regulatory. Some worship styles or traditions will inevitably be left out or unfairly rebuked when a single author prescribes how worship *should* be done out of his or her convictions. Alternatively, discussing how worship works in a particular tradition or

---

[8]The Old Testament has several words for praise and thanksgiving, including *halal, shabakh, tehillah, zamar, yadah*, and *todah*. The New Testament also utilizes several words such as *ainesis, epaineō, eulogia, hallēlouia*, and *hymneō*. These words are all closely related to the concepts described above, but for our discussion here, we will look specifically at how the Bible describes worship.
[9]Brooks, *Worship Quest*, 22-23.

community avoids unnecessary prohibitions and allows us to take a step back and recognize formative roles in worship. Because these roles are unavoidably contextualized, we have a better view of what these worship practices mean for that culture. Practical suggestions and normative propositions can henceforth be determined as fitting within the narrative framework of the worshiping community. But what does a hermeneutical approach to study worship entail? To answer this, let's first define hermeneutics.

Hermeneutics is the field of study that deals with interpretation. When one thinks of hermeneutics one might think of "biblical hermeneutics," which utilizes exegetical techniques and principles to uncover the meanings of biblical texts. The broader *field* of hermeneutics, however, is utilized when interpreting *any* meaningful human action or byproduct. Anything can be "read" as a text. When people choose particular styles of clothing, for instance, they are helping us determine how to read or categorize them. If an American male wears a cowboy hat, belt buckle, and boots he has put himself in a narrative of "cowboy" or "southwesterner." He has chosen, knowingly or not, to be in dialogue with all the formal aesthetic, history, social impact, and presentational awareness that goes along with that sort of dress. In other words, he has chosen which narrative he'd like to be associated with. The same can be said for someone wearing a cashmere sweater with flats and a Gucci bag, or a LeBron jersey with Jordans and a snapback hat. Hermeneutics looks at all of these clues to see how *meaning* is made in a culture. These particular examples are about fashion, but hermeneutical approaches or methods can be applied to *any* cultural phenomenon.

When looking at Christian worship through a hermeneutical lens, we are first seeking to understand the worship practice before we prescribe any commendations or suggest any corrections. Theologian David Tracy sees the hermeneutical work of a theologian as one who seeks to "retrieve, interpret, translate, mediate the resources—the questions and answers, form and content, the subject matter—of the classic events of understanding of those fundamental religious questions embedded in the classic events, images, persons, rituals, texts and symbols of a tradition."[10] Put differently, theologians

---

[10]David Tracy, *The Analogical Imagination: Christian Theology and the Culture of Pluralism* (New York: Crossroad, 1981), 104.

seek to interpret all the sources, practices, and materials that surround the most pivotal events that define the Christian faith. In our case, we are seeking to understand the Christian response of worship to classic events such as Christ's redemption, the universal outpouring of the Spirit at Pentecost, and the commission of the church to extend the kingdom of God as we await the coming king. We are seeking to understand these events on theological terms from a particularly Pentecostal perspective and examine how they are embodied in Pentecostal spirituality.

Another issue with prescriptive books is that they often claim to be *the* biblical approach to worship. The problem with this claim, however, is that biblical theologies derive from scriptural interpretations. Biblical texts are understood through several unavoidable contextual lenses like our traditions and religious experiences.[11] Even the language we use to read the texts contextualize our understanding of them. As David Taylor points out, "Starting points in Scripture are never neutral; terms are never neutral; exegesis is never neutral. And to say that worship must be in 'accord' with Scripture is far from self-explanatory."[12] So, what is it that makes one approach to worship more biblical than another if the starting point (the biblical passage) was interpreted, and the worship practice derived from that particular interpretation? One could arguably find, after all, a biblical basis for every varying worship practice across Christian traditions. There is a biblical basis for full immersion baptism (Mt 3:13-16), and for sprinkling (Ezek 36:25). There is a biblical basis for transubstantiation (Jn 6:54), consubstantiation (1 Cor 10:15-18), and for symbolic understandings of the Eucharist (Mt 26:26-28; Mk 14:22-25). There is a biblical basis for spontaneous musical worship (Ps. 96:1), and for the restriction of instruments in the church (Hab 2:20). There is a biblical basis for high church, sacerdotal liturgies (Rev 4–5), and for low church, evangelical traditions (Acts 2:42-44). There is a biblical basis for fostering spiritual gifts in and through worship (1 Cor 12:4-11), and for the cessation of the extravagant gifts (1 Cor 13:8). And the list goes on. While some biblical interpretations are certainly stronger than others, this book does not make arguments for a particular tradition's superior reading of a text. Nor does it compare the

---

[11]W. David O. Taylor, *Glimpses of the New Creation: Worship and the Formative Power of the Arts* (Grand Rapids, MI: Eerdmans, 2019), 23.

[12]Taylor, *Glimpses of the New Creation*, 21.

liturgies of different traditions and determine which practices are more biblical. Instead, our hermeneutical approach begins by *acknowledging at the start*
the biblical lens that shapes renewal worship and its practices. In other words,
we are not arguing for but assuming an exegetical lens from start to finish.
We will see in the following chapters that Pentecostals and charismatics, while
engaging the whole Bible, particularly view the gospel narrative through
the lens of Acts 2. It is here where the Spirit is poured out on all flesh and the
church is empowered and mobilized to spread the gospel to the ends of the
earth. This biblical lens shapes all the worship practices of renewal worship,
and so will predicate the theological method used throughout this book.

When we seek to understand the worship practices of a particular worshiping community, in our case Pentecostal and charismatic worship, we can look
at which particular biblical passages are interpreted and emphasized, and
how the worship practices reinforce those biblical ideas. After assessing the
cultural artifacts of renewal worship, commendations can be offered if the
worship practices line up with the implications of the passages they're based
on, and corrections can be suggested if the practices veer away from the
renewal interpretations of the text. This is not merely a prescriptive approach
to a theology of worship, however, because it uses a methodological measuring stick that's evaluated against the tradition's own narrative lens. By adopting
Acts 2 as the biblical lens of our theology of renewal worship, I am following
a general consensus (among contemporary Pentecostal scholars) that Pentecostal theologies are characterized by a biblical hermeneutic that's informed
by Luke-Acts, and Acts 2 in particular.[13] Nevertheless, my findings will bear

---

[13]For the 50th anniversary of the Society for Pentecostal Studies, *Pneuma* published a commemora-
tive double-issue, and the essays sought to forecast the future of global Pentecostalism and Pentecostal scholarship. The editors Nimi Wariboko and Bill Oliverio saw Acts 2 as the major
commonality in all the essays of the issue: "The key insight in their prognoses of the future is this:
Pentecostals need to transform their practices, ideas, institutions, and theologies to live into a
multicultural future in the light of the pentecostal narrative of Acts 2. Each of the authors reached
this conclusion from different starting points" (Nimi Wariboko and L. William Oliverio, "The
Society for Pentecostal Studies at 50 Years: Ways Forward for Global Pentecostalism," *Pneuma* 42
[2020]: 328). Many other scholars have made similar points in prior works. See Martin Mittelstadt,
Reading Luke-Acts in the Pentecostal Tradition (Cleveland, TN: CPT Press, 2010); Amos Yong, *The
Spirit Poured Out on All Flesh: Pentecostalism and the Possibility of Global Theology* (Grand Rapids,
MI: Baker Academic, 2005); Wolfgang Vondey, *Pentecostal Theology: Living the Full Gospel* (London:
Bloomsbury, 2017); Frank Macchia, *Baptized in the Spirit: A Global Pentecostal Theology* (Grand
Rapids, MI: Zondervan, 2006); Kenneth Archer, *A Pentecostal Hermeneutic for the Twenty First
Century: Spirit, Scripture and Community* (London: Bloomsbury, 2004).

my own inevitable biases as an interpreter. I am, in fact, an insider of this discourse—a Pentecostal scholar, educator, and practitioner. As a theology, this book is ultimately confessional. But to avoid off-the-cuff prescriptions on matters of renewal worship, we'll use a theological method for renewal worship as a measuring stick for gaining the meaning of the "texts," both scriptural and cultural.

PENTECOSTALISM AND THE GLOBAL LANDSCAPE

So, why renewal worship? To answer that question, let's begin by defining some key terms, including the *Christian renewal movement*, *Pentecostalism*, and *renewal worship*. Clarifying terms up front aids our understanding by helping us avoid vagueness and ambiguity later on. The Christian renewal movement consists of interdenominational Christian groups around the world that place special emphasis on a direct personal experience of God. The term *renewal movement* can be interchanged synonymously with Pentecostalism *if* Pentecostalism is defined broadly as the global movement, comprising denominational "classical" Pentecostals, Neo-Pentecostals, and charismatics. In other words, the renewal movement refers to any stream of Christianity that exhibits Pentecostal and charismatic features in their worship, doctrine, and spirituality. Whenever I use the terms "renewal" and "Pentecostal," they will be used in this manner unless otherwise stated or qualified. Renewal worship refers to the worship and liturgical practices of Pentecostal and charismatic communities around the world, which are particularly attentive to the renewing power of the Holy Spirit.

Some would argue that the major stream of renewal in world Christianity comes from the global Pentecostal movement.[14] In fact, Pentecostalism has been identified as one of today's fastest-growing global religious phenomena,[15] and many reasons have been cited for the advancement of Pentecostalism around the globe. For instance, Allan Anderson writes that Pentecostalism's main expression is pneumatological (centered around the doctrine of the

---

[14]Wariboko and Oliverio, "Society for Pentecostal Studies," 327.
[15]Pew Research Center, *Spirit and Power—A 10-Country Survey of Pentecostals*, October 5, 2006, www.pewforum.org/2006/10/05/spirit-and-power; Philip Jenkins, *The Next Christendom: The Coming Global Christianity* (New York: Oxford University Press, 2011); Yong, *Spirit Poured Out*, 19.

Holy Spirit), making its interpretation broad and ecumenical[16] as it pertains to the whole Christian church.[17] As such, Pentecostalism is easily adopted and adapted throughout the world.[18] William K. Kay suggests that Pentecostalism "assumes that practice *is* theology" in its ability to combine belief and practice.[19] It is experiential and practical, making it more approachable than formal dogmatic approaches to Christianity.[20] As the popular moniker states, Pentecostal experience is "better caught than taught."[21] Amos Yong states that its message of Spirit empowerment is attractive to diverse and marginalized groups around the world. Pentecostalism offers a desperately needed message of hope to people who struggle through lower socioeconomic statuses.[22] Recent literature, however, presents the embodied worship culture of Pentecostalism as another possible reason for its global impact.[23] Anderson, Kay, and Yong's assessments are not wrong because there are many factors that determine the reasons behind the rapid growth of any religious or social phenomenon. Likewise, there are many ways to evaluate religious identity and its impact on human experience on a global level.

Nevertheless, I suggest understanding the movement's nature and appeal by examining Pentecostalism not through creedal formulae, but by its culture of worship. Instead of shoehorning the actual praxis of the faith back into an earlier doctrinal formula, this approach allows the renewal practices themselves to guide the way we come to understand Pentecostal spirituality. Because *renewal* spirituality, by definition, seeks a fresh, replenished expression of the historic Pentecostal traditions, studying the contemporary culture of worship hermeneutically elucidates the Spirit's present activity in the

---

16 Ecumenism is the promotion and fostering of Christian unity throughout the world.

17 Allan Anderson, *An Introduction to Pentecostalism: Global Charismatic Christianity* (Cambridge: Cambridge University Press, 2004), 14.

18 Yong, *Spirit Poured Out*, 18.

19 William K. Kay, *Pentecostalism* (London: SCM Press, 2009), 7.

20 Anderson, *An Introduction to Pentecostalism*, 14.

21 Daniel Albrecht, *Rites in the Spirit: A Ritual Approach to Pentecostal/Charismatic Spirituality* (Sheffield: Sheffield Academic Press, 1999), 205.

22 Yong, *Spirit Poured Out*, 39.

23 Michael Wilkinson and Peter Althouse, eds., *Annual Review of the Sociology of Religion*, vol. 8, *Pentecostals and the Body* (Leiden: Brill, 2017); Mark Cartledge and A. J. Swoboda, eds., *Scripting Pentecost: A Study of Pentecostals, Worship and Liturgy* (Surrey, UK: Ashgate, 2017); Monique Ingalls and Amos Yong, eds., *The Spirit of Praise: Music and Worship in Global Pentecostal-Charismatic Christianity* (University Park: Pennsylvania State University Press, 2015).

movement. That's not to say that doctrinal formula should altogether be avoided; there are still guiding motifs in renewal spirituality that must be identified (I will contend that the universal outpour of the Holy Spirit motif is the prevailing renewal guiding narrative). Rather, this hermeneutical approach seeks to understand what dogmas arise from the communal (worshipful) confessions of the guiding narrative.

A great part of what defines Pentecostalism is how its doctrinal and liturgical distinctives flow from religious experience. Religious or spiritual experiences are subjective encounters that cannot be comprehended through the five senses and are thus interpreted through religious frameworks. Pentecostal theologian Keith Warrington defines Pentecostalism's "heartbeat" as the experiential encounter of God.[24] Many other distinctives have been suggested to define Pentecostalism,[25] but Warrington believes that they are too restrictive because they are either too closely related to a particular denomination or tradition, or too vague because they are variously interpreted around the world.[26] A focus on spiritual encounter avoids confinement to a particular denominational understanding of Pentecostalism and makes room for diverse interpretations of other characteristics commonly associated with Pentecostalism. This does not prevent us from approaching common theological distinctives like Spirit baptism or speaking in tongues; rather it allows us to speak of those distinctives broadly without foregrounding any reading that is too closely tied to a particular tradition within the global Pentecostal movement.

I will primarily consider the global Pentecostal movement as it is today in the twenty-first century. Numerous excellent books tracing the revivalist origins of Pentecostalism already exist,[27] so my primary focus will be to

---

[24]Keith Warrington, *Pentecostal Theology: A Theology of Encounter* (London: T&T Clark, 2008), 20.

[25]Common suggestions include speaking in tongues as initial evidence, the fourfold or fivefold gospel, and Spirit baptism.

[26]For example, the "fourfold gospel," which views Jesus as Savior, Healer, Baptizer, and Coming King, and the "fivefold gospel," which also includes Jesus as Sanctifier, are good models for describing classical North American Pentecostalism, but may not be a good depiction of the more diverse global "Pentecostalisms" that are prevalent around the world now (see Warrington, *Pentecostal Theology*, 18).

[27]See Vinson Synan, *The Holiness-Pentecostal Tradition: Charismatic Movements in the Twentieth Century* (Grand Rapids, MI: Eerdmans, 1997); Donald Dayton, *Theological Roots of Pentecostalism* (Grand Rapids, MI: Baker Academic, 1987); Cecil Robeck Jr., *The Azusa Street Mission and Revival: The Birth of the Global Pentecostal Movement* (Nashville: Thomas Nelson, 2006); Henry Knight III,

exegete the contemporary worship practices that are culturally significant today. A major premise of this book is that renewal worship incubates and cultivates the experiential spirituality that defines Pentecostalism. Thus, studying Pentecostalism's culture of worship allows us to see what formational mechanisms already exist and how the stimuli implicitly or explicitly support a Pentecostal community's lived spirituality and doctrinal positions. In this way, we can see the Pentecostal ethos at work as it highlights the impact of its religious experience. I will be exegeting the worship culture of Pentecostalism, which will, in turn, help us to better understand the movement in general.

So, let's try answering the question again: Why renewal worship? Studying renewal worship allows us to grasp the meaning and significance of both the global Pentecostal movement and of Pentecostalism's influence on contemporary worship. Consequently, this theology will not only be important for Pentecostals, but for anyone engaging in contemporary forms of worship of which Pentecostalism has a significant impact.

THE STRUCTURE OF THE BOOK

Numerous practical and theological consequences arise when addressing what renewal worship is and how it works. To properly address these issues, the remainder of the book is broken up into two parts. Part one is titled "Profiling Renewal Worship," and answers the "what," "who," and "how" of renewal worship by mapping out a theological method and addressing pertinent implications. Part two is titled "Renewal Worship in Context," and fleshes out further implications that concern structure and spontaneity in renewal worship, the narrative and prophetic aspects of renewal worship, and the reconciling witness and global appeal of renewal worship. Finally, there is a conclusion that brings all the themes discussed in the book together.

Each chapter begins with a short exegesis of a pertinent scriptural passage. An important principle of Pentecostal theology is for it to be biblically based, and one of the main reasons this book adopts a hermeneutical approach to understand worship is to see how the renewal worshiping community bases

ed., *From Aldersgate to Azusa Street: Wesleyan, Holiness, and Pentecostal Visions of the New Creation* (Eugene, OR: Pickwick, 2010); Allan Anderson, *Introduction to Pentecostalism*; and Anderson, *To the Ends of the Earth: Pentecostalism and the Transformation of World Christianity* (Oxford: Oxford University Press, 2013).

its worship practices on Scripture. Scripture thus informs and catalyzes the concepts that follow. Each chapter also ends with a doxology in the form of a poetic stanza that captures the ideas presented. Taken all together, these doxologies form a nuanced "Pentecostal doxology" that gives insight into a pneumatological theology of renewal worship.

Chapter one begins part one with a chapter titled "What Renewal Worship Is: A Biblical and Theological Method." This chapter establishes our study's theological method by identifying the Acts 2 account of Pentecost as the guiding biblical narrative. The implications of this passage see worship experientially as an inbreaking of what is to come. This inbreaking comes to us as a *charism*, or gift given for the good of the church, from God when the Spirit is poured out on all flesh.[28] This pouring out flows from the initial outpouring at Pentecost and is perpetually reciprocated as a response from God's people. Because this response is active and not passive, real affective hope is possible. This is indebted to the theological idea that the kingdom of God is "already and not yet"—already present since Jesus inaugurated the kingdom while on earth, but not yet fulfilled as we await the second coming of Christ. This rightly points Christian hope to the return of Christ and allows us to let that future hope proleptically[29] break into and form our present circumstances. This model emphasizes the pneumatological component involved, especially as it pertains practically to a theology of abundance.

Chapter two, titled "Who Renewal Worship is For: The Object of Worship," discusses the relational nature of renewal worship by advancing a theology of abundance. This chapter maintains that renewal theology and renewal worship focus on the Spirit as abundant Gift. This suggests that God is both the operating Giver and the Gift that is given to humanity. Not only does God foster divine relationality through God's own nature, but God also invites us into relationship with God and each other through the revelation of the Son

---

[28]Peter, quoting Joel 2:28-32, sees Pentecost as a partial fulfillment of Joel's prophecy. While the Spirit was poured out in particular to those gathered in the upper room on the day of Pentecost, the designation "all flesh" is typically interpreted by Pentecostals to mean that they (those in the upper room) were the first recipients of the perpetual and continuous outpouring of the Spirit that is available to everyone from there on out.

[29]*Prolepsis* is the representation of something in the future (in this case, the second coming of Christ), as if it has already occurred. So the second coming, which has yet to occur, shapes our reality in the present day.

and by the mediation of the Spirit. God's presence is available abundantly as the Spirit is poured out on all flesh, and it is through this gracious Gift that we are drawn back to God. In this way, we understand that the object of renewal worship is the relational God.

Chapter three, titled "How Renewal Worship Works: Worship as a Shaping Narrative," explores the ways in which the Pentecostal worship experience is emplotted and interpreted by the worshiping community.[30] In particular, this chapter looks at how music demonstrates and reinforces the Pentecostal story aesthetically, helping people discover their own part in the broader narrative. From Pentecostalism's birth as a revivalist movement, music has been ubiquitous to every expression of its worship. Music is so important to Pentecostal spirituality that it is regarded sacramentally as an occasion to encounter God in the midst of the people's praises.[31] Music scores the other liturgical elements of renewal worship, adding a powerful affective dimension to the ritual reinforcement of the Pentecostal narrative.

The book then switches gears with chapter four, titled "How Renewal Worship Flows: Between Word and Spirit." As part two of the book seeks to hermeneutically approach particular practices within renewal worship, all of the remaining chapters help to uncover what these worship practices mean and how they affect renewal communities and Pentecostals worldwide. Chapter four explains the "flow" of renewal worship and how worship is navigated spiritually in a service. Renewal worship oscillates between the creative (formational) power of the Word, and the refining (deconstructive) power of the sanctifying Spirit. Although distinguished here by role, Word and Spirit are unified and work together in the life of a Christian and are always in tandem in worship, but renewal worship is unique in the way that this oscillation plays out through notions of structure and spontaneity, and triumph and lament.

---

[30] The term *emplotted* is coined by philosopher Paul Ricoeur. It refers to being placed in a narrative. See Paul Ricoeur, *From Text to Action: Essays in Hermeneutics, II*, trans. Kathleen Blamey and John Thompson (Evanston, IL: Northwestern University Press, 2007), 3. This concept will be fleshed out in chap. 3.

[31] The term *sacrament* is not often used in Pentecostal and charismatic contexts (see Daniel Albrecht, "Worshiping and the Spirit: Transmuting Liturgy Pentecostally," in *The Spirit in Worship—Worship in the Spirit*, ed. Teresa Berger and Bryan Spinks [Collegeville, MN: Liturgical Press, 2009], 224), but refers to a ritual or ceremony that imparts divine grace. While many renewal traditions view rituals like baptism and the Eucharist as merely symbolic gestures of deeper truths, those who hold to sacramental views consider these rites to be true channels of God's grace.

These ideas were inspired by Irenaeus's understanding of the Son and Spirit as the "hands of God" and how the formational power of the right and the deconstructive power of the left work in tandem to bring about growth and renewal.[32] In renewal worship, ambient music and improvisational words and prayer often create that charged space where spiritual formation takes place. Because renewal worship is sensitive to the Spirit, ministers have the ability to navigate the spiritual needs of the community through the inspiration of the Holy Spirit.

The main point of chapter five, "What Renewal Worship Says: The Prophetic Functions of Renewal," is to discuss the ways in which renewal worship functions prophetically in both the local and global church. This chapter discusses how spiritual alignment through worship is necessary for understanding God's will for worshipers and for worshiping communities. Once aligned, worshiping communities come to understand the Spirit's ministry in their community and the world. This requires both knowing the worshiping community's social context and discerning what new work the Spirit is doing in the public arena. Because the Spirit indwells the church, the prophet no longer acts as God's only mode of communication to the people. Pentecostals believe Christ's sacrifice allows every believer to have the ability to communicate directly to God through the ever-present Spirit. Renewal worship also works prophetically on a global scale. In recent years, some renewal worship songs have broadcasted singular messages to the universal church. Global distribution and the mimetic quality of songs allow unifying messages to shape whole generations.

Chapter six, "Who Renewal Worshipers Are: The Renewed Global Community," claims that the universal outpour motif demonstrates the Spirit's work for global unity and reconciliation as the Spirit is poured out on *all* flesh. Reconciliation is made available by Christ's redemption, and the Spirit creates the appropriate space for people to be reconciled back to God and with each other. This chapter argues that Pentecost and the Azusa Street Revival both demonstrate how a universal outpour of the Spirit must precede true reconciliation, and how renewal worship helps spread this unifying message. This

---

[32]Irenaeus was a second-century Greek bishop of the church who played a key role in the development of Christian theology during the patristic era. Some of his ideas will be addressed in chap. 4.

chapter also looks at some ways renewal worship has approached global engagement, promoting unity while respecting cultural differences. The main argument of this chapter is that renewal worship must be understood as a global reality, and we should celebrate its diversity, acknowledging the different ways people around the world honor God.

The conclusion, "Where Do We Go from Here?," draws together all the themes of the book and succinctly outlines the book's theology of renewal worship. By answering the "what," "who," and "how" of renewal worship, part one introduces a theology of renewal worship that sees God's Spirit flowing abundantly from the universal outpour. Worship in a theology of renewal is both the reception of and response to the Spirit's overflow, and the visualization of what is to come. Part two shows how this theology works out practically in a worship service (chap. 4), how this theology speaks to and affects the local and global community (chap. 5), and how the church has implemented these ideas around the world to foster reconciliation and unity (chap. 6).

Studying renewal worship is a worthy pursuit whether you consider yourself a devoted constituent of the Pentecostal movement or an inquisitive outsider. Because Pentecostalism is one of the fastest growing religious movements in the world, and because its influence spreads far beyond denominational lines, it is vital that anyone concerned with the global church come to know the biblical and theological commitments behind renewal worship practices. Doing so will help you learn a little more about your own worshiping community, and it will help you understand what God is doing today through the renewal movements. While we are united by the same Spirit, and every part of the body of Christ is significant, let us, then, come to understand and celebrate what the Spirit is doing through the renewal worship practices of Pentecostalism.

PART 1

PROFILING RENEWAL WORSHIP

1

WHAT RENEWAL WORSHIP IS

A BIBLICAL AND THEOLOGICAL METHOD

In the last days it will be, God declares,

that I will pour out my Spirit upon all flesh,

and your sons and your daughters shall prophesy,

and your young men shall see visions,

and your old men shall dream dreams.

Even upon my slaves, both men and women,

in those days I will pour out my Spirit;

and they shall prophesy.

ACTS 2:17-18

THE PASSAGE ABOVE takes place on the day of Pentecost after the Spirit came upon those who gathered in the upper room (Acts 2:1-4).[1] As crowds gathered, Peter stood and declared the partial fulfillment of Joel 2's prophecy concerning the Day of the Lord,[2] and more than three thousand people

---

[1]It is important to note that Pentecost was already a holy day in Judaism, which is why many Jews were gathered in Jerusalem in the first place. Also known as Shavuot or the Feast of Weeks, Pentecost is a harvest feast that celebrates the wheat harvest and takes place fifty days after the Feast of Firstfruits.

[2]In Matthew, Jesus makes the kingdom of God concern the renewal of Israel, but pictures it as being related to people being baptized in the Spirit (Mt 3:7-12; 19:28-29). In this way he sees the kingdom of God as entering history through the Spirit before a cataclysmic Day of the Lord event. He seems to indicate an "already and not yet" understanding of the kingdom of God when he refers to the blessings of this life and in the age to come (Mk 10:30; Mt 12:28-32; Lk 17:20-37). This means that Joel's prophecy of the Day of the Lord was partially fulfilled at the cross and through Pentecost, and will be totally fulfilled in the age to come at Christ's second coming.

welcomed the message and were baptized (Acts 2:41). This is Pentecost—the culmination of Christ's earthly ministry and the birth of the church.[3] Peter's discourse ties together at least three pertinent themes that we see expressed again and again in renewal theology and spiritualty. First, we see priority given to the outpoured Spirit. This is God impelled upon creation to mobilize and motivate the increase of God's ministry on earth. Second, we see an emphasis on the egalitarian distribution of charismatic gifts. Everyone—man and woman, young and old, slave and free—will be enlisted and equipped to become God's active agents to carry out this ministry. And third, this whole event bears an eschatological imprint. The outpour occurs in the "last days," presumably to usher in the kingdom of God. Every part of this—the outpour of the Spirit, the commissioning of God's people, and the expansion of the kingdom—was inaugurated by Christ during his time on earth and points forward to his return. The goal of this book is to mine this account and see how renewal worship is both informed by and reinforces this narrative and its many implications.

The whole biblical narrative rises to a crescendo with Christ, and while some may see Christ's ascension as the crux of this apex, Pentecostal theologian Frank Macchia reasons convincingly that the biblical narrative actually climaxes at Pentecost because it is here where Christ pours the Spirit out on all flesh.[4] Through Pentecost, redeemed people become agents of the kingdom of God. Macchia writes that Pentecost "is the event where the Spirit Baptizer pours forth the Spirit on all flesh and incorporates us into himself—into the life and mission of the triune God."[5] If theology is the study of God in relation

---

[3] Frank Macchia, *Jesus the Spirit Baptizer: Christology in Light of Pentecost* (Grand Rapids, MI: Eerdmans, 2018), 40.

[4] Frank Macchia crafts a Christology that's biblical, Pentecostal, conversant with the church fathers, and expands logically from Wolfhart Pannenberg's Christology from below. Macchia states that Pannenberg stops short by concluding the revelation of Christ's deity with the resurrection. Pannenberg believes that the claims of Jesus' deity were vindicated at the resurrection, which then can be traced back to prove every aspect of Jesus' life, including his incarnation (Wolfhart Pannenberg, *Jesus—God and Man* [Philadelphia: Westminster, 1978], 24-25). Macchia believes that while the resurrection *implies* a vindication of Jesus' assumption, Pentecost rendered Jesus' lordship *explicit* (*Jesus the Spirit Baptizer*, 40). This is because Jesus reveals his unity with the self-imparting Lord when he pours out the Spirit at Pentecost. Only God can *give* God. Macchia's Christology is a sophisticated corrective from the misgivings of creedal Christology, and a powerful answer to the challenges brought by those who sought to reconstruct the historical Jesus.

[5] Macchia, *Jesus the Spirit Baptizer*, 64. James Dunn makes a similar point: "The climax and purposed end of Jesus' ministry is not the cross and the resurrection, but the ascension and Pentecost." James D. G. Dunn, *Baptism in the Holy Spirit* (London: SCM Press, 1970), 44.

to humanity, the Pentecost event should be seen as supremely theological because humanity is brought back into God's life and mission. At Pentecost, Christ pours out the Spirit on the newly commissioned humanity to help bring about God's redemptive plan for creation.

For Macchia, what began as a biblical theology of the account of Pentecost in Acts turned into a theological method for understanding Christian, and particularly Pentecostal, faith and doctrine through the lens of Pentecost. The benefit of such an approach is that we can fix our theological interpretations to a centralized point of narrative contact. It helps us comprehend our Pentecostal spirituality in light of a greater, cohesive, biblical narrative. Such a method would be appropriate for rooting a renewal theology of worship. Even though Christian worship can be understood as a social phenomenon, concepts that pertain to faith traditions cannot merely be understood sociologically. Sociology helps us understand social relations between peoples and cultures but cannot adequately explicate the spiritual and theological significance of religious concepts. As Pentecostal theologian Mark Cartledge points out, *"Theological texts need theological contexts to make sense of them."*[6] In order to *truly* understand how a community worships, we must get a sense of what worship means theologically for that community and how this meaning fits within the community's contextual framework. To this end, this chapter seeks to determine a theological method that is biblically based and pays close attention to the hermeneutical, text-context negotiation that concerns the meaning and practice of renewal worship. Beginning with the Acts 2 account of Pentecost, our method makes the "universal outpour" motif the keynote biblical image through which everything else is observed.

As the title of this chapter suggests, we will answer the question "What is renewal worship?" by articulating a theological method for renewal worship that is biblically rooted in the Acts 2 account of Pentecost. Following Frank Macchia, this method connects the universal outpour of Acts 2 to the return of Christ and helps us understand future hope as proleptically breaking into

---

[6]Mark Cartledge, "Locating the Spirit in Meaningful Experience: Empirical Theology and Pentecostal Hermeneutics," in Kenneth Archer and L. William Oliverio Jr., eds., *Constructive Pneumatological Hermeneutics in Pentecostal Christianity* (New York: Palgrave Macmillan, 2016), 255; emphasis original.

and forming our present circumstances. This chapter also differentiates the Pentecostal understanding of worship from evangelical and sacramental views, especially as it concerns the immediate presence of God in worship and the gifts that are bestowed by God through worship. Finally, this chapter demonstrates practical considerations of this method, highlighting the significance of healing in renewal worship, and displaying how this might work out in individual, communal, and societal levels. It is my hope that this theological method will be thoroughly biblical, thoroughly Pentecostal, and useful for understanding Christian worship in a renewal context.

GROUNDING A BIBLICAL THEOLOGICAL METHOD

The expression *biblical theological method* is not a highbrow term for merely reading Scripture but denotes a method for interpreting Scripture and evaluating the doctrinal implications of the interpretation. Developing a theological method for renewal worship that is biblically based must, therefore, be indicative of the *way* Pentecostals read Scripture. That's not to say Pentecostals read a different Bible or practice things that are extrabiblical, but it does mean that Pentecostals bring some theological commitments to the text *before* reading a passage. This shouldn't be alarming, though, because every Christian tradition brings some of their own theological commitments to the biblical texts. This is an inescapable fact of our bounded reality. No one comes to a text from a totally neutral or completely objective position. Pre-text commitments are often inherently formed through the religious practices of the Christian tradition.[7] What's unique about Pentecostalism is that worship, and particularly musical worship, is one of the great determining factors of Pentecostal theology. In other words, renewal worship helps shape the Pentecostal pre-text. While many theologians have historically viewed a faith tradition's emotions and attitudes (pathos) as flowing from Christian action (praxis) that was initially informed by belief (doxa), Pentecostal theologian Kenneth Archer flips the script, claiming that worship is the primary way Pentecostals *do* theology. Archer writes,

> Our theological explanations can become a critical reflection upon our doxology with our acts of worship always informing and transforming our official

---

[7]For further reading, see Daniel Treier, *Introducing Theological Interpretation of Scripture: Recovering a Christian Practice* (Grand Rapids, MI: Baker Academic, 2008), chap. 1.

dogma; and, in turn, our dogma informing our doxology. Orthodoxy has more
to do with our primary way of doing theology, which is worship, than the
secondary critical reflective activity—the production of official dogma or right
believing (*orthopistis*).[8]

What this means is that we can't look at the foundations of renewal theology
through a strictly linear lens. Doxa does not necessarily come before praxis
and pathos in Pentecostal traditions. Rather, these modes of conduct com-
mingle and inform each other through communal expression. When discussing renewal worship, we can appreciate belief and action together in concert,
eschewing any chronological priority. Taking this into account, we can take
a closer look at how theology informs worship and vice versa.

Uncovering theological commitments. The aural makeup of a liturgy is
formative for a community's theology.[9] What is expressed, verbally and
artistically, accents particular theological commitments of the community's
outlook. We often hear of worship scholars, particularly ones writing prescriptively, discussing the "theological soundness" of a worship song. Soundness, in logic, refers to a statement being both valid and true, so if something
is theologically sound it makes sense *and* speaks truly of the Christian faith.
The problem with finding the theological soundness of a song is that often
people disregard a song's implicit theology because it does not agree with
their own theological commitments. But theologically *different* does not
mean theologically *unsound*. In fact—and this is important—most published worship songs *are* theologically sound; they just portray contrastive
theological commitments.

A theologically unsound song must deny or at least confuse primary doctrinal beliefs. Primary Christian beliefs are fundamental and broad—the types
of beliefs one *must* confess in order to be considered a Christian. These primary beliefs are creedal, having been mostly scrutinized and formalized by
the fourth century. Many of these beliefs were nicely encapsulated in the
Nicene-Constantinopolitan Creed and affirm basic Christian beliefs: God is
the Creator of all things, Christ and the Spirit are coeternal with the Father,

---

[8]Kenneth Archer, *The Gospel Revisited: Towards a Pentecostal Theology of Worship and Witness* (Eugene,
OR: Pickwick, 2011), 11.
[9]Don Saliers, *Worship as Theology: Foretaste of Glory Divine* (Nashville: Abingdon, 1994), 162.

Christ died and rose again for the redemption of fallen humanity, the Scriptures are holy, Christ will return to judge and set all things right, Christ inaugurated the kingdom of God, which has no end, and God established the confessional church for witness. If a worship song denies or confuses any of these statements, then indeed, it is theologically unsound. But most songs affirm these statements, either outright or implicitly. The matters of theological difference in these songs are usually secondary or even tertiary issues that illustrate particular theological traditions. To make this point, let's consider three ways contemporary worship music expresses theological commitments lyrically and by its structure.

Keith Getty and Stuart Townend's contemporary hymn "In Christ Alone," for instance, is about finding one's identity in Christ, but like many hymns this song traces the whole gospel message from the incarnation through the death, resurrection, ascension, and second coming of Christ. But the line "Till on that cross, as Jesus died, the wrath of God was satisfied,"[10] suggests a particular commitment to the penal substitutionary theory of atonement. This is a theological view of atonement that's held by many evangelicals today but rejected by several mainline traditions. In a nutshell, this view states that Jesus' sacrifice satisfied divine justice and that God was unable to forgive sin without someone or something assuming its penalty. My point here does not concern the theory's theological propriety; I simply want to demonstrate the presence of a theological pre-text commitment in a worship song. In this case, the implicit commitments of penal substitution align with Reformed theology. Reformed theologians will likely want to include penal substitution as a primary belief, but that would mean millions of Christians around the world that hold to a different view of the atonement are denying a primary Christian doctrine, which leads, inevitably, to heterodoxy, or at worst heresy. But, as stated above, primary Christian beliefs are broader and more foundational. The creedal, primary belief that's affirmed here is simply that Christ atoned for our sins, not which theory of atonement explains this assertion best. In other words, people who reject the particular theory of penal substitutionary

---

[10]"In Christ Alone," words and music by Stuart Townend and Keith Getty, CCLI 3350395 © 2001 Thankyou Music (administrated by Capitol CMG Publishing). It should be noted that some versions of the song update the lyrics to avoid the implicit commitment of penal substitution.

atonement have not committed heresy, but people who reject the broader belief that Christ has atoned for our sins have.[11]

Similarly, Hillsong Worship's song "So Will I (100 Billion X)," is about creation bowing down and worshiping God. Although the song's main theme isn't controversial, one of the lines is

And as you speak
A hundred billion creatures catch your breath
Evolving in pursuit of what you said
If it all reveals your nature so will I.[12]

The lyrics are poetic and do not offer an explicit commitment to the theory of evolution in God's act of creation, but by using the word *evolving* in a context that also describes nature and science in the line prior, Hillsong has left open the possibility for concepts like theistic evolution, which is popular in theologically progressive and post-evangelical traditions. The creedal, primary belief that's affirmed here is simply that God created all things, not the manner in which God created. Those who profess a particular theory of *how* God created everything have not committed heresy, but people who reject the broader belief *that* God created everything have.

One final example can be found with gospel artist Tasha Cobbs Leonard's song "I'm Getting Ready" through lyrics that state,

Eyes haven't seen
And ears haven't heard
The kind of blessings
The kind of blessings
That's about to fall on me.[13]

---

[11] I often make the distinction for my students of being "theologically wrong" and "theologically heretical." Everyone holds to particular theological commitments, and when someone commits to a belief, that person has rejected, outright or in part, every other theory on the same subject. This is perfectly normal, and simply what it means to hold beliefs. It is perfectly normal and justifiable to believe that the rejected beliefs are wrong. It is not justifiable, however, to say they are heretical unless they reject or distort a creedal, primary Christian belief.

[12] "So Will I (100 Billion X)," words and music by Joel Houston, Benjamin Hastings, and Michael Fatkin, CCLI 7084123 © 2017 Hillsong Music Publishing Australia (administered by Hillsong Music Publishing, Capitol CMG Publishing).

[13] "I'm Getting Ready (Ready for Overflow)," words and music by Tasha Cobbs Leonard and Todd Galberth, CCLI 7099373 © 2017 Meadowgreen Music Company, Tasha Cobbs Music Group,

One could see a commitment to the prosperity gospel or at least to a theology of abundance.[14] This sort of theology is expressed across many charismatic traditions, but also viewed (and rejected) by many other traditions, including some Pentecostal traditions, as a justification for greedy consumerism.[15] To really understand the positive and negative implications of this theology we must handle these commitments with more nuance—a task that will commence in the next chapter. For now, let's settle on the less contentious notion that worship song lyrics are not theologically neutral, but expressive of a particular faith community's theological tradition.

While worship song lyrics regularly demonstrate and reinforce theological commitments, the structure of worship also helps to shape theology. To shed light on how worship influences spiritual and communal formation, worship scholar Glenn Packiam differentiates between a service's "espoused" and "operant" theology.[16] Espoused theology considers the words that are expressed through songs, preaching, prayers, and so on, whereas operant theology is what is encoded in the worship. Uncovering what's encoded requires analyzing the structure and form of the worship practice, and the way it's performed or enacted.[17] For instance, when worship is sacramental, the presence of God is emphasized through a covenantal understanding of ritual. When the worship service utilizes a lot of intercessory prayer and focuses on healing and abundance, the community's theology is shaped by paradigmatic lived experiences. What a community *does* when they gather to worship demonstrates and shapes the community's theological commitments as well.[18] And not only

---

Integrity First Music Publishing (administered by Capitol CMG Publishing, Kobalt Music Publishing America, Inc.).

[14]As a biblical basis, the prosperity gospel emphasizes that God cares for us (Jer 29:11), provides for us (Rom 8:28), supplies us with more than we need (2 Cor 9:8), and calls us to live life abundantly (Jn 10:10).

[15]See Costi Hinn, *God, Greed, and the (Prosperity) Gospel: How Truth Overwhelms a Life Built on Lies* (Grand Rapids, MI: Zondervan, 2019); David Jones and Russell Woodridge, *Health, Wealth, and Happiness: How Prosperity Gospel Overshadows the Gospel of Christ* (Grand Rapids, MI: Kregel, 2017); Daniela Augustine, *The Spirit and the Common Good: Shared Flourishing in the Image of God* (Grand Rapids, MI: Eerdmans, 2019).

[16]Glenn Packiam, *Worship and the World to Come: Exploring Christian Hope in Contemporary Worship* (Downers Grove, IL: IVP Academic, 2020), 105.

[17]Packiam, *Worship and the World to Come*, 108.

[18]Additionally, I have argued elsewhere that the worship space itself displays theological commitments. See chap. 8 of Steven Félix-Jäger, *Spirit of the Arts: Towards a Pneumatological Aesthetics of Renewal* (New York: Palgrave Macmillan, 2017).

are theological commitments implied and shaped by worship, theological principles for understanding worship are also implicit in the worship service.

Differentiating evangelical, sacramental, and Pentecostal worship. Gordon Smith, in his book *Evangelical, Sacramental & Pentecostal*, constructively distinguishes between the evangelical, sacramental, and Pentecostal principles[19] found in worship, arguing that the universal church should synchronously inhabit all three attributes. While each tradition affirms a holistic approach to worship, each of these principles emphasizes a different aspect of God's "ecology of grace."[20] We will look at how these principles are defined and use them typologically to organize pertinent theological outlooks in and around the renewal movements. It should be noted that any form of codification has drawbacks because the categories are inevitably painted with broad strokes. Worshiping communities will undoubtedly reflect multiple facets of each of these principles. Nevertheless, organizing these experiences by abstraction will help us recognize to which proclivities a worshiping community is drawn.

The evangelical principle affirms Scripture as the "animating role in the life of the church."[21] Scripture here becomes a primary means by which God is present in the church. Evangelicals, therefore, seek a dynamic theology of the Bible.[22] This principle highlights the emphasis on the Bible, especially in didactic forms found in evangelical worship, where worship songs are evaluated by their ability to faithfully articulate biblical truths. For instance, consider how evangelical worship leader Matt Boswell describes the role

---

[19]In his book Smith refers to this as the "Pentecost principle," but I will retain the adjectival form of "Pentecostal" to tie it to the renewal movements. This should not be confused, however, with Nimi Wariboko's "Pentecostal principle" from his book *The Pentecostal Principle: Ethical Methodology in New Spirit* (Grand Rapids, MI: Eerdmans, 2012). Here Wariboko distinguishes a Pentecostal social ethic viewed through a theology of play. I use the term "Pentecostal principle" merely to refer to the precepts surrounding the way Pentecostals and charismatics worship.

[20]Gordon Smith, *Evangelical, Sacramental & Pentecostal: Why the Church Should Be All Three* (Downers Grove, IL: IVP Academic, 2017), 44. Similar arguments for unifying liturgical and charismatic worship can be found in Andrew Wilson, *Spirit and Sacrament: An Invitation to Eucharismatic Worship* (Grand Rapids, MI: Zondervan, 2019), and an argument for different theological distinctives flowing together ecumenically can be found in Richard Foster, *Streams of Living Water: Celebrating the Great Traditions of Christ* (San Francisco: HarperCollins, 2010).

[21]Smith, *Evangelical, Sacramental & Pentecostal*, 53.

[22]Smith, *Evangelical, Sacramental & Pentecostal*, 53.

of the worship leader: "If we are to teach and admonish one another through song, then the people choosing or writing the songs need to be well-versed in the emphasis, movement, and contours of the Bible. We must become singing theologians whose aim is to teach and proclaim the truth of God with accuracy and skillfulness."[23] This agenda regards Scripture highly but is didactically geared toward the edification of the mind, conceivably at the expense of engaging the holistic, formational powers of worship and the arts. Rather than forming people's affections through the liturgical arts, the arts are used secondarily as a tool to convey biblical truths. Furthermore, when this principle is followed dogmatically, poetic and contextual expressions of biblical truths in worship can be disregarded or even derided.[24] In a worst-case scenario, the Bible can take precedence over the Spirit, leaving no room for a direct, experiential encounter with God. This is particularly dangerous because anything that takes precedence over God becomes an idol.[25] The idolatrous homage of the Bible is called "bibliolatry." As Richard Foster notes, "To avoid the heresy of bibliolatry, we would do well to remember the classical formulation of Christian theology: *Christus Rex et Dominus Scripturae*. 'Christ is King and Lord of Scripture.'"[26] We cannot allow the Bible to be proclaimed more than Christ who is Lord of *all*, even Scripture. We also cannot allow the Bible to precede the actual presence of God. As will be discussed further in chapter three of this book, even something good like the Bible can become an idol.

---

[23]Matt Boswell, "Doxology, Theology, and the Mission of God," in *Doxology & Theology: How the Gospel Forms the Worship Leader*, ed. Matt Boswell (Nashville: B&H, 2013), 19.

[24]This unfortunate and divisive tendency will be discussed further in chaps. 5 and 6 of this book.

[25]Many times, it is a lack of linguistic clarity that leads to statements where the Bible implicitly takes precedence over God. For example, evangelical worship leader Matt Papa stated three ways worshipers can see God is through the eyes of the heart, through Scripture, and in the gospel (Matt Papa, "The Worship Leader and Mission," in *Doxology & Theology: How the Gospel Forms the Worship Leader*, ed. Matt Boswell [Nashville: B&H, 2013], 66-67). But when Papa described seeing God in the Bible, he conflated Jesus as the Word of God with the Bible. He writes, "We see God and His glory in the Bible. The Word of God is the revelation of Himself to mankind. Period. It's how we see God. It is Revelation. The Scriptures are the foundation of all Christian worship" (66). While the Word of God is the revelation of God to humanity, as John 1 clearly states, Jesus is the Word of God. Jesus is the Revelation of the Revealer God (to use Barthian language). The Bible is a record of the Word of God. As can be seen, the evangelical biblicism here resulted, perhaps unintentionally, in an equivocation of Scripture *as* God.

[26]Richard Foster, *Streams of Living Water: Essential Practices from the Six Great Traditions of Christian Faith* (San Francisco: HarperSanFrancisco, 2001), 231.

Conversely, the sacramental principle emphasizes ritual as a symbolic means for receiving God's grace and animating the Christian faith in the lives of believers.[27] The rich Christian symbols of baptism and Eucharist "integrate heart and mind in our bodies."[28] The sacraments engage us holistically, and are significant because they are symbols directly ordained by Christ. These symbols also carry spiritual power as they "locate Christ's presence here and now."[29] The presence of Christ is, in a mysterious way, enfleshed through the sacraments. The sacramental principle seeks to faithfully practice the rituals of worship described and authorized in Scripture. The sacramental principle becomes dangerous, however, when the rituals fossilize and become mere tradition. When this happens, the relational principium behind the sacrament is lost, and the symbols become the ends rather than the means that point to deeper realities. In a worst-case scenario, the rituals themselves are worshiped rather than God. Once again, the basest pitfall of all is idolatry, but instead of bibliolatry, this principle can perpetuate the idolization of ritual.

Finally, the Pentecostal principle affirms the church in the power of the Spirit. Here the Spirit is viewed as being immediately and graciously present in worship.[30] While the evangelical principle claims to experience the presence of God primarily through Scripture, and the sacramental principle claims to experience the presence of God primarily through the sacraments, the Pentecostal principle claims to experience the presence of God directly through the constant and gift-giving Spirit. The worshiping community experiences what Packiam calls an "I-You encounter" with God, where the person and community (the collective I) meets God in song and prayer.[31] This direct, experiential encounter of the Spirit epitomizes what Pentecostals see as renewal worship. The Bible is not disregarded, nor are the sacraments neglected, but each is understood as a testament to the actual, concomitant relationship a believer has with God. Christ's promise of the Spirit (Jn 15:26; 16:7-15; Lk 24:49) is taken at face value, and believers experience God as Spirit in worship. All Pentecostals believe that God still reveals new things to

---

[27]Smith, *Evangelical, Sacramental & Pentecostal*, 73.

[28]Smith, *Evangelical, Sacramental & Pentecostal*, 76.

[29]John Rempel, *Recapturing an Enchanted World: Ritual and Sacrament in the Free Church Tradition* (Downers Grove, IL: IVP Academic, 2020), 14.

[30]Smith, *Evangelical, Sacramental & Pentecostal*, 99.

[31]Packiam, *Worship and the World to Come*, 45.

believers today, but typically Pentecostals believe that these revelations should align with Scripture.

The Pentecostal principle becomes dangerous when experience trumps Scripture. In this regard, a Pentecostal or charismatic may believe a personal conviction is *as* significant as Scripture, or worse they may defend a personal conviction that goes against Scripture because they're convinced it came as a special and personal revelation. Since God is not duplicitous, personal revelations should always be in sync with what God has already revealed through Scripture. The worst-case scenario for the Pentecostal principle is similar to the evangelical and the sacramental principles. Instead of idolizing the Bible (evangelical) or idolizing ritual (sacramental), the biggest snare of the Pentecostal principle is the idolization of experience. Pentecostal biblical scholar Melissa Archer warns against this: "For Pentecostals, the temptation towards false worship might seem irrelevant; after all, Pentecostals seek above all an authentic and experiential encounter with God. Pentecostals, however should constantly discern whether or not they are unwittingly engaging in false worship."[32] For Pentecostals, idolatry might come in the guise of propping up charismatic pastors or leaders to a status of devotion, or elevating a technologically equipped physical atmosphere or style of worship to a point of veneration.[33] In these cases something has taken precedence over God, even if the intention was, ironically, to foster the atmosphere for encountering God.

While the Pentecostal principle puts the worshiper's personal and communal relationship with God front and center, Scripture and sacrament are still necessary for rightly knowing God. As Smith writes, "In our worship, it should be clear—evident and obvious—that both Word and sacrament are supremely charismatic events, means and moments wherein the Spirit of the Living God is present to the world."[34] As Scripture and sacrament render the Spirit present in the world, the Spirit is personally and directly present in the lives of the believers before and outside Scripture and sacrament. Since the Pentecostal principle reveals a theological commitment to experiential encounter, renewal worship renders every encounter of the Spirit an act of worship.

---

[32]Melissa Archer, *"I Was in the Spirit on the Lord's Day": A Pentecostal Engagement with Worship in the Apocalypse* (Cleveland, TN: CPT Press, 2015), 311.

[33]Archer, *"I Was in the Spirit on the Lord's Day,"* 311.

[34]Smith, *Evangelical, Sacramental & Pentecostal,* 116.

Deeming worship as every encounter of the Spirit means that both the extravagant and the "mundane" experiences with God constitute worship. While
renewal worship is experienced through ecstatic praise, miracles, and tongues,
it is also experienced by hearing God's voice in the quiet of prayer, devotion,
and Scripture reading. Worship can happen in solitude, at the table, and in the
streets—whenever and wherever God is present. Anywhere God is present
becomes "holy ground," and is thus fit for worship. This sentiment can be found
in the lyrics of Christopher Beatty's praise chorus "Holy Ground," which affirms
that holy ground is wherever the Lord is present, and "where He is, is holy."[35]
There is no sacred space apart from God, and any space becomes sacred when
God is present. Of course, God is omnipresent, so part of what makes a space
sacred is the worshiper recognizing the presence of God in the space. Sacred-
ness is thus dependent on a reciprocal acknowledgment of God's presence in
a space. In other words, sacred spaces occur at the location where the worshiper
turns his or her heart toward the ever-present God.

It should be noted that stating worship happens wherever God is present
is not saying "all of life is worship." Stating all of life is worship becomes a
mere platitude when it is not understood theologically.[36] To say that one thing
is entirely something else renders the initial term meaningless. Words embody
difference in meaning, or else distinctions could never be made. So, while it
is tempting to say all of life is worship because it seemingly elevates worship's
significance, its lack of contextual framework makes the phrase ambiguous
and unclear. If all of life is worship, then worship is both *everything* (all of life)
and *nothing* because there is no distinction between it and anything else. If
that same phrase is articulated through a theological lens, however, then the
phrase will be limited to a theological context, and its meaning can begin to
make sense. Nevertheless, renewal worship does not state "all of life is worship," but it does proclaim "every encounter of God is worship." Pentecostals
do not believe every place is sacred by its own measure, but any place becomes
sacred when God is present and worshiped.

---

[35]"Holy Ground," words and music by Christopher Beatty, CCLI 19526 © 1982 Universal Music—
Brentwood Benson Publishing, Birdwing Music (administrated by Brentwood-Benson Music
Publishing, Inc., Capitol CMG Publishing).

[36]Harold Best, *Unceasing Worship: Biblical Perspectives on Worship and the Arts* (Downers Grove, IL:
InterVarsity Press, 2003), 9.

Along these lines, Wolfgang Vondey sees "the altar" as a sacramental symbol, essentially symbolizing the charged, sacred space where encountering God is expectant.[37] The altar is the holy ground where people come and are vulnerably submitted to the will of God and ready to receive spiritual transformation. Vondey writes,

> At the heart of the Christian liturgy celebrated in its place, Pentecostals find the outpouring of the Holy Spirit and its physical manifestations that together create a sacramental environment in the church. Characteristic of this environment are the active participation and transformation of all people in a Spirit-filled encounter with God. The most widely used symbol for this environment among Pentecostals is the altar.[38]

As the altar call is an invitation into a sacramental environment, the human response is a physical manifestation of active participation.[39] The worshiper can publicly respond to the Spirit's prompting through the preached word or musical worship. Vondey sees the altar space as a threshold to the presence of God, so "the altar" functions symbolically as any place involving the invocation of the Spirit.[40] While Communion is the historical communal response to the preached word, Constance Cherry states that there should at least be some intentional response to the word in a worship service when Communion is not offered.[41] If worship truly is relational, then there must be a flow of reception and a response. The emotional, spiritual, and symbolic response to God at the altar keeps the relational flow active in renewal worship. Pentecostal worship largely avoids the language of sacramentality, but if we understand the altar symbolically as that responsive meeting place of the Spirit, then we can begin to understand how Pentecostals too have, at least in some sense, a sacramental theology.[42]

---

[37]Wolfgang Vondey, "Pentecostal Sacramentality and the Theology of the Altar," in *Scripting Pentecost: A Study of Pentecostals, Worship and Liturgy*, ed. Mark Cartledge and A. J. Swoboda (London: Routledge, 2017), 104.

[38]Vondey, "Pentecostal Sacramentality," 98.

[39]Vondey, "Pentecostal Sacramentality," 100.

[40]Vondey, "Pentecostal Sacramentality," 100-101.

[41]Constance Cherry, *The Worship Architect: A Blueprint for Designing Culturally Relevant and Biblically Faithful Services* (Grand Rapids, MI: Baker Academic, 2010), 99.

[42]For further reading see Andrew Wilson, *Spirit and Sacrament: An Invitation to Eucharismatic Worship* (Grand Rapids, MI: Zondervan, 2019).

The evangelical, sacramental, and Pentecostal principles reveal the importance of Scripture, ritual, and experience, respectively, for determining whether the worship practices of the faith community are theologically sound. As expressed above, each of these principles utilizes Scripture, ritual, and experience as sources for theology, but they all emphasize different sources as starting points for their theology. The most appropriate way to approach any of these principles is to give priority to God so as to avoid idolatry, but to hold Scripture alongside sacrament and experience so that the communal expression of worship is scripturally sound (evangelical), obedient (sacramental), and heartfelt (Pentecostal). Now that we have a sense of what a biblical theological method is and what this means for a Pentecostal interpretation of Scripture, let us outline a theological method for renewal worship by anchoring our system to the Acts 2 account, which typifies the Pentecostal narrative.

OUTLINING A METHOD FOR RENEWAL WORSHIP

When outlining a theological method, we are essentially clarifying how theological claims are made. We've already discussed the Pentecostal bent toward experience as a pre-text for renewal theology. A Pentecostal's encounter with the Spirit in worship (broadly defined as any experience of God) fundamentally affects the way a Pentecostal reads, interprets, and applies Scripture. As will be discussed further in chapter three, Pentecostals read their own stories into the greater Pentecostal narrative that begins in Acts. Pentecostals are not merely reading biblical history, but the origin story of their own spiritual lineage. The Pentecostal principle in renewal worship sees the direct encounter of the Holy Spirit as informing the Pentecostal's theological outlook, as each encounter with the Spirit adds something personal to the overarching story that began in Acts 2. Considering all this, our theological method for renewal worship takes the guiding narrative of Acts 2, and teases out two key themes that will help us situate any associated theological claims. These themes are that worship can be viewed as a continuous outpour, and that worship can be viewed as a foretaste of what is to come. As we will see, these themes must be taken together in order to gain a proper sense of what renewal worship means theologically.

Worship as continuous outpour. For Harold Best, the concept of worship touches on all of life when it is understood theologically as a "continuous outpouring." This phrase puts forward a biblically complete model of worship because it begins with God's initial outpour of Godself, and then accounts for the human response to this outpour, which is itself also a continuous outpour.[43] Best writes, "As God eternally outpours within his triune self, and as we are created in his image, it follows that we too are continuous outpourers, incurably so."[44] So for Best, because humans are made in the image of the revelatory God who eternally outpours, humans are also continuous outpourers.

Humans by nature pour out their devotion to something, and because of the fall, idols are often on the receiving end of endless adoration. Best writes, "At this very moment, and for as long as this world endures, everybody inhabiting it is bowing down and serving something or someone—an artifact, a person, an institution, an idea, a spirit, or God through Christ. Everyone is being shaped thereby and is growing up toward some measure of fullness, whether of righteousness or of evil."[45] The key is for worship to be directed toward God, the initial continuous outpourer. Even before creation God was relational through a triune ontology, pouring out immeasurable love to each interpenetrating person of the Trinity.[46] God's outpour to humanity is a gift and an invitation to participate in a continual relationship with the triune God.

While Best has expertly navigated what it means theologically for worship to be a continual experience, his theology approaches the triune God, strangely, exclusively through a christological lens, only brushing past the Spirit. He writes that Christ's sacrifice is a "once-for-all pouring out of his incarnate self on the cross."[47] While this is certainly true, the notion is incomplete as it fails to acknowledge the role of the universal outpour of the Spirit found in Pentecost as quoted at the beginning of this chapter. Consider Best's articulation

---

[43]Best, *Unceasing Worship*, 19.
[44]Best, *Unceasing Worship*, 10.
[45]Best, *Unceasing Worship*, 17. James K. A. Smith compellingly makes this same argument and highlights the role of ritual in personal and communal formation in James K. A. Smith, *Desiring the Kingdom: Worship, Worldview, and Cultural Formation* (Grand Rapids, MI: Baker Academic, 2009).
[46]Best, *Unceasing Worship*, 21.
[47]Best, *Unceasing Worship*, 20.

of God's continual outpouring through Christ: "Thus right now, and for as long as God himself decides it to be so, creation is being held together by the outpouring Word of his Son, in whom and through whom all things come into being and consist (Col 1:16-17; Heb 1:3)."[48] The Word is indeed the organizing principle of creation, but where is the Spirit in God's continuous outpour? Paul recognizes the Spirit's agency as the one through whom God's love is continually poured into our hearts: "And hope does not disappoint us, because God's love has been poured into our hearts through the Holy Spirit that has been given to us" (Rom 5:5). Without the Spirit, the continuous outpour of Christ from the cross cannot be grasped by the church. As the Spirit of life, the Spirit universalizes the redemptive consequence of the cross. For all of Best's talk about the continuous outpour as a triune act, he is remarkably silent about the Spirit.

A Pentecostal understanding of the continuous outpour would not only emphasize the role of the Spirit but would also see the event of Pentecost as pivotal for understanding the fullness of the Christian life. For instance, Macchia sees the Pentecost event as uniting christological, pneumatological, ecclesiological, and eschatological components. One can trace a unified notion of Spirit baptism that makes sense of God's continual outpour through Christ's mission. Christ's mission on earth was to bring people, and creation in general, back into life in the Spirit, which is a restored relationship with God. As Macchia writes, "His entire journey, from his incarnation to his crucifixion and resurrection, creates the means by which he incorporates all flesh into his life in the Spirit, his life with the Father. Mediating a river of the Spirit for others on behalf of the Father reveals Christ's very identity and mission."[49] Since the whole mission of Christ was aimed at bringing the created order fully back to life in the Spirit, it is clear that Christ would become the Spirit baptizer. The cross liberated fallen humanity through God's mercy, but God's grace was rendered accessible through Christ's resurrection. Macchia writes, "Christ's entire mission may be viewed as a baptism in fire (culminating in the crucifixion) and a baptism in the Spirit (culminating in the resurrection)—not two separate baptisms, mind you, but one in

---

[48]Best, *Unceasing Worship*, 21.
[49]Macchia, *Jesus the Spirit Baptizer*, 27.

Spirit-and-fire for our redemption."[50] The resurrected Christ, the firstborn
among many brothers and sisters (Rom 8:29), is the one who can baptize
others in the Spirit, imparting the Spirit in unity with the Father.[51] Because
Christ is the only true bearer of the Spirit, only he can mediate the Spirit.[52]

Christ's mediation of the Spirit extends beyond the individual believer.
Pentecost saw the Spirit being poured out on *all flesh* (Acts 2:17).[53] The universal outpour of Acts 2 implies that redemption extends to the whole created
order. Everything is in some state of redemption until Christ proclaims, "See,
I am making all things new" (Rev 21:5). While Christ established the kingdom
of God on earth during his earthly ministry, Pentecost is truly where our
communal confession of Jesus as Lord began.[54] At Pentecost the people of
God were gathered to form the confessing church, and the church was commissioned to extend the kingdom of God until its consummation at Christ's
return. At Pentecost the ministry of the kingdom of God—the extension of
the "Father's cause in the world"—was transferred to the church.[55]

Macchia's Christology posits that Pentecost should be our vantage point
for our theological deliberations. Every christological event including the
incarnation, crucifixion, and ascension should be discussed in light of Pentecost, "with Pentecost at the horizon."[56] Because Christ is glorified at the
ascension, it's tempting to view this event as the pinnacle of the gospel message.
However, we can only know the full meaning of the ascension once it's comple-
mented by the gift of Pentecost and the outpouring of the Spirit on the church.[57]
As Smith states, "The ascension is the triumph of God—Jesus is made Lord
and Christ as he returns to the right hand of the Father. But it is not the culmination. Pentecost follows, and it must follow for the purposes of the ascension to be fulfilled."[58] It is through Pentecost and the subsequent universal

---

[50]Macchia, *Jesus the Spirit Baptizer*, ix.

[51]Macchia, *Jesus the Spirit Baptizer*, 5.

[52]Macchia, *Jesus the Spirit Baptizer*, 55.

[53]This will be fleshed out further in chapter 5, but we should note that this is a quote of Joel 2.
Pentecostals believe that when Peter was quoting Joel 2 he was proclaiming the partial fulfillment
of Joel 2's prophecy.

[54]Macchia, *Jesus the Spirit Baptizer*, 35.

[55]Macchia, *Jesus the Spirit Baptizer*, 4.

[56]Macchia, *Jesus the Spirit Baptizer*, 64.

[57]Smith, *Evangelical, Sacramental & Pentecostal*, 27.

[58]Smith, *Evangelical, Sacramental & Pentecostal*, 25.

WHAT RENEWAL WORSHIP IS

outpour of the Spirit that the ascended Christ is present to each believing individual and the community of believers.[59] The universal outpour is, therefore, necessarily pneumatological. This vantage point is also eschatological because Spirit baptism drives the church toward eschatological fulfillment.[60] When reading the whole biblical narrative, we see strong themes that elicit a kingdom theology. Everything culminates in Christ, and Christ proclaims the kingdom of God as already present and not yet consummated.

Worship as a foretaste of what is to come. The eschatological hope of the church is renewal, and the mission of the church is to bring it about. In this way the righteousness of the kingdom of God is both now and not yet. We can view Christ's proclamation of the kingdom as God's inbreaking into human history, but the total consummation of the kingdom is yet to be fulfilled.[61] In Matthew 3:7-12, the kingdom of God is pictured as renewal through Spirit baptism; it is the reality where creation is reconciled back to God. The blind are healed, the oppressed are liberated, and the good news is proclaimed to the poor (Lk 4:18-35). Forgiveness of sins and Spirit empowerment are signs of the age to come already taking effect now, in the present,[62] and all this is made possible by the universal outpour of the Spirit. The ministry Christ inaugurated while on earth was carried out by the church after Pentecost and persists today. The church is commissioned to be God's agent in ushering in the already proclaimed but not yet consummated kingdom of God. As the church heralds the coming kingdom, real future hope proleptically enters into and forms our present circumstances. In Acts, God is characterized as the King who restores and reinterprets the present in light of the future.[63] So the eschatological hope in Peter's proclamation at Pentecost is real, efficacious hope, and not mere wishful thinking. God's promise of tomorrow transforms the realities of today.

For Macchia, this hope stems from Pentecost. Through the resurrection of Christ, the Spirit exceeds the limits of death, and then through Christ's

---

[59]Smith, *Evangelical, Sacramental & Pentecostal*, 26.

[60]Frank Macchia, *Justified in the Spirit: Creation, Redemption, and the Triune God* (Grand Rapids, MI: Eerdmans, 2010), 98.

[61]Macchia, *Jesus the Spirit Baptizer*, 214.

[62]Saliers, *Worship as Theology*, 58.

[63]Michael Salmeier, *Restoring the Kingdom: The Role of God as the 'Ordainer of Times and Seasons' in the Acts of the Apostles* (Eugene, OR: Pickwick, 2011), 79.

ascension and through Pentecost, the Spirit overflows the limits of death by being poured out on all creation. This overflow reaches eschatologically to the renewal of creation.[64] New life is thus given to all who partake in the Spirit's overflow. As Macchia states it, "This divine reign is actualized now among those who drink of the Spirit from him."[65] As much as this eschatological motif is addressed in various theologies of worship, the renewal perspective offers distinctive insight on how such a theological commitment manifests in practice. Packiam points out that hope is elicited by the charismatic expectation of God's presence made manifest by the Spirit. Experiencing the presence of God in worship is a foretaste of God's presence "filling all in all."[66] This means that renewal worship does not necessarily see hope defined through eschatologically themed lyrics; rather, hope is understood theologically as the Spirit's inbreaking through worship.[67] As Packiam writes, "For this experience of hope to occur, the songs need not be specifically about that hope; they simply need to be songs of worship that make the worshiper aware of God's presence."[68] The eschatological component of renewal worship is not an espoused theology, but an encoded theology that encrypts the eschatological implications of the universal outpour in the encounter of the Spirit during worship. In this way, renewal worship is unique in its approach to eschatological hope.

This eschatological motif can be elucidated further by revisiting the evangelical, sacramental, and Pentecostal principles, paying close attention to how these various approaches define the eschatological outlook of worship.[69] The evangelical principle points to biblical portrayals of worship as models for what we are to do and how we are to worship. As R. C. Sproul states succinctly, "Pleasing God is at the heart of worship. Therefore, our worship must be informed at every point by the Word of God as we seek God's own instructions for worship that is pleasing to Him."[70] Though we

---

[64]Macchia, *Jesus the Spirit Baptizer*, 296.

[65]Macchia, *Jesus the Spirit Baptizer*, 313.

[66]Packiam, *Worship and the World to Come*, 181.

[67]Packiam, *Worship and the World to Come*, 181.

[68]Packiam, *Worship and the World to Come*, 182.

[69]While Smith's distinctions raised this topic initially, what follows are observations that combine some implications drawn from Smith's text with other practical considerations.

[70]R. C. Sproul, *How Then Shall We Worship: Biblical Principles to Guide Us Today* (Colorado Springs, CO: David C Cook, 2013), 11.

can certainly craft biblical portraits of worship from passages throughout the Bible, one of the best-known biblical depictions of worship comes from the book of Revelation. Revelation 5:11-12 pictures representatives from all of creation surrounding Christ's throne in heaven proclaiming the worthiness of the sacrificed Lamb of God. Then in Revelation 5:13 every living creature sings:

> To the one seated on the throne and to the Lamb
> Be blessing and honor and glory and might
> Forever and ever!

This image is the quintessential eschatological experience of worship. For many evangelicals, this is the perfect view of heavenly worship and the prime example of how our worship should be modeled. In this view worship is ultimate and without end as we join "every creature in heaven and on earth and under the earth" to sing praises to Christ the King. Worship becomes the vision of the new creation.[71] In fact, several evangelical worship songs use Revelation 5 as a lyrical basis. The most famous of these is Jennie Lee Riddle's "Revelation Song."[72] For the evangelical, when a worshiper sings the words of Scripture through a song like "Revelation Song," the worshiper joins all the saints from every moment—all of creation is joined in song. The worship of the visible church takes part in the eternal worship of the invisible church. As ethnomusicologist Monique Ingalls points out, evangelicals often frame their musical worship experience through an eschatological discourse, encouraging worshipers to "understand their singing as participation with the heavenly community, as an aural contribution to the 'sound of heaven.'"[73] Worshipers join the choirs of heaven by singing together. This is the evangelical way to "perform the eschaton," as worshipers imagine their gathered community being part of the ideal heavenly community.[74] The evangelical principle

---

[71]Robert Webber, *Worship Old and New*, rev. ed. (Grand Rapids, MI: Zondervan, 1994), 192.

[72]"Revelation Song" was covered by many artists and helped propel Kari Jobe's career as a worship artist.

[73]Monique Ingalls, *Singing the Congregation: How Contemporary Worship Music Forms Evangelical Community* (Oxford: Oxford University Press, 2018), 74. Ingalls traces this sort of discourse from evangelical worship conferences, and since the conferences model what worship is like in heaven, local churches tend to adopt these styles of worship as well. This moral argument explains some of the stylistic, performative, and organizational choices made by evangelical churches.

[74]Ingalls, *Singing the Congregation*, 81.

envisions today's worship through the lens of eternity, which encompasses every act of worship—past, present, and future.

While the evangelical principle sees its eschatological outlook of worship as the present participation of eternal worship that is known only fully to God, the sacramental principle articulates the present-future phenomenon through a kingdom theology. The sacramental principle sees ritual and artistic expression as eschatological inbreakings of the kingdom of God. Theologian Don Saliers, for instance, posits that baptism and Eucharist are eschatological signs that bring about reconciliation:

> So it is that Baptism and Eucharist as the initiating and continuing sacramental actions carry a radical theological claim: Christ is present, the rule of God is very near, in fact the gifts given in the water bath and in the holy meal obliterate the conditions that keep us separated and alienated. We are reconciled to God and to neighbor. The communion is a foretaste of glory divine and a foreshadowing of the new Jerusalem.[75]

In baptism we are publicly initiated into the faith and reconcile with God by participating in Christ's death and resurrection.[76] When we submerge into the water, we participate in a physical mimesis of burial, and as we emerge from the water, we act out the promise of being resurrected at Christ's return.[77] The Eucharist helps us gain solidarity with those who are suffering in the world as we are united with the suffering Christ through his broken body and blood.[78] A glimpse of our ultimate reconciliation at the eschaton is on view as we are filled with Christ's pathos in the midst of a distressed world. So the presence of Christ at baptism reconciles us to God, and the presence of Christ at the Eucharist table reconciles us to each other. However, we will not need sacraments in eternity because faith becomes sight; but for the time being, "sacraments are the densest signs given to us for the ambiguous interim we inhabit on earth between the breaking in of God's reign and its consummation. In the sway of the Holy Spirit, the animator and medium of life, God's reign becomes tangible."[79] The sacraments in worship make the presence of

---

[75]Saliers, *Worship as Theology*, 60.
[76]Saliers, *Worship as Theology*, 56.
[77]Saliers, *Worship as Theology*, 57. Mimesis is the artistic and literary imitation of real life.
[78]Saliers, *Worship as Theology*, 42.
[79]Rempel, *Recapturing an Enchanted World*, 22.

God tangible to the worshiper in our age of already and not yet. The sacramental principle, therefore, sees God's eschatological inbreaking as taking place through the sacraments.

The liturgical arts also play a sacramental role in worship. Theologian David Taylor points out that an eschatological perspective is always intrinsically tied to a pneumatological reading of worship and the liturgical arts. The formational end of any act of worship is the "perfecting work of the Spirit."[80] As such, Taylor recounts the eschatological function of the liturgical arts through their ability to foster the Spirit's sanctification in the lives of believers. By the Spirit, the arts help form us to reach our eschatological goal in Christ. The arts aid in spiritual formation, helping us become more fully ourselves in Christ.[81] So like baptism and the Eucharist, the arts play a sacramental role in making the presence of God tangible to the worshiper.

Although the Pentecostal principle shares many characteristics with these approaches, it departs significantly from each position at crucial points. While the Pentecostal principle certainly agrees with the evangelical principle that our earthly worship participates in eternal heavenly worship, renewal theology seems best articulated as a kingdom theology. Renewal worship is eschatological when it sees God breaking into our present through experiential encounters of the Spirit. These divine encounters often yield spiritual gifts (tongues, healings, prophecies, miracles, etc.) as charisms of the age to come. Tongues give us a token of the deep and perfect communication that's available to us at the eschaton, healings give us a preview of our perfected spiritual bodies when we're glorified, prophecies announce and decree the reconciled future God has for us, and miracles foreshadow our renewed cosmos. Spiritual gifts are, therefore, foretastes of the coming kingdom. The Pentecostal principle's kingdom theology is unreservedly pneumatological, and spiritual gifts take center stage.

The sacramental principle, on the other hand, locates its kingdom theology liturgically in the sacraments. The presence of Christ is made manifest through the sacraments, so the foretaste of the coming kingdom is known primarily

---

[80]W. David O. Taylor, *Glimpses of the New Creation: Worship and the Formative Power of the Arts* (Grand Rapids, MI: Eerdmans, 2019), 219.

[81]W. David O. Taylor, "Mother Tongues and Adjectival Tongues: Liturgical Identity and the Liturgical Arts in a Pneumatological Key," *Worship Journal* 92 (2018): 68.

through the reconciling effects of the sacraments. As mentioned above, Pentecostals tend to be skeptical of rituals, seeing them as "merely formal, empty route activity, overly rigid, or a way of acting that is antithetical and impervious to the Spirit."[82] Like other Protestant traditions, baptism and Communion are the only sacraments acknowledged in the Pentecostal tradition, but they are typically viewed as symbolic public expressions of faith within the person's community. That's not to say, however, that these sacraments do not convey significant spiritual enrichment. While any act of worship is potentially sacramental in renewal worship, the Spirit mediates the presence of Christ through baptism and Communion. The rituals have no power in themselves, but the Spirit is present in them, and through them the Spirit points us back to the redeeming power of Christ.

Baptism, Communion, and Pentecostal sacramentality. According to Pentecostal theologian Andrew Ray Williams, one of the main reasons Pentecostals and charismatics have neglected robust accounts of water baptism is because they struggle to see its connection to Spirit baptism, which is largely regarded as the crown jewel of Pentecostal theology.[83] Early twentieth-century Pentecostals, for instance, talked about the importance of identifying with Christ in water baptism, but did not explicitly tie water baptism to Spirit baptism. They understood water baptism as ritually participating in Christ's death—being "buried" with Christ.[84] These early Pentecostals were taught to remember that resurrection can only occur after death, so to really identify with Christ, they must allow their old selves to die and be buried with Christ. Just as the Spirit raised Christ from the dead, so too will the Spirit raise believers up out of the baptismal waters.

To continue thinking about the Spirit's role in water baptism, Williams suggests we look beyond water baptism's judicial, ceremonial character, and recognize that it also has a relational character. Williams states that the "relational Spirit of God baptizes us into the *person* of Christ, enacting

---

[82]Donna Lynne Seamone, "Pentecostalism: Rejecting Ritual Formalism and Ritualizing Every Encounter," *Journal of Ritual Studies* 27, no. 1 (2013): 73.

[83]Andrew Ray Williams, *Washed in the Spirit: Toward a Pentecostal Theology of Water Baptism* (Cleveland, TN: CPT Press, 2021), 232.

[84]Williams, *Washed in the Spirit*, 43. For this point, Williams specifically cites the words of Aimee Semple McPherson in *The Bridal Call*, but many early Pentecostals borrowed the language of Rom 6:3-4 to identify with the death of Christ.

transformation from death to life."[85] Baptism, therefore, is not merely an outward profession of an inward change, but also an inward imparting of identity.[86] Through baptism, the Spirit leads us to share in Christ's death, burial, and resurrection.[87] So it is the Spirit through baptism who firmly establishes our new identity in Christ. To give water baptism a stronger connection to the reception of the Spirit, Williams suggests Pentecostals think about how the Spirit is active in the water of baptism: "Pentecostals ought to consider summoning the Spirit in the waters of baptism, thus bearing witness to 'the promise' of the gift of the Spirit for every new believer (Acts 2:39)."[88] Acts 2:38 states that once believers repent and are baptized, they will "receive the gift of the Holy Spirit." While this does not mean the solitary act of baptism confers salvation,[89] or that believers can *only* receive the Spirit through baptism, it does indicate clearly the Spirit's presence in and through the rite of baptism. So while Pentecostals would not equate water baptism with Spirit baptism,[90] they would see the rite of water baptism as a foretaste of a Spirit-baptized reality. The two are tied together as they both point to a future where all of creation is enraptured by the life-giving Spirit (1 Cor 15:45). Water baptism simultaneously looks back to the death and resurrection of Christ *and* looks forward in anticipation of the eschatological transformation of all creation.[91]

Communion can likewise be understood through a lens of renewal. Pentecostal theologian Chris Green articulates the importance of Communion in Pentecostal spirituality as centering around a posture of thanksgiving and communal inclusivity. The Eucharist symbolizes a participation in Christ's death (Mt 26:26-27), spiritual nourishment (Jn 6:53-57), and unity with Christ (1 Cor 10:17). But the Eucharist does not *just* symbolize what Christ has done for us on the cross. It reasserts the covenant of renewal we have entered into

---

[85]Williams, *Washed in the Spirit*, 196.

[86]Williams, *Washed in the Spirit*, 196.

[87]Williams, *Washed in the Spirit*, 197.

[88]Williams, *Washed in the Spirit*, 225.

[89]Throughout the book of Acts baptism is accompanied by a confession of faith.

[90]Pentecostals typically affirm Spirit baptism as subsequent to salvation.

[91]Peter Althouse, "Ascension—Pentecost—Eschaton: A Theological Framework for Pentecostal Ecclesiology," in *Toward a Pentecostal Ecclesiology: The Church and the Fivefold Gospel*, ed. John Christopher Thomas (Cleveland, TN: CPT Press, 2010), 245.

upon our salvation. It is in this remembrance that we rejoice in God's promise of renewal. As Green writes,

> Insofar as our Eucharist is a faithful thanksgiving, then the event is nothing less than a rite of covenant renewal. As we give thanks for God's covenant-making acts, offering up and receiving these gifts of bread and wine—gifts carried along by and embodying the sacrifice of our praise—we are also promising that we will continually offer *ourselves* to God, as *living sacrifices* (Rom. 12.2). At the Table . . . we are dialoguing with God, saying our Amen to his promise, our Yes to his graceful command.[92]

Covenant meals, like a Passover Seder, were annual renewals of a covenant that reminded participants of their allegiance to their Lord. Communion is a covenant meal—one that Jesus describes as a new blood covenant (Mt 26:28). There is a relational, two-way covenant at play in the Eucharist, and one could say in baptism. Both are more than mere acknowledgments of inward changes, but an anamnestic[93] recollection of how renewal is even possible. So for Green, Communion is a relational engagement with God's covenant of renewal, and in this sense there is a personal and corporeal encounter with Christ through the Spirit who seeks Communion with us.[94]

This sacramental view of the Eucharist and baptism points forward eschatologically to our ultimate renewal, but also stretches back to the cross and engages the long history of the "great tradition" of the church. This view fulfills Green's desire for a liturgy that is both received historically from the great tradition and speaks to our Pentecostal spirituality.[95] The key difference between this Pentecostal sacramental view and that of the sacramental principle highlighted above, is that the latter sees the actual rites as mediating the presence of God, whereas the former sees baptism and Communion as yet another way that the Holy Spirit is present in the lives of worshipers. The Spirit's work in baptism and Communion is to repetitiously synchronize

---

[92]Chris Green, *Toward a Pentecostal Theology of the Lord's Supper: Foretasting the Kingdom* (Cleveland, TN: CPT Press, 2012), 261-62.

[93]"Anamnestic" refers to remembering things from a previous existence, like placing yourself in and with Christ at his sacrifice.

[94]Green, *Toward a Pentecostal Theology*, 266.

[95]Chris Green, "Saving Liturgy: (Re)imagining Pentecostal Liturgical Theology and Practice," in *Scripting Pentecost: A Study of Pentecostals, Worship and Liturgy*, ed. Mark Cartledge and A. J. Swoboda (London: Routledge, 2017), 114.

worshipers to the redeeming work of Christ. So while Pentecostals expect the Spirit to be regularly present in every aspect of their lives and worship, they believe the Spirit is present in baptism and Communion in a special, chris-tomorphic way.[96] So while *any* encounter with God and manifestation of spiritual gifts are always, already sacramental, the spiritual presence of Christ is specially present in baptism and Communion.

Pentecostals enact a "ritual dynamic" that ties together important staple acts of a Pentecostal worship service such as music, testimony, prayer, and of course baptism and Communion.[97] Throughout this ritual dynamic, Pente-costals define their ecclesial practices in the context of Spirit baptism, so even baptism and Communion reflect the outpour of the Spirit. Baptism displays an initiatory response to Christ's gift of the Spirit as believers symbolically die to their sin and rise in the Spirit, and Communion displays a continuation of a life in the Spirit as the church unites in solidarity with Christ. These rites, and every rite, exists in order for us to be drawn back into life in Spirit.

Pentecostals link eschatology and pneumatology because they see Christ inaugurating the kingdom of God by the power of the Holy Spirit. The universal outpour of the Spirit in Acts 2 is the fulfillment of Christ's promise of the Spirit (Jn 16:7), and empowers the church for kingdom ministry. The continuous outpour of the Spirit qualifies renewal worship, and renewal worship then prevails as a foretaste of the coming kingdom. Spirit baptism is a theological metaphor that gets at the "pneumatological substance of eschatology."[98] As Macchia writes, "Eschatology is helpful for showing the expansive reach of pneumatology, because eschatology implies participa-tion in God that is both purifying and empowering, presently at work and still unfulfilled, and life-transforming and demanding in terms of how we will respond to the reign of God in our times."[99] The significance of the already and not yet in renewal spirituality requires our full theological appreciation of the Spirit of the last days. A theological method of renewal

---

[96]Christomorphism means to take on Christ's death paradigmatically in the Christian life.

[97]Seamone, "Pentecostalism," 79. Also, see Daniel Albrecht, *Rites in the Spirit: A Ritual Approach to Pentecostal/Charismatic Spirituality* (Sheffield: Sheffield Academic Press, 1999). Here Albrecht looks at the formational "rites" of the corporate Pentecostal/charismatic worship service. Like Seamone, Albrecht sees aspects of worship as existing in a Pentecostal ritual field.

[98]Macchia, *Baptized in the Spirit*, 91.

[99]Macchia, *Baptized in the Spirit*, 41.

worship is necessarily pneumatocentric and eschatological, and seeing worship as a continuous outpour of the Spirit and as an inbreaking of what is to come is, I believe, a fruitful framework for understanding renewal worship. For the final section of this chapter, let us flesh out our theological method a bit by briefly analyzing some ways that the Spirit heals and reconciles people and communities, bringing about the kingdom of God through renewal worship.

HEALING AND RENEWAL WORSHIP

For the Pentecostal, the ultimate inbreaking of the kingdom of God is the actual presence of God in the lives of believers. The presence of God is made tangible in worship principally through experiential encounters with the divine, and then through the blessings those encounters bestow. Pentecostals affirm sacraments as symbols of the age to come because Christ is spiritually present in and through them, but the sacraments are regarded as acts of worship observed through reverence and done out of obedience. Experiential encounters in worship, on the other hand, are viewed as direct, unmediated experiences with God. Worship does not make way for a divine encounter; the encounter itself constitutes worship. Worship is a response to the presence of God, and spiritual gifts come to believers reciprocally as gifts from God to the believer. When worshipers experience God in worship, they experience the God who is love and the source of all life. People are healed and reconciled spiritually, emotionally, and physically as a natural consequence of drawing close to God in worship. As God reconciles us in worship, we receive a foretaste of the total reconciliation that awaits all of creation at the eschaton. Spiritual gifts are, therefore, foretastes of what is to come, and this is particularly evident with miracles and the gift of healing.

Healings and other signs and wonders were necessary for Jesus' inauguration of the kingdom of God during his earthly ministry. As Macchia writes, "Miraculous signs and wonders were not incidental or nonessential to Jesus' ministry. Rather, these signs were at the very substance of his mission to inaugurate the reign of God in the world and to overthrow the reign of death, sin, and the devil."[100] Jesus performed signs and wonders in his

---

[100]Macchia, *Baptized in the Spirit*, 146.

ministry as a foretaste of the ultimate renewal of creation. The healings that occurred in Jesus' ministry were signs of redemption, healing, and reconciliation.[101] These ideas are held widely by adherents of kingdom theology, but what distinguishes the Pentecostal account of the kingdom of God is how these gifts are still applicable today, and specifically how they manifest in worship. For Pentecostals, "miracles represent nature in the power of the Spirit reaching for a glimpse of its future renewal."[102] Not only do miracles happen today, they carry eschatological significance as premonitions of future renewal. Healings should be seen in the same light. As Catholic theologian Francis Sullivan states, "Charismatic healing is a foretaste of the resurrection of the body, which God now freely grants, when and where he chooses, as a sign of his power to raise the dead to eternal life."[103] Thus healing is understood as a realization of our final states when we are glorified and resurrected with spiritual bodies (1 Cor 15:35-50). When we are healed physically and emotionally, we experience a small part of the ultimate healing that awaits us at the eschaton.

A kingdom perspective on healing properly situates the role of healing in Pentecostal spirituality. When healing is understood as a promise of the coming kingdom, then our eschatological reality becomes the goal of faith rather than a temporary healing in the here and now. Healings are essential to Pentecostal spirituality, but they are signs that point to God's *eschatological* aim of renewal. Some Pentecostals and charismatics vest so much interest in the present moment of healing that they lose sight of its ultimate, eschatological meaning. Healings happen when God chooses to break into our present lives and gives us a glimpse of what's to come. Healings happen on God's timing and for God's purposes; they are transformations that occur "when humans encounter God at the point of their need."[104] While God desires for all to be healed (Ex 23:25-26), ultimate healing occurs at the eschaton. And while it is important for believers to pray for present healing (Jas 5:14-15), they must trust that God's healing may come in this age or the next. Healings that

[101]Macchia, *Baptized in the Spirit*, 146.
[102]Macchia, *Baptized in the Spirit*, 147.
[103]Francis Sullivan, *Charisms and Charismatic Renewal: A Biblical and Theological Study* (Eugene, OR: Wipf & Stock, 1982), 165.
[104]Ruth Duck, *Worship for the Whole People of God: Vital Worship for the 21st Century* (Louisville, KY: Westminster John Knox, 2013), 235.

happen in this age are not ultimate, but point toward the ultimate healing that takes place at the eschaton. Nevertheless, Pentecostals believe in the efficacy of these signs, and know how important the gift of healing is for witness and spiritual edification.

Healings happen in renewal worship because God is present when the people gather to worship. Worship creates a charged space for God to bestow blessings upon people in the form of healings and miracles. As J. Rodman Williams writes, "Wherever people become channels of the divine power, extraordinary healings may be expected to occur."[105] Because Pentecostals believe worship is broadly sacramental, they have an expectancy for the Spirit of God when they worship. The Holy Spirit is the Comforter who "comes alongside us and dwells in us to provide God's solace, healing and power."[106] Since the Spirit is ever-present, the notion of "God showing up" is more a matter of worshipers turning their hearts toward God who is already present, and when worshipers are in tune with the life-giving Spirit, healings happen.

As the phrase suggests, *renewal* worship keeps its sights set on renewal, and healing is part and parcel of this notion. The theme of healing shows up lyrically time and time again in renewal worship and is often presumed to be in anticipation of the coming kingdom. Consider lyrics from the bridge of Tasha Cobbs Leonard's "This Is a Move":

> *Healing is coming in this room*
> *Miracles happen when you move*
> *Heaven is coming.*[107]

Leonard portrays miracles happening as a consequence of the presence of God. It is the Spirit who moves and brings healing. While the lyrics portray an expectancy of God in the here and now ("in this room"), the line "heaven is coming" gives a nod to God's movement as an eschatological inbreaking

---

[105]J. Rodman Williams, *Renewal Theology: Systematic Theology from a Charismatic Perspective* (Grand Rapids, MI: Zondervan, 1996), 256.

[106]Mark Labberton, *The Dangerous Act of Worship: Living God's Call to Justice* (Downers Grove, IL: InterVarsity Press, 2007), 56.

[107]"This Is a Move," words and music by Brandon Lake, Nate Moore, Tasha Cobbs Leonard, and Tony Brown, CCLI 7123068 © 2018 Bethel Worship Publishing, Brandon Lake Music, Mouth of the River Music, Tony Brown Music Designee, Meadowgreen Music Company, Tasha Cobbs Music Group (administrated by Bethel Music Publishing, Capitol CMG Publishing).

of God's reign. A similar idea is also evident in Hillsong Worship's "Cry of the Broken," written by Darlene Zschech:

> *I come boldly to your presence*
> *Lord I bow before your throne*
> *You're my healer* [108]

Like in "This Is a Move," the immediate presence of God makes healing possible and elicits eschatological hope. In both cases, healing is a charism of the age to come.

Healing is also regularly tied to the sanctifying power of the Spirit. For instance, in "Just One Touch" by Kim Walker-Smith, the presence of the Holy Spirit reveals beauty, joy, and freedom:

> *My joy overflows*
> *From all of Your beauty revealed to me*
> *I will not move*
> *Speak for Your Spirit is life to me.* [109]

Then later in the bridge, Walker-Smith associates the Spirit's healing with sanctifying refinement, as fire *leads* to healing. "Fire" in these lyrics should be understood metonymically [110] as the sanctifying grace of the Spirit, which is closely related to the image of a refiner's fire. Because healing here is tied to refinement, one can look to beauty as the telos of the process of sanctification and ultimate healing. In just a few lines, Walker-Smith has laid out a fairly complex theology of renewal worship: there is a continuous outpour ("joy overflows"), a divine revelation of an eschatological end ("Your beauty revealed to me"), a pneumatological emphasis ("Your Spirit is life to me"), sanctification ("Your fire"), and healing. Taken all together, we can see healing as a work of the Spirit, which comes to pass when worshipers come in contact with God's presence.

---

[108] "Cry of the Broken," words and music by Darlene Zschech, CCLI 5894220 © 2010 Wondrous Worship (administrated by Music Services, Inc.).

[109] "Just One Touch," words and music by Jordan Frye, Kim Walker-Smith, and Skyler Smith, CCLI 7084175 © 2017 Capitol CMG Genesis, Jesus Culture Music (administrated by Capitol CMG Publishing).

[110] Metonymy refers to the substitution of a thing's attribute to refer to its total meaning. The famous phrase "The pen is mightier than the sword" from Edward Bulwer-Lytton's play *Richelieu* uses two metonyms: the "pen" refers to winning mass appeal through writing, and the "sword" refers to subjugating people through war.

So far, we've focused specifically on individual healing through worship, but the gift of healing is not only for a person's physical, mental, and emotional health. When the Spirit is at work, the church as a whole benefits from social and communal healing as well. This is significant because worship has the power to reshape and heal the whole worshiping community, not just the individual. Social and communal healing may take the form of racial reconciliation, social and educational reform, efforts toward gender equality, the reintegration of former offenders into society, the acceptance and reception of disabled and marginalized people into a church community,[111] and the general striving for a just and peaceful society. This is a healing of society and social structures—the things that organize our communities. This message permeates Brooke and Scott Ligertwood, Cody Carnes, and Kari Jobe's song "Heal Our Land," which talks about God's healing affecting both the individual and society. Consider the lyrics of the bridge:

So God we pray to You
Humble ourselves again
Lord would You hear our cry
Lord will You heal our land[112]

Referencing 2 Chronicles 7:14, this song shows that "healed land" comes when we humble ourselves. Later in the bridge the lyrics state that once the land is healed, every person ("ev'ry eye" and "ev'ry heart") will know that healing and reconciliation were made possible by the cross. If we adopt a holistic approach to worship, we must recognize the role worship plays in communal reconciliation.

For Macchia, the universal outpour of the Spirit reveals Christ as our brother who takes others in.[113] The Spirit is poured out indiscriminately to people from every age, race, and gender so everyone can be drawn back into God's family. Worship reconciles us to God and to each other, and our

---

[111]Amos Yong, "Disability and the Gifts of the Spirit: Pentecost and the Renewal of the Church," *Journal of Pentecostal Theology* 19 (2010): 90.

[112]"Heal Our Land," words and music by Brooke Ligertwood, Cody Carnes, Kari Jobe, Scott Ligertwood, CCLI 7070516 © 2016 Kari Jobe Carnes Music, SHOUT! Music Publishing Australia, Worship Together Music, Writer's Roof Publishing (administrated by Capitol CMG Publishing, Hillsong Music Publishing).

[113]Macchia, *Jesus the Spirit Baptizer*, 28.

relationships are truly mended and healed when we stand in familial solidarity with others, especially with those who are suffering. Communities are healed and we are truly reconciled when we fight for justice in the lives of our suffering brothers and sisters. Jesus baptizes us all into the same Spirit, and worship unites us and conforms us to the heart of Christ who came to

> bring good news to the poor.
> He has sent me to proclaim release to the captives
> and recovery of sight to the blind,
> to let the oppressed go free,
> to proclaim the year of the Lord's favor. (Lk 4:18-19; Is 61:1-2)

It is God's vision for all of creation to be reconciled back to God and to live harmoniously together in God's presence. Since worship aligns us to God's heart, this communal sense of healing will emerge in our desires. Worship without action is inadequate. As Saliers puts it, "Our lives and our liturgies are incomplete until we learn solidarity with others who suffer, and allow others to touch our suffering."[114] Something is seriously wrong if worship does not result in actionable reconciliation. As mentioned earlier, the eschatological hope of worship is active, so true renewal worship will always elicit real change in the hearts of believers, and in the structures of community.

As worship helps to reconcile us back to God and to our communities, worship also reconciles communities to other communities. Unnecessary cultural boundaries are broken in worship. While each community carries its own cultural linguistic system, to use George Lindbeck's term,[115] these systems can exclude others to a point of discrimination. It's one thing when shared experience creates deep, particular solidarity within a culture, but it's quite another when cultural embargos are implemented to prevent inclusive engagement and meaningful dialogue between people. Part of the Pentecost narrative is that the Spirit was poured out on *everyone*—young and old, rich and poor, man and woman—so that all can *join* in the Spirit's witness. This crucial concept is repeated by Paul in Galatians 3:28: "There is no longer Jew

---

[114]Saliers, *Worship as Theology*, 135.

[115]George Lindbeck, *The Nature of Doctrine: Religion and Theology in a Postliberal Age* (Louisville, KY: Westminster John Knox, 1984), 33. Lindbeck describes a cultural-linguistic system as a framework that shapes the entirety of life and thought for a particular culture.

or Greek, there is no longer slave or free, there is no longer male and female; for all of you are one in Christ Jesus." The body of Christ is baptized into one Spirit, so in a legitimate sense—not one that is riddled by mere potboiler clichés—we are one family.

The boundaries that are broken by the Spirit are those that group people in castes and determine a person's worth by privilege. Macchia states it well: "The Christ who became flesh in order to pour forth the Spirit of life *upon all flesh* implies an understanding of humanity that lives from the Word of the Father's love and the liberation of the Spirit's witness, rather than from its own resources apart from God. All humanly conceived and exploited hierarchies of privilege are shattered."[116] In worship, people from every walk of life join together to humbly and vulnerably sing praises to God. As we lift our voices together in chorus, our pride and dissimilarities are checked at the door. Our status and fabricated hierarchies vanish when we join each other around Christ's table. We become what we've always been: brothers and sisters. The gift of healing is about making things right and making things whole, and this works individually, communally, and globally. God is present when the people praise (Ps 22:3, Mt 18:20), and when the Spirit of life is present, healing happens.

CONCLUSION

This chapter answered the question "What is renewal worship?" by establishing a theological method for a renewal theology of worship that is rooted in the Acts 2 account of Pentecost, utilizing, particularly, the universal outpour as a guiding motif. We sought to establish a Spirit-centered, eschatological model of theology that sees worship as a continuous outpour of the Spirit and as an inbreaking of what is to come. Worship begins when the unmerited gift of the Spirit is poured out on all flesh. Worship then continues as God's people respond to God's self-impartation. As mentioned in this book's introduction, this response is active and not passive, which gives worshipers a glimpse of the coming kingdom of God that has already broken into the present. This inbreaking of the kingdom of God produces physical, emotional, and spiritual healings in the lives of worshipers, and all this happens because of the

---

[116]Macchia, *Jesus the Spirit Baptizer*, 111.

immediate presence of the Holy Spirit in renewal worship. Since it is common in hymns for the final stanza to take on the form of a doxology, let us follow suit as we close out each chapter and consider doxologies that I've written to recapitulate the concepts discussed:

> *Praise God who fills our breath*
> *Renewing us afresh*
> *Praise God whose Spirit pours out on all flesh.*

2

WHO RENEWAL WORSHIP IS FOR

THE OBJECT OF WORSHIP

On the last day of the festival, the great day, while Jesus was standing
there, he cried out, "Let anyone who is thirsty come to me, and let
the one who believes in me drink. As the scripture has said, 'Out of
the believer's heart shall flow rivers of living water.'" Now he said
this about the Spirit, which believers in him were to receive; for as
yet there was no Spirit, because Jesus was not yet glorified.

JOHN 7:37-39

THE TEXT ABOVE is part of Jesus' teaching that took place during the Feast of Tabernacles, a harvest celebration where Jewish men and women remembered God's provision for the Israelites who wandered through the wilderness in the book of Numbers. Just as God offered water to the Israelites in the desert, Jesus offers the Spirit to believers after the ascension at Pentecost. But unlike the Israelites' water, which would eventually dry up or be consumed, the Spirit flows eternally as "rivers of living water." The Spirit never dries up and always flows in abundance. This came as a promise for God to once again "tabernacle" among believers, first through Christ the redeemer, and then forever through the abundant Spirit. Here the Spirit is the eternal Gift that believers receive.[1]

When God gives us the Gift of the Spirit, this is a kenotic gesture of God *giving* God to believers.[2] The Gift we are given is the eternal, abundantly

---

[1] *Gift* here is a name for God and so is capitalized and recognized as a proper noun.

[2] *Kenotic* is the adjectival form of the Greek word *kenosis*, which means "self-emptying" and refers to Christ relinquishing some of his divine attributes when he became human, which also allowed

flowing God. Knowing this about God is significant when we try to articulate a theology of renewal worship. The God we worship is the Gift-Giver *and also* the Spirit who is poured out as the Gift of God. At the same time, the Gift of God is the active agent that draws us back to God. Renewal worship understands this "drawing back" as part of the reciprocal nature of worship, which is part of a theology of abundance that characterizes our understanding of renewal spirituality. Christian worship in general is relational with aims to glorify God and to draw people into God's presence, but renewal worship focuses on a "theology of abundance" that sees God's Spirit being liberally poured out on all flesh. In other words, while all Christian worship recognizes the work of the Spirit in divine-human interaction, renewal worship *emphasizes* the Spirit in every aspect of its spirituality.

This chapter discusses the relational nature of renewal worship by advancing a theology of abundance. Since renewal theology focuses on the Spirit as the abundant Gift that was poured out on all flesh, this chapter looks at the sorts of relationships that are fostered through renewal worship. What is meant by a "theology of abundance" will be differentiated from prosperity teaching, though this chapter retains the notion that God desires us to live prosperously. This message is repeated and reinforced in musical worship, and particularly in spoken forms of worship, including testimony, preaching, and tongues. It is through this lens that we come to understand the object of renewal worship as the relational God.

THE SPIRIT AS GIFT

On the surface, the answer to the question "Who is worship for?" is an easy one to answer: God! Christians worship God alone, and anything propped up before God becomes an idol.[3] Although we can easily state God is the

---

him to suffer death. This idea is rooted in Phil 2:7-8 which states, "but emptied himself [*kenosis*], taking the form of a slave, being born in human likeness. And being found in human form, he humbled himself and became obedient to the point of death—even death on a cross." So as Jesus poured out his divine attributes at the incarnation, Jesus pouring forth the Spirit at Pentecost is once again a kenotic gesture.

[3] As will be discussed in further detail next chapter, worshipers can fall into idolatry. They can idolize themselves, or each other, or anything else including the experience of worship itself. But no Christian scholar will argue that anyone or anything besides God *should* be worshiped. Idolatry is regularly, and rightly, condemned by Christians as worshipers seek to offer God true and undefiled worship (Jn 4:23).

rightful recipient of our worship, the answer becomes more complex (and interesting) when we dig deeper and see how exactly this occurs concerning God's self-giving and relational character. Since God is self-emptying (universal outpour) and a generous Gift-Giver, there is a reciprocity involved in worship that must be noted. The concept of "gift-exchange" was popularized as a topic of academic concern by French sociologist and anthropologist Marcel Mauss who championed the idea of "the gift" by applying the concept of gift-exchange to social life. Gift-exchange regards the transfer of goods or services that necessitate giving, receiving, and returning. Mauss highlighted the social rather than economic functions of the gift, claiming that reciprocal social relations build up relationships between humans.[4] This means that gifts are in a way never free because there is always some expectation of reciprocal exchange. When someone is given a gift, something is expected in return for the gift. It might be as simple as gratitude, but something is always exchanged on a social level. Worship is not reciprocal in the sense that we the worshipers are also worshiped. But something *is* returned in worship—namely, love. Because God is relational, our worship is not a mere performance of love, but a loving exchange with the God who is love (1 Jn 4:8, 16).

Furthermore, when we recognize God as both Giver *and* Gift, then we begin to understand the kind of God we are worshiping. Gifts can be given as expressions of love, gratitude, friendship, solidarity, honor, and so on. While gift-giving is always a relational act between at least two parties, the Spirit is also the Gift that is given, and the gift-exchange is the act of love. Love is both an object (God is love) and an action (God loves) when the Spirit is given to worshipers. One of the earliest theologians to articulate the notion of "Spirit as Gift" was Augustine in the fourth century. Reading the Gospel of John, Augustine noticed that the Spirit given to believers as "living water" must be the "gift of God" from earlier passages.[5] In John 7 Jesus calls the Spirit the living water, but earlier in John 4:10, Jesus calls the living water the "gift of God": "If you knew the gift of God and who it is that asks you for a drink, you would have asked him and he would have given you living water" (NIV).

---

[4]Marcel Mauss, *The Gift: The Form and Reason for Exchange in Archaic Societies* (London: Routledge, 2010), 25.

[5]Augustine, *On the Holy Trinity; Doctrinal Treatises; Moral Treatises*, ed. Philip Schaff and Anthony Uyl (Woodstock, VA: Devoted, 2017), 232.

This led Augustine to conclude the following: "Because this living water, then, as the evangelist has explained to us, is the Holy Spirit, without doubt the Spirit is the gift of God."[6] Augustine also understands the gift of the Spirit to be love: "Wherefore, if Holy Scripture proclaims that God is love, and that love is of God, and works this in us that we abide in God and He in us, and that hereby we know this, because He has given us of His Spirit, then the Spirit Himself is God, who is love."[7] So, following Augustine, the important thing to take away here is that we worship a God who is fundamentally relational, and the gift we reciprocate in worship is love.

Calling God relational is not merely saying that God *acts* relationally. Rather, it's making the claim that God is relational *by nature*. The theological concept of *perichoresis* sees the persons of the Trinity as co-indwelling and mutually interpenetrating in a divine community of being. As such, not only does God foster divine relationality through God's own nature, but also draws us into relationship with God and each other through the revelation of the Son and by the Gift of the Spirit. As Don Saliers writes, "This dance around (*perichoresis*) of honor and blessing in the very heart of God will not rest content until it is also shared in brokenness and in the actualities of life."[8] God's great concern for us is marked by a desire for reconciliation and renewed relationships.

Renewal worship can be seen as a layered response to God's relational invitation of love through the Spirit. The first relationship fostered through worship is an up-down relationship, where the Spirit is poured out on all flesh as the abundant Gift of love. Worship, therefore, begins with God, as God graciously gives the Spirit to the people. Accordingly, this is a revelation that reveals God's worthiness to creation. After that, the second relationship fostered through worship is the down-up relationship where believers respond to God's revelation by turning their hearts toward God. Both of these relationships happen continually but are initially responses to God's self-revelation. Finally, the third relationship fostered through worship is a lateral relationship as the community reconciles and unites with each other and with God. As Frank Macchia states, "God in Christ, and through the presence of the Spirit,

---

[6] Augustine, *On the Holy Trinity*, 232.
[7] Augustine, *On the Holy Trinity*, 233.
[8] Don Saliers, *Worship as Theology: Foretaste of Glory Divine* (Nashville: Abingdon, 1994), 41.

reconciled the world to the divine life freely given, self-offered, and abundantly poured out on all flesh."[9] Just as an overflowing cup spills out over its surroundings, the relational experience of the abundant God in worship spills out over the individual and permeates the community.

Because God is relational by nature, there is already relationship *within* God's substance.[10] This means that God is not in need of others in order for God to experience relationship—God already experiences relationship between the persons of the Trinity. The first up-down layer of relation in renewal worship described above does not necessitate any sort of need for God's fulfillment. People are drawn into relationship with God as a grace and as a consequence of God's abundance. In other words, God did not create us in order to satisfy a pressing relational lack. As such, the reciprocal nature of renewal worship renders problematic the popular evangelical expression that people are "created to worship." Monique Ingalls points out that this slogan has become a "multivalent signifier of identity" for young evangelicals,[11] which attests to their true identity and purpose on earth. Ingalls writes,

> In this narrative, God is the author of the individual's story as it is lived out on a daily basis. Singing provides an embodied way of performing this identity, identifying with the divinely purposed roles and actions in the song lyrics of worship, love, surrender, and belief. Through musical performance and performative consumption, the worshiper aligns herself with this particular identity, embodying through song and dress her sincere intentions to be transformed into who she was "meant to be."[12]

At first blush, this notion sounds noble because it significantly elevates the importance of worship in a Christian's life, and helps young people form their identities as impassioned disciples. However, this notion disregards the reciprocity of worship when taken uncritically. Harold Best points out that creating something *to* worship might suggest God is in need of something external

---

[9]Frank Macchia, *Jesus the Spirit Baptizer: Christology in Light of Pentecost* (Grand Rapids, MI: Eerdmans, 2018), 298.

[10]The creedal Trinitarian formula states that God is one divine substance (*mia ousia* [Greek] or *una substantia* [Latin]), and three divine persons (*treis hypostaseis* [Greek] or *tres personae* [Latin]).

[11]Monique Ingalls, *Singing the Congregation: How Contemporary Worship Music Forms Evangelical Community* (Oxford: Oxford University Press, 2018), 66.

[12]Ingalls, *Singing the Congregation*, 66.

(worship) to bring God some sense of completion.[13] In other words, when worship is understood perfunctorily in this light, God is not fully self-reliant and people are made with a functional rather than relational purpose. Moreover, when worship is not understood through a framework of relationship, the notion of being "made to worship" can appear one-sided, as if worship is unilaterally directed to God by desireless automatons. Like robots, people will have been made merely to enact a specific function.

For an example of how this evangelical expression is regularly communicated, consider the words of worship leader and songwriter Matt Papa: "God created humanity to worship and obey Him (Gen. 2:15; Col. 1:16). . . . God, infinitely holy and worthy of adoration, has been 'set aside' (Rom. 4) by His quintessential creation as unsatisfying, unreliable, and at best useful."[14] Before critiquing Papa's choice of language, I do want to point out that the heart of his quote is exactly right. Papa is essentially saying that many people have chosen to worship other things instead of God, the only being actually worthy of worship. That point is perfectly accurate. But his phrase that "God created humanity to worship and obey Him" is problematic for the reasons cited above. I should also point out that the biblical passages he used to back up his remark don't actually convey what he's claiming. For instance Genesis 2:15 states, "The LORD God took the man and put him in the garden of Eden to till it and keep it." This only states that God gave Adam the vocation of caring for the land.[15] Although the concept of the image of God does carry the weight of representation of God, the function of "caretaker," nevertheless, comes *after* the creation of humans in the image of God (Gen 1:27). Furthermore, Colossians 1:16 states, "For in him all things in heaven and on earth were created, things visible and invisible, whether thrones or dominions or rulers or powers—all things have been created through him and for him." This states that everything was created by God "through him and for him." That phrase looks like it might indicate that we were created to worship, but creating

---

[13]Harold Best, *Unceasing Worship: Biblical Perspectives on Worship and the Arts* (Downers Grove, IL: InterVarsity Press, 2003), 23.

[14]Matt Papa, "The Worship Leader and Mission," in *Doxology & Theology: How the Gospel Forms the Worship Leader*, ed. Matt Boswell (Nashville: B&H, 2013), 56.

[15]One could argue that "till and keep" indicates Adam's priestly role in the garden, which would then make the garden a temple. Because those two words are only ever used together when referring to a priest, perhaps Adam's work carried a liturgical function as well.

something for Christ does not necessarily imply worship. That passage *does* imply relationship, however. When something is created *for* someone, the assumption that the creator will be in relation to the creation is obvious, but to state that the quality of the relationship is *necessarily* worship is a stretch of logic. Of course, we can take a more nuanced approach to this idiom, where "made to worship" actually means "made to be in a loving relationship with God." This might very well be what Papa has in mind, but it's not usually the connotation of the "made to worship" expression in evangelical circles. Perhaps it is best to say, "I was made for relationship with God," which is itself reciprocal and results in worship that reciprocates love. In this sense, relationship with the relational God takes precedence and worship is the anticipated consequence of the bond.

If you recall in the introduction of this book, we defined worship as "turning our hearts toward God as a response to God's self-revelation." This definition substantiates the initial universal outpour of the Spirit (the up-down relation) and the human response (the down-up relation). The down-up layer of relation in renewal worship concerns the human response of love to God's outpour of the Spirit. If love is what's reciprocated in worship, we should distinguish what is meant by love. The ancient Greeks had at least seven different words that could mean "love,"[16] but the Greek words most used throughout the New Testament are the nouns *philia* and *agapē*, which form the verbs *agapaō* and *phileō*. *Agapē* is commonly understood as a divine love, as God's selfless, sacrificial love. *Philia*, on the other hand, also means love, but connotes the more human "brotherly love," like friendship.[17] The passages that describe the love of God almost exclusively use these two words.

Another common Greek word for love is *erōs*, which signifies human desire that reaches toward fulfillment. *Erōs* is usually equated with romantic or erotic love. Often in the Christian imagination *erōs* is contrasted against *agapē* as a

---

[16]These are typically listed as *eros* (erotic love), *philia* (friendly love), *storge* (familial love), *agapē* (unconditional love), *ludus* (playful love), *pragma* (enduring love), and *philautia* (self-love). *Mania* (obsessive love) is sometimes included on this list as an eighth Greek word for love. See John Alan Lee, *Colours of Love: An Exploration of the Ways of Loving* (New York: New Press, 1973); and C. S. Lewis, *The Four Loves* (New York: HarperCollins, 1960).

[17]Considering the work of charity, one could also argue that *agapē* refers to assistance between unequals, whereas *philia* refers to assistance between equals.

vulgar form of love, like a lustful desire.[18] This notion is given a bit of credence since *erōs* is actually never used in the New Testament, and the only times it is used in the Greek translation of the Hebrew Bible (Septuagint), it typically connotes sexual desire. For instance, Esther 2:17 states, "The king loved Esther more than all the other women; of all the virgins she won his favor and devotion." In other books like Hosea and Jeremiah *erōs* translates from *'ahavah* as *eraston*, which is used to convey illicit love. However, other texts give *erōs* a positive connotation. For example, in Proverbs 4:6, Solomon tells us to love the anthropomorphized woman known as "Wisdom": "Do not forsake her, and she will keep you; love her, and she will guard you." Here *erōs* merely connotes a passionate desire, not lust. We should passionately pursue Wisdom, and our desires and motivations should be to know her more. This sense of *erōs* is not at all vulgar. In fact, I have argued elsewhere that this sense of *erōs* and *agapē* work together to form a full and holistic expression of love in renewal worship.[19]

For theologian Adam Cooper, *erōs* is the "fundamental disposition of all things to move towards their proper good and perfection."[20] This means that *erōs* is a dynamic, cosmic force—the innate drive for completion or fulfillment. If this is how *erōs* can be understood, then the down-up experience of worship entails *erōs*. In renewal worship, worshipers desire to know God more, so they pursue the experience of God. This desire is only momentarily quenched when worshipers dwell in the unmitigated presence of God. But since the nature of *erōs* is desire, then the longing for the presence of God perpetually returns with a fresh yearning for the Spirit. Fortunately, the Spirit indwells worshipers with "rivers of living water" (Jn 7:38) that will never run out and continually satisfy our pursuit of God. So renewal worship can be seen as a constant flow of desire and fulfillment as worshipers experience the abundant love of God.

These ideas are commonly present in renewal worship songs too. Consider some of the lyrics from Hillsong Young & Free's song "Pursue":

---

[18]See Anders Nygren, *Agape & Eros*, trans. Philip Watson (1953; repr., Chicago: University of Chicago Press, 1982).

[19]Steven Félix-Jäger, *Spirit of the Arts: Towards a Pneumatological Aesthetics of Renewal* (New York: Palgrave, 2017), 79-80.

[20]Adam Cooper, *Holy Eros: A Liturgical Theology of the Body* (Kettering, OH: Angelico Press, 2014), 18.

I'm desperate for Your presence
Longing to be with You
Lead me to a new place
More of You.[21]

Here the worshiper is in a desperate, longing pursuit of God. The worshiper
recognizes that one must surrender to God, so there is also a sense of sacrificial
love. What's significant about this is that *erōs* is not disconnected from *agapē*—
the love of desire is also a sacrificial love. *Erōs* and *agapē* must be taken
together to get a full sense of the reciprocal nature of renewal worship. It
should also be noted that God's love for us is not devoid of *erōs*. God may be
relationally complete apart from us, but God still desires to be in relationship
with us. It is not out of necessity, but out of grace that God desires a relationship with us. For instance, Cory Asbury's song "Reckless Love" demonstrates
both God's sacrificial love (*agapē*) and God's desire (*erōs*). By stating, "When
I was Your foe, still Your love fought for me," the verse demonstrates God's
agapic, sacrificial love. In fact, later in the verse, sacrifice is explicitly refer-
enced when it affirms that God paid everything out of goodness.

The chorus, however, depicts God's passionate pursuit of us with the line,

Oh, the overwhelming, never-ending, reckless love of God
Oh, it chases me down, fights 'til I'm found, leaves the ninety-nine.[22]

Then the chorus resolves, showing us that God's love was not earned but
received as a divine grace. Taken all together, "Reckless Love" is an excellent
example of the abundant, reciprocal love of God. There is a passionate pursuit
on both sides, which is best described as an expression of *erōs*.

The final layer of relation in renewal worship is the lateral relation. If
you can imagine each worshiper in a worship service experiencing the
up-down and down-up layers of relation with God, then perhaps you can
imagine the infinite God who gives abundantly, giving us love beyond
measure—a love that *over*flows. To stay with the continuous outpour motif,

---

[21]"Pursue," words and music by Aodhan King and Hannah Hobbs. CCLI 7032394 © 2014 Hillsong
Music Publishing Australia (administrated by Hillsong Music Publishing, Capitol CMG Publishing).
[22]"Reckless Love," words and music by Caleb Culver, Cory Asbury, and Ran Jackson, CCLI 7089641
© 2017 Cory Asbury Publishing, Richmond Park Publishing, Watershed Worship Publishing,
Bethel Music Publishing (administrated by Bethel Music Publishing, Essential Music Publishing
LLC, Watershed Music Publishing).

worship is the continual sharing of the Spirit. Worship is like a stream that always flows (continual outpour), but communal times of worship, along with intense individual encounters of God through personal acts of worship, are like the river overflowing. This overflow yields crops that nourish us spiritually, and what is yielded can also be seen as a foretaste of what is to come. Life in the Spirit sustains our reconciled relationship with God *and* others, and worship enacts the constant renewal the worshiping community needs and lives in, while pointing to a future where the promise of renewal is realized. So, because God's reconciling love spills out from the individual worshiper, the community collectively experiences the love of God too. Since God created all things and desires for all things to be reconciled back to God, one must view the individual's relationship with God in the context of the greater community, which God is constantly reconciling. As theologian Andy Lord writes, "Relationships involve responses to the love offered and experienced; it is not just a case of receiving without responding in transforming love to others. This is the case within a fellowship and yet cannot stop there as worship is of the God who created the whole world."[23] So, love that is reciprocated back to God is also reciprocated outward to the worshiping community.

Moreover, as the whole worshiping community shares God's love laterally, it becomes a true witness and testament of God's love to the world. We are called to evangelize by showing the love of God to others. This is what Jesus was talking about when he addressed the disciples: "I give you a new commandment, that you love one another. Just as I have loved you, you also should love one another. By this everyone will know that you are my disciples, if you have love for one another" (Jn 13:34-35). It is by reciprocating the love of God in worship that God's love is extended out beyond us. What's interesting is that this witness causes others to enter into worship as well. Consider what Jesus said in the Sermon on the Mount: "In the same way, let your light shine before others, so that they may see your good works and give glory to your Father in heaven" (Mt 5:16). Here it is our witness that shines, the witness which is evidenced by love (Jn 13:34-35), that causes others to "give glory to

---

[23] Andy Lord, "A Theology of Sung Worship," in *Scripting Pentecost: A Study of Pentecostals, Worship and Liturgy*, ed. Mark Cartledge and A. J. Swoboda (London: Routledge, 2017), 91.

[our] Father in heaven." Giving glory to God is part of what it means to reciprocate the love of God. In other words, people are compelled to worship God
when our witness of love is on display. Worshiping the relational God entails
all of the following: God's love poured out on us as Spirit, our response of love
to God and others, and the reconciliation of communities back to God so
that all can enter into a loving relationship with God. Key to all of this is
understanding God as ultimate Gift-Giver, an essential concept that animates
a theology of abundance.

A THEOLOGY OF ABUNDANCE

Right at the start of their book *For Life Abundant*, Dorothy Bass and Craig
Dykstra describe what a theology of abundance entails: "God in Christ promises abundant life for all creation. By the power of the Holy Spirit, the church
receives this promise through faith and takes up a way of life that embodies
Christ's abundant life in and for the world. The church's ministers are called
to embrace this way of life and also to lead particular communities of faith
to live in their own situations."[24]

Here we can see how abundant living is God-given, rooted in Christ,
empowered by the Spirit, and ministered through and by the church. I would
also add an eschatological component to abundant living that sees God's
generous Gift as a foretaste of what is to come. A theology of abundance does
more than merely recognize our God-given abundance, it also stresses how
the people of God become people that practice a "life-giving way of life."[25] In
addition to the Gift of the Spirit, the church is given provisions that can be
used to help others and promote life, and are given spiritual gifts to continually extend the kingdom of God on earth. A theology of abundance encompasses a way of life, not a one-sided reception of divine blessing.

As stated above, the up-down and down-up levels of relation overflow with
God's love, and it is from this overflow that one graciously gives. We cannot
ignore the fact that a theology of abundance entails blessing and prosperity
for those who are in God. The logic is simple: in order to give out of our

---

[24]Dorothy Bass and Craig Dykstra, "Introduction," in *For Life Abundant: Practical Theology, Theological Education, and Christian Ministry*, ed. Dorothy Bass and Craig Dykstra (Grand Rapids, MI:
Eerdmans, 2008), 1.

[25]Bass and Dykstra, "Introduction," 6.

God-given blessings, we must first be blessed. This biblical concept is even evident as the people of God were envisaged in Genesis 12:1-2. Consider what was said to Abraham when God called him to leave Haran and settle in Canaan: "Now the LORD said to Abram, 'Go from your country and your kindred and your father's house to the land that I will show you. I will make of you a great nation, and I will bless you, and make your name great, so that you will be a blessing.'" While this promise depends on Abraham's obedience, God promises to bless Abraham holistically—even with material sustenance—so that he can be a blessing to others. If we take a holistic approach to our spirituality, the notion of blessing must concern materiality along with spiritual and emotional well-being. Our response should neither be an ascetic rejection of materiality, nor should it permit a gross indulgence of the finer things in life. Instead we must articulate a nuanced interchange concerning prosperity in a theology of abundance. When dealing with material prosperity, there are two equal and opposite snares one must sidestep: scarcity and greed. Let's look at each of these pitfalls.

What a theology of abundance is not. Old Testament scholar Walter Brueggemann points out that the Bible begins with a "liturgy of abundance," and that Genesis is a "song of praise for God's generosity."[26] In Genesis 1 God lovingly puts everything in order and calls it good. God gives life to plants and animals and then breathes life into humankind. God then commands humans to be fruitful and multiply (Gen 1:28). This means that the *very first* commandment God gave humanity was one of abundance. God calls "everything in its kind . . . to multiply the overflowing goodness that pours from God's creator spirit."[27] The command to "be fruitful" is an injunction to share in and bring forth God's abundance. Finally, God rested and marked the Sabbath because six days of work is more than enough! Sabbath observation preserves our experience of the abundance God has given us.

As Pentecostal pastor and theologian A. J. Swoboda writes in his book *Subversive Sabbath*, "Without a day of Sabbath, we are not able to enjoy our abundance. In other words, we make a living but have no time to live . . . Sabbath is not only a day to recharge for the six days of challenging work

---

[26]Walter Brueggemann, "The Liturgy of Abundance, The Myth of Scarcity," *The Christian Century* 116, no. 10 (1999): 342.

[27]Brueggemann, "Liturgy of Abundance," 342.

ahead. It is also the reason we endure six days of hard work."[28] Sabbath was never established as a rule for its own sake, but as another provision that helps us keep right perspective of God's bountiful sustenance for our lives. As such, Sabbath observance became an integral aspect of ancient Hebrew worship (Ex 20:8-11; 35). In Exodus, families were instructed to gather enough manna the day before Sabbath so that they would have enough food to eat on Sabbath day without having to gather anything additionally. This kept Sabbath day free from any sort of work and preserved it as a true day of rest. These "rules" were not to be implemented legalistically so as to burden the people; actually, the opposite is true. These guidelines were supposed to be observed as a means to safeguard our rest in God. This is what Jesus meant when he corrected the Pharisees in Mark 2:27-28: "Then he said to them, 'The sabbath was made for humankind, and not humankind for the sabbath; so the Son of Man is lord even of the sabbath.'" Gathering provisions prior to the Sabbath was to keep the spirit of Sabbath intact, namely, to rest in God's abundance. Sabbath, above anything else, is a day of rest so we can remember and enjoy the abundant provisions God has given us.

However, Brueggemann points out, as we continue reading Genesis, the "myth of scarcity" creeps up and threatens the notion that God has indeed given us more than enough. This is evident when, in the face of famine, Pharaoh greedily takes all the land and resources he can gather (Gen 47).[29] Pharaoh's mindset is a common one that is still with us today. The fear of there not being enough opposes generosity and drives us to exclude people. As Miroslav Volf writes, "We exclude because in a world of scarce resources and contested power we want to secure possessions and wrest the power from others." But as Volf and Brueggemann point out, there is more than enough to go around in our world, so the idea of scarcity is the fantasy that ironically drives greedy consumption. The fear of shortage feeds a "theology of scarcity" that says there is not enough, and we must fight tooth and claw to survive. Most people do not knowingly subscribe to a theology of scarcity, but many dutifully live by its tenets. A theology of abundance, on the other hand, says that God has generously given us life and love.

---

[28] A. J. Swoboda, *Subversive Sabbath: The Surprising Power of Rest in a Nonstop World* (Grand Rapids, MI: Brazos, 2018), 84.

[29] Brueggemann, "Liturgy of Abundance," 343.

Abundant living situates us in victory. So when times are tough and we experience suffering, or even when our lives on earth end, our well-being cannot be taken from us.[30] God's abundance is eternal, and in Christ and by the power of the Holy Spirit, there's always more than enough. In times of famine or persecution, the sustaining wellspring is necessarily spiritual, as the posture of worship and gratitude changes perspectives and makes every circumstance teem with grace in preparation for deliverance. Perhaps this is what drove Paul and Silas to pray and sing hymns to God while in jail (Acts 16:25-31). Their worship miraculously delivered them out of jail, and their extension of grace led to the salvation of the jailer and his household. Our circumstances, good or bad, are what they are and are many times out of our control, but our responses to these circumstances are ours alone. So let's allow the abundance of God to compel us to respond well in crisis.

Theologies of abundance are also often contrasted with atonement theologies. Unlike that of scarcity, however, these theologies do not oppose each other. Rather, these theologies are differentiated in their application for evangelism. Theologian Ronald Nydam, for instance, thinks that a theology of abundance is the best starting point for sharing the gospel, especially given our global, pluralistic age. Because the modern mind believed all truth could be uncovered and explained, empirical modes of knowledge superseded any kind of arational religious or spiritual beliefs. Empirical thinking was perceived to be clear-cut and rationalistic—uncompromising. As a response, Christians developed rational approaches to evangelism, and the best method for showing someone they needed salvation was to challenge their optimistic self-reliance and show them that they were deeply flawed. In other words, we had to convince people that they were sinners before we could share the good news of salvation with them. In modernity, therefore, evangelism started with the fall and ended with salvation, which incidentally are the same parameters that mark the doctrine of atonement.[31]

Atonement can only be used as a gateway to salvation if the person seeking atonement is well aware of his or her own sin. Put differently, the acknowledgment of sin precedes the want of atonement. In his book *A History of Sin*,

---

[30]Brueggemann, "Liturgy of Abundance," 343.

[31]Ronald Nydam, "The Relational Theology of Generation Y," *Calvin Theological Journal* 41 (2006): 327.

theologian John Portmann defined atonement as "heartfelt contrition coupled with a genuine intention to avoid sin."[32] Hence, sin and atonement go hand in hand. While the idea of sin was particularly tangible in modernity, this is not necessarily the case for people living in a pluralistic age surrounded by competing worldviews. Because of technology, increased international travel, and advanced global interactions, competing worldviews are on display and readily approachable. These worldviews exhibit complete ways of living with their own religious impulses, norms, and ethical standards. Thus, cultural relativism is part of the reason why sin is not so easily defined today, and atonement theologies have progressively grown ineffectual as starting points for evangelism. Portmann sees this theological shift as ignominious,[33] claiming that Western society is merely "tired" of sin. Portmann writes, "Forgiveness now often amounts to a weary resignation that what's done is done. . . . These psychological responses indicate sin fatigue. If we weren't tired of sin (or of trying to figure it out), we wouldn't bend atonement to fit our busy schedules or scoff at it altogether. Sin fatigue has ushered in atonement fatigue."[34] Likewise, the late Reformed theologian Gordon Clark viewed this shift as a major crisis.[35] He claimed that a new paradigm of abundance was "nonsense" and that the Western church was inadequately prepared for it.[36] To combat this, Clark called for a resurgence of strict fundamentalist biblicism and a full-throttle rejection of postmodernism.[37] What Clark is missing is that a mere awareness of sin is not the same thing as salvation. We should be less concerned about which doctrine brings people to the door of salvation, and more concerned about people actually hearing the gospel and turning to God. Clark's call to reemphasize the doctrine of atonement for evangelism is really a call to return to outmoded approaches for reaching the modern mind.

The times have changed, but the gospel has not. The best thing to do now is to find appropriate ways to minister the same gospel in new circumstances. To use an analogy, modern-minded people have gone through the front door marked "atonement" to enter salvation. People today might have wandered

---

[32]John Portmann, *A History of Sin* (Lanham, MD: Rowman & Littlefield, 2007), 33.
[33]Portmann, *History of Sin*, 3.
[34]Portmann, *History of Sin*, 33.
[35]Gordon Clark, *The Atonement* (Jefferson, MD: The Trinity Foundation, 1987), 167.
[36]Clark, *Atonement*, 169.
[37]Clark, *Atonement*, 169.

away from that door, but they're still by the building. As people hang out near a side door marked "abundance" it would be wise for someone to crack open the door and invite them in. Inside the door, they enter the same house. The house is salvation, and once inside, the person will repent out of a desire to reciprocate God's abundant love. Their sins *will* be washed away by the blood of Christ, and atonement *will* be actualized. Revisiting the overflowing cup analogy, what's the fastest way to get all of the air out of an empty cup? Is it to put the cup in a vacuum and somehow extract the air little by little? No. The fastest way is to fill the cup with water and let it overflow. In the same way, the fastest way to get sin out of our lives is to allow the Spirit to be poured over us and to let the love of God overflow in us. This sentiment makes much more sense to people in a global, pluralistic age because people today have a desire to experience the abundant love of God. It's no wonder that songs that emphasize God's abundant love like "Reckless Love," "There's an Overflow," and "The Blessing" have quickly garnered international recognition.

A theology of abundance essentially reverses the emphasis of sin's prospect as a guiding motive for spirituality. Theologian Sallie McFague says it perfectly: "We learn how we should *not* live ('sin') by becoming aware of how we *should* live ('salvation'). When we accept that we were created by love and for love, that all things come from overflowing divine abundance and are intended to flourish through interdependence with God and others, then we begin to sense what salvation is."[38] Instead of letting a fear of sin drive our motives, a theology of abundance allows the blessings that come from salvation guide us. Salvation means we have been liberated from the bondage of sin, so if we are truly liberated, we must also allow our minds and instincts to be liberated as well. We cannot live in a fear of retracting back to the life we left, but we must live in the Spirit—in the new life that God has bestowed upon us. The choice of adopting an atonement theology or a relational theology of abundance as a guiding system can be likened analogically to a marriage. Is it better for a couple to get married because they have a fear of being alone, or because there is an abundance of love between both parties that calls for eternal commitment? This is the life of blessing presented to us by God's abundant love.

---

[38]Sallie McFague, *Life Abundant: Rethinking Theology and Economy for a Planet in Peril* (Minneapolis: Fortress, 2001), 21.

Differentiating prosperity from abundance. Renewal worship and theology focuses on the Spirit as abundant Gift, but the concept of abundance should be distinguished from the so-called "prosperity gospel." While a theology of abundance also encloses the notion of prosperous living, the prosperity gospel is a much narrower outlook that espouses capitalistic commitments, which can distort the ideas of spiritual holism that are central to abundance. A theology of abundance speaks of a life of rich provision that's gratefully received *and* generously given. Abundance is part and parcel of the life and teachings of Jesus. This is apparent in John 10:10 when Jesus says, "The thief comes only to steal and kill and destroy. I came that they may have life, and have it abundantly." What's evident is Jesus' desire for all to have abundant life. Christ makes this possible through his incarnation and sacrifice, calling us away from lives of scarcity and destruction and toward lives of fullness and vivacity. Furthermore, Paul echoes these sentiments in his second letter to the Corinthians: "And God is able to provide you with every blessing in abundance, so that by always having enough of everything, you may share abundantly in every good work" (2 Cor 9:8). Paul sees God's free gift of abundance as a means and mandate to share the blessing. God's good gifts are meant to be extended so that all can be blessed by them. When prosperity teachings turn completely insular, forgetting the key notion of sharing out of one's abundance, they betray the communal commitments of the Gift.

For our theology of renewal worship, I have opted to use the term "theology of abundance" instead of "prosperity gospel" because I believe it more accurately portrays the holistic nature of God's Gift-Giving as people are blessed spiritually, physically, and emotionally. It also allows us to avoid the many negative connotations that can be found through some of the more fanatical expressions of the doctrine. Though easily abused, there are some tenets of the prosperity gospel that are biblically sound, so the doctrine must be taken critically instead of rejected wholesale. At its core, the prosperity gospel teaches that God desires for Christians to be blessed and prosper in all facets of life.[39] God's children are given health and prosperity because God desires good for those who love God and are called to God's purposes

---

[39]Katherine Attanasi, "Introduction: The Plurality of Prosperity Theologies and Pentecostalisms," in *Pentecostalism and Prosperity: The Socio-Economics of the Global Charismatic Movement*, ed. Katherine Attanasi and Amos Yong (New York: Palgrave Macmillan, 2012), 3.

(Rom 8:28). To support the idea that God wants believers to prosper, adherents look to verses that describe God's desire for people to be blessed abundantly (Jn 10:10). To propagate health and prosperity, the doctrine cites the principle of sowing and reaping (Gal 6:7). By emphasizing material well-being, the prosperity gospel is sometimes called the "health and wealth gospel."

Yet, some renditions of the doctrine claim that health and prosperity come to believers in a manner commensurate to their faith. This line of thinking regularly takes on the moniker "word of faith" teaching, which claims a person has power over health and provision through faith. While these notions are helpful for impoverished and marginalized groups that need empowerment over dire circumstances,[40] to the already affluent this mentality can perpetuate greedy consumerism and anticommunal individualism. Furthermore, word of faith teachings could imply that those with material wealth have demonstrated more faith than those who are impoverished. This reasoning is sometimes used to justify a minister's request for more financial giving. Hence, the term "prosperity gospel" is often used pejoratively to refer to teachings that perpetuate materialism and capital gains through emotional manipulation.

Most expressions of the prosperity gospel, however, do not view prosperity only in financial terms. Prosperous living also includes spiritual, physical, and emotional health,[41] so a holistic abundant life is not limited to financial success. To this point Macchia writes, "Not all such churches distinguish themselves by a narrow accent on prosperity, but they all typically share the conviction that faith in Christ should lead to material well-being. Their preaching has highlighted divine healing of the body as well as well-being and prosperity through faith in Christ."[42] Moreover, non-Western expressions of the prosperity gospel are usually responses to context-specific problems of poverty; they do not merely take part in a universal drive for material consumption.[43]

---

[40]Edward Suh argues that while the exploitative renditions of the prosperity gospel require critique, many versions actually promote empowerment and human flourishing for marginalized groups. See Suh, *The Empowering God: Redeeming the Prosperity Movement and Overcoming Victim Trauma in the Poor* (Eugene, OR: Pickwick, 2018), 3.

[41]Attanasi, "Plurality of Prosperity Theologies," 4.

[42]Frank Macchia, "A Call for Careful Discernment: A Theological Response to Prosperity Preaching," in *Pentecostalism and Prosperity*, 226.

[43]Macchia, "Call for Careful Discernment," 228.

But although there are situations where the prosperity gospel is helpful and even necessary, the doctrine is often maligned as a false doctrine of consumeristic materialism wherein shepherds "fleece their flocks,"[44] promising exponential returns from tithes because God is *bound* by the laws of prosperity. If material wealth does not return exponentially to a giver, some prosperity teachers attribute it to a lack of faith on the part of the giver. While this is just one side of prosperity teaching, there are many examples of these abuses and bombastic rhetoric (I will highlight some below). These abuses begin and end with consumerism, thus bearing capitalistic interests. Perhaps we can view these abuses as a form of prosperity teaching that has been contextualized to wealthy capitalistic Westerners. When more prosperity is promised to the already wealthy, the rhetoric can perpetuate the ever-expanding consumption of goods and bolster greed. These abuses seem to go against Paul's call to bless others out of our divinely blessed abundance. Abusive prosperity teachings see the blessed "other" as the church or parachurch institution that directly profits from the gifts. The benefits reaped are used to fund buildings, new technologies, and even the lavish lifestyles of prosperity ministers. The people who reap the benefits are the adherents themselves, not their surrounding communities. But again, it must be noted that this mentality is not indicative of every expression of prosperity teaching around the world. Because prosperity gospels are globally contextualized and take on many forms, what is needed is a greater sense of discernment to determine what ways these prosperity teachings go along with a theology of abundance and in what ways they do not.

Historian Kate Bowler makes a helpful distinction between *hard* and *soft* prosperity in her book *Blessed*. She contends that while all prosperity teachings hold to notions of faith, victory, and wealth, the teachings vary in how forcefully they adhere to prosperity principles that are considered laws (such as the principle of reaping and sowing, for instance). Describing hard prosperity, Bowler writes, "Hard prosperity drew a straight line between life circumstances and a believer's faith. Faith operated as a perfect

---

[44]Femi Adeleye, "The Prosperity Gospel and Poverty: An Overview and Assessment," in *Prosperity Theology and the Gospel: Good News or Bad News for the Poor*, ed. J. Daniel Salinas (Peabody, MA: Hendrickson, 2017), 19.

law, and any irregularities meant that the believer did not play by the rules."[45] Thus, proponents of hard prosperity state that financial failures demonstrate a lack of faith on the part of the giver since God desires for believers to always succeed.

Conversely, Bowler says soft prosperity "appraises believers with a gentler, more roundabout, assessment."[46] While soft prosperity teachers hold to general precepts concerning abundant living, they do not hold to the rigid and formulaic principles of hard prosperity. This optimistic assimilation of soft prosperity is what has entered many mainstream churches around the globe and is the expression of prosperity that most influences renewal worship.[47] Bowler's distinction helps discern between teachings that express the biblical truths of abundance from those that make materiality the central focus of the message.[48]

To nuance the theological notion of prosperity even further, Pentecostal theologian Amos Yong created a typology that distinguishes five theological justifications for prosperity teachings. At one pole are those that argue "for prosperity," stating "the Bible portrays God's desire to bless his people with spiritual, physical, and material abundance."[49] Because Christ's ministry holistically affected both the spirit and body of all those he encountered, we should strive for holistic prosperity in our own lives. For those who find themselves in dire poverty, this stance can give them the hope needed to gradually overcome poverty.[50] At the opposite pole are those that argue "against prosperity," positing the gospel renounces motivations for material gain. Here adherents do not oppose prosperous living per se but believe we should strive for spiritual, not material, gain. Yong points out, however, that this view may be duplicitous, since many of these adherents tend to already be financially wealthy.[51] This view says that any motivation for prosperity is permitted but should be theologically neutral. Considering these opposing

---

[45] Kate Bowler, *Blessed: A History of the American Prosperity Gospel* (Oxford: Oxford University Press, 2013), 97.

[46] Bowler, *Blessed*, 8.

[47] Bowler, *Blessed*, 237.

[48] Macchia, "Call for Careful Discernment," 232.

[49] Amos Yong, "A Typology of Prosperity Theology: A Religious Economy of Global Renewal or a Renewal Economics?," in *Pentecostalism and Prosperity*, 19.

[50] Yong, "Typology of Prosperity Theology," 17.

[51] Yong, "Typology of Prosperity Theology," 21.

views, the disunion between them seems too clear-cut and univocal. They both make important points, but adhering to either one or the other can easily result in the demonization and outright dismissal of the other view. Instead of falling into easy reductions of opposing views, perhaps it would be best to consider other perspectives that fall somewhere between these two.

Yong also suggests three median positions that consider ministerial and social factors the other arguments might have overlooked. Yong calls the first of these positions the "missional argument." This view states that wealth is neutral, neither good nor bad, but can be used to extend God's mission in the world. A person's wealth ultimately belongs to God anyway, so if God blesses someone with riches, it should be used for godly purposes. A person's resources should be used for evangelization, not merely for personal pleasure.[52] Since a person's true treasure is in heaven (Mt 6:19-20), wealth on earth should be used now missionally to extend both temporal and eternal blessings.

Yong names the next argument the "contextual argument." This argument claims prosperity and holistic well-being are integral parts of a person's salvation.[53] This is one of the most prevalent forms of the prosperity gospel among the impoverished areas of the Global South. In order to differentiate the missional and contextual arguments, Yong writes, "Whereas the missional argument presents the perspective of those who are engaged in missionary or evangelistic work, the contextual argument emphasizes the viewpoint of those who are being missionized and evangelized."[54] In other words, a person's financial position and ministerial calling determine in large part to which of these views they are drawn. These two arguments together encompass the mindset of many Christians engaged in global missions throughout the world.

The fifth and final argument presented by Yong is called the "balanced argument." This view attempts to look at the whole biblical witness to articulate a normative stance on prosperous living, and in doing so it rejects some aspects of the prosperity gospel.[55] This view states the Bible extends three guiding themes regarding prosperity. First, a person's prosperous living should never be a stumbling block to others (1 Cor 8:13). Does the prosperity teacher

---

[52]Yong, "Typology of Prosperity Theology," 21.
[53]Yong, "Typology of Prosperity Theology," 23.
[54]Yong, "Typology of Prosperity Theology," 23.
[55]Yong, "Typology of Prosperity Theology," 25.

live abundantly or immodestly? Does the teacher's living testimony hurt the fidelity of the prosperity gospel's potential message of hope? If one's subsistence is overtly lavish and materialistic, one could become stumbling blocks to the very people one is trying to help. Second, adherents should strive for shared, communal prosperity. Once a person is prosperous, that person should extend philanthropic giving to help others prosper. Third, and finally, a person's prosperity should be measured by how much the person can give away to help others, not by how much that person can store up. These principles together demonstrate what looks like a global renewal adaptation of the Protestant ethic that values hard work and godly stewardship.[56] This balanced argument can also work in conjunction with the missional and contextual arguments. In fact, all three of these views seem to nuance the initial "for prosperity" argument, shifting it more toward the center.

While Yong's typology provides greater understanding of various prosperity teachings, it also shows us that we cannot merely adopt a reductionistic account of the prosperity gospel. There are many different prosperity gospels expressed in many different ways throughout the world. Yong's distinctions can help us discern when we should reject overtly consumeristic expressions of the prosperity gospel and when the approach is helpful for fostering holistic living among those in need. McFague states that the church should categorically reject the type of abundance late-capitalistic consumerism supports, but offer a different view of abundance. The abundant living the church must support is a sacrificial, cruciform lifestyle of generosity,[57] one that envisions fruitful ways of living and worshiping that benefit others as much as we have benefited from God's abundance. This is very much in line with the "balanced approach" of prosperity teaching from Yong's typology.

If the integral notion of "giving away" is missing in the prosperity teaching, then that teaching should be dismissed. And by "giving away" I do not mean giving to a prosperity ministry in order to raise one's chances of being prosperous. That's only a loosely veiled attempt at a quid pro quo with God. That is—let me state this bluntly—an effort to manipulate God and others for selfish gains. Many televangelists use this very line of reasoning, twisting the biblical

---

[56]Yong, "Typology of Prosperity Theology," 17.
[57]McFague, *Life Abundant,* 198.

principle of sowing and reaping for their own gains. This is crudely exemplified in televangelist Gloria Copeland's oft-cited book *God's Will is Prosperity*,
originally published in 1978: "You give $1 for the Gospel's sake and $100
belongs to you; give $10 and receive $1000; give $1000 and receive $100,000. . . .
In short, Mark 10:30 is a very good deal."[58] The worst aspect of this quote is
Copeland's reading of Mark 10, implying believers get a handshake "deal" from
God when they follow Christ. Consider the immediate context of v. 30:

> Peter began to say to him, "Look, we have left everything and followed you."
> Jesus said, "Truly I tell you, there is no one who has left house or brothers or
> sisters or mother or father or children or fields, for my sake and for the sake of
> the good news, who will not receive a hundredfold now in this age—houses,
> brothers and sisters, mothers and children, and fields, with persecutions—and
> in the age to come eternal life. But many who are first will be last, and the last
> will be first." (Mk 10:28-31)

The whole point of this passage is Jesus affirming that while it *is* costly to follow him, the blessings far outweigh the losses. The blessings would come in
"this age" and "in the age to come." This is not a quid pro quo, but a realistic
point that following Christ requires giving up something transitory, albeit
costly, but results in gaining something eternal and priceless. And let's not
forget that Jesus said one of the "blessings" we'll receive is persecution (Mk
10:30). This is a clear indication of the cost of discipleship. That word alone
upends Copeland's reading of the passage.

Copeland's hard prosperity concept of giving away betrays the very heart
of a theology of abundance that sees God's blessing in all things, including
persecution. This is precisely why one of Jesus' Beatitudes states, "Blessed are
those who are persecuted for righteousness' sake, for theirs is the kingdom
of heaven. Blessed are you when people revile you and persecute you and
utter all kinds of evil against you falsely on my account. Rejoice and be glad,
for your reward is great in heaven, for in the same way they persecuted the
prophets who were before you" (Mt 5:10-12). The price of following Christ is
costly, but the return is eternal. Because Copeland's poor exegesis is so closely

---

[58]Gloria Copeland, *God's Will Is Prosperity* (Tulsa, OK: Harrison House, 1978), 54. As readers might
    have guessed, Kate Bowler cites this passage as perfectly illustrating "hard prosperity" (*Blessed*,
    99).

tied to the popular understanding of the term "prosperity gospel," I have deliberately avoided adopting the term for our theology of renewal worship, electing instead the broader and more appropriate phrase "theology of abundance." In fact, it is the hard prosperity concept that God is contractually bound to bless us if we follow certain rules or principles that utterly opposes a true theology of abundance. At the start of this chapter, we saw that abundance entails the relational act of God pouring out the Spirit so we may be drawn back into relationship with God. The hard prosperity understanding of God is not relational, but transactional. God, here, is merely an investment manager that keeps tally of giving, spending, and dividends, and worse, God is impersonally bound by "laws" or "principles." Not only do these ideas derive from poor exegesis, but they also fail theologically by fundamentally misunderstanding the relational nature of God. Since relationship with God is the substance of worship, giving generously to be a witness and to bless others is an act of worship. This is in line with what Femi Adeleye, the director of the Institute for Christian Impact in Ghana, asserts: "Prosperity theology deliberately fails to see that all forms of giving to God—be it tithes or offerings— should be acts of *worship*. Instead, it teaches that tithing or giving to God is an *investment*."[59] Adeleye's assessment really only serves to critique hard prosperity, but his point is well taken. If the acts of giving and receiving are not relational, then they are not acts of worship.

While hard prosperity's perception of giving away is deeply flawed, a fitting concept of giving away entails graciously giving from every aspect that God has abundantly bestowed upon us. God's love is abundantly bestowed, so we graciously give love back to God and to all those around us. God gives us spiritual gifts, so we graciously use these gifts for the benefit and edification of others, and to strengthen and build up the church (1 Cor 14:12). God blesses us in health and finances, so we help and give to those in need. We grow in Christian maturity, so we testify about God's work in our lives and help others grow as well. This concept of giving away is comprehensive, and not merely focused on monetary wealth. God has blessed us in every aspect of life, so we turn around and give from every aspect of our life. In Christ, God experienced death on our behalf, and at Pentecost Christ gave us the Spirit. Thus Christ,

[59] Adeleye, "Prosperity Gospel and Poverty," 16.

the revelation of God, gave us both his life (at the crucifixion) and his Spirit (at Pentecost). This means that God literally gave *everything* to those God loves, and so must we (Jn 15:13). To be more like God is to become a giver like God, and the telos of a theology of abundance is to flourish from a receiver to a giver. The Christian walk entails us continually growing to be more and more like Christ, so let's not forget that God is the supreme Gift-Giver as Christ pours out the Spirit upon all flesh.

The appropriate notion of giving away is evident in Israel Houghton's song "More Than Enough":

> *Your promise is pouring over me*
> *Eternally I'm blessed to be a blessing*
> *Exceeding, abundantly more than enough.*[60]

As the song states, God's blessing is "abundantly more than enough," allowing the blessed one to be a blessing to others. What's so interesting about this song in particular is that it evidences a marked theological change in Houghton's worship music. As worship leader and scholar Wen Reagan traces, Houghton's early work portrays an indebtedness to soft prosperity teaching.[61] For instance, consider some lyrics from the song "New Season" from Israel and New Breed's 2001 album of the same name:

> *A fresh anointing is flowing my way*
> *It's a season of power and prosperity* [62]

This song proclaims a new season of power and prosperity, essentially calling prosperity into existence. Incidentally, this album was released the same year that Houghton joined the staff of Joel Osteen's Lakewood Church in Houston, Texas. This is significant because Osteen has long been regarded as the "lead

---

[60]"More Than Enough," words and music by Aaron Lindsey, Israel Houghton and Martha Munizzi, CCLI 5174816 © 2008 Integrity's Praise! Music, Sound Of The New Breed, Martha Munizzi Music (administered by Capitol CMG Publishing, Integrity Music, David C Cook, Say the Name Publishing).

[61]Wen Reagan, "Blessed to Be a Blessing: The Prosperity Gospel of Worship Music Superstar Israel Houghton," in *The Spirit of Praise: Music and Worship in Global Pentecostal-Charismatic Christianity,* ed. Monique Ingalls and Amos Yong (University Park: Pennsylvania State University Press, 2015), 222-23.

[62]"New Season," words and music by Derick Thomas and Israel Houghton, CCLI 2927262 © 1997 Need New Music, Integrity's Praise! Music, Sound Of The New Breed (administered by Capitol CMG Publishing, Integrity Music, David C Cook).

ambassador" of soft prosperity teaching,[63] which might have influenced Houghton's lyrics. Although Houghton did not leave Lakewood until 2016,[64] there was already a theological shift present in his music since the release of his album *The Power of One* in 2009. Houghton, inspired by Amos 5, began to see that great songs mean nothing to God if the "the poor, the widow, the orphan, the voiceless," are not emphasized.[65] Houghton's music began to acknowledge matters of social justice, recognizing that it is the responsibility of those who are blessed to turn around and bless those who are in need. In Houghton, therefore, we see a theology of abundance at work as he develops from a receiver ("New Season") to a giver ("More Than Enough"). The "season of power and prosperity" has led to Houghton being "blessed to be a blessing." So a theology of abundance, rightly understood, acknowledges God's desire for us to prosper so that in our blessed state we can become givers that emulate the generous Gift-Giving God.

UTTERING ABUNDANCE THROUGH TESTIMONY, PREACHING, AND TONGUES

Before we consider the formational power of communal worship next chapter, I'd like to spend some time discussing how a theology of abundance is evidenced in verbal forms of worship such as preaching, testimony, and tongues. My goal for this section is not to trace a full-fledged theology of renewal preaching, testimony, or tongues—there already exist many exceptional studies concerning these topics.[66] Rather, I am merely locating the implications of a theology of abundance as they pertain to verbal forms of

---

[63]Reagan, "Blessed to Be a Blessing," 223.

[64]Houghton stepped down from his position as worship pastor of Lakewood Church after a case of infidelity in his marriage years prior became public. Although they tried reconciling, Houghton and his wife got divorced, which also prompted his stepping down. See Christine Thomasos, "Israel Houghton Returns to Joel Osteen's Lakewood Church After Engagement to Adrienne Bailon," CP Entertainment (2016), www.christianpost.com/news/israel-houghton-returns-to-joel -osteens-lakewood-church-after-engagement-to-adrienne-bailon.html (accessed August 9, 2020).

[65]Reagan, "Blessed to Be a Blessing," 225.

[66]Lee Roy Martin, ed., *Toward a Pentecostal Theology of Preaching* (Cleveland, TN: CPT Press, 2015); Steven Studebaker, ed., *Pentecostal Preaching and Ministry in Multicultural and Post-Christian Canada* (Eugene, OR: Pickwick, 2019); Mark Cartledge, *Testimony in the Spirit: Rescripting Ordinary Pentecostal Theology* (London: Routledge, 2017); Robert Menzies, *Speaking in Tongues: Jesus and the Apostolic Church as Models for the Church Today* (Cleveland, TN: CPT Press, 2016); Cartledge, *Charismatic Glossolalia: An Empirical-Theology Study* (London: Routledge, 2016); Cartledge, ed., *Speaking in Tongues: Multi-Disciplinary Perspectives* (Eugene, OR: Wipf & Stock, 2006).

worship so we can better recognize the language of abundance that's uttered in renewal worship.

PREACHING

Both testimony and preaching are proclamatory, but in different ways. While preaching consists of the *objective recounting* of the biblical gospel message, testimony is the *subjective recounting* of the gospel message as it applies to the life of a believer. Preaching requires the proper exegesis and exhortation of biblical texts and principles, so congregants can affectively be moved from biblical comprehension to life application. Conversely, testimony begins at the point of application, citing specific ways God has affected the life of the believer. Both of these proclamatory forms of worship testify of God's abundant love for the church. The gift of tongues, on the other hand, is not necessarily proclamatory, although declarations are possible when accompanied by interpretations. Speaking in tongues is a common act of renewal worship where worshipers speak in languages unknown to the speaker. The very notion of tongues comes as an *overflow* of human expression. As we will see, each of these verbal forms of renewal worship exhibits the traits of abundance.

While preaching is highly valued in renewal spirituality, it is not always recognized as a form of worship. Pentecostal churchgoers often identify worship exclusively as the musical portion of the service, seeing preaching as a persuasive form of teaching. However, worship really encapsulates any form of honoring God, so preaching should appropriately be understood as an act of worship.[67] Because preaching reveals God's character, it is essential to the worship service.[68] Furthermore, if you recall, in the last chapter, we found that renewal worship sees every encounter of God as an act of worship. Preaching should be understood in this same context since "encounters with the Holy Spirit are expected during the preparation, delivery, and response to the sermon."[69] This line of reasoning refocuses the

---

[67] Jeffrey Arthurs, "John 3:16 in the Key of C," in *The Art & Craft of Biblical Preaching: A Comprehensive Resource for Today's Communicators*, ed. Haddon Robinson and Craig Brian Larson (Grand Rapids, MI: Zondervan, 2005), 42.

[68] Arthurs, "John 3:16 in the Key of C," 43.

[69] Mark Cartledge, "Practical Theology: Attending to Pneumatologically-Driven Praxis," in *The Routledge Handbook of Pentecostal Theology*, ed. Wolfgang Vondey (London: Routledge, 2020), 164.

point of preaching, recognizing the object of preaching as the same object of worship, namely, the relational God. When preaching is understood as an act of worship, the unneeded pressures of preaching a good sermon that connects with people are diminished by the primary desire to worship God through preaching.

Renewal preachers seek a special anointing from God, and their work is deemed successful when the congregants experience the power of the Spirit through their spoken words. Historically, Pentecostal preaching was considered quality when it "encouraged participants to drink from this holy and potent fount."[70] Put differently, Pentecostal preachers carry a divine mandate to lead people to the life-giving Spirit. The preacher's proclamation should be exciting and charismatic, but above all faithful to the Spirit and Scriptures. As the sermon is conveyed, there is an expectation of reciprocity between the preacher and the congregant. As Wolfgang Vondey points out, preaching requires "a narrative of speaking, hearing and then, again, speaking and hearing."[71] This means that preaching is a back-and-forth proclamation and reception of the gospel until the congregation's desires are completely turned toward God.[72] Sermons attempt to engage a person's affections rather than merely his or her intellect, so a successful sermon results in the transformation of a person's desires. As Vondey writes,

> Preaching as an appeal to the affections is a transformational practice in which the initial proclamation of the outpouring of the Spirit (by the preacher) and the hearing of the message (by the audience) shifts in the actual baptism to a speaking by the audience (in tongues and exaltation) by the preacher. Preaching is thus seen as a charismatic ritual evidenced in the transformation of the practice itself, involving the joining of Word and Spirit beginning with the proclamation of the gospel through the anointing of the preacher, directed to a re-experiencing of the biblical event, shifting to the anointing of the audience, the outpouring of the Spirit, and the response of the recipients.[73]

---

[70]Leah Payne, "'New Voices': Pentecostal Preachers in North America, 1890–1930," in *Scripting Pentecost: A Study of Pentecostals, Worship and Liturgy*, ed. Mark Cartledge and A. J. Swoboda (London: Routledge, 2017), 19.

[71]Wolfgang Vondey, *Pentecostal Theology: Living the Full Gospel* (London: Bloomsbury, 2017), 88.

[72]Vondey, *Pentecostal Theology*, 88.

[73]Vondey, *Pentecostal Theology*, 88-89.

Quality preaching penetrates the soul and tears down walls that separate the worshiper from the heart of God.[74]

As renewal preachers lead congregants to the life-giving Spirit, they participate in a theology of abundance in at least two ways. First, preachers proclaim the good news of the resurrected Christ *and* the outpoured Spirit, which is a message of hope *and* abundance. Bearing a kingdom perspective in mind, the church is in between the already and not yet of the kingdom of God, so the good news proclaimed is not only that Christ bought our redemption on the cross, but also that God has empowered the church through the universal outpour of the Spirit. Renewal preachers regularly carry this encouraging message of hope and abundance to the pulpit, reminding the church that it has taken up the ministry of Christ until his triumphant return. Second, preachers facilitate the flow of worship, connecting the intellectual and affective formation of the congregants. A typical service flow in renewal worship integrates preaching with music. The service usually begins with music, and when prayer, announcements, and Scripture readings occur, they are typically underscored by music to keep the flow of the service intact. Toward the end of the musical portion of the service, preachers often approach the stage for a "ministry time" with the congregation. Here the preachers do the connecting work of the service, linking the sung worship with the message that will be preached. Over gentle keyboard music or a vamping band, preachers offer encouragement, uniting the people to adopt particular ways of looking at an idea or biblical passage. The preachers pray, often discerning the Spirit's prompting in case there is anything in particular God is leading them to pray over. Finally, when the people are spiritually unified, the preacher is able to transition out of the ministry time and into the sermon.

The description above demonstrates the preacher's role as mediator. The preacher mediates the flow of the Spirit while facilitating the flow of the worship service. God pours out the Spirit abundantly on all flesh, and preachers mediate the Spirit's flow toward communal unity. The renewal preacher's mediation is not that of a barrier like a dam that withholds water in order to regulate its flow—the sort of mediation that is sometimes, if unfairly,

---

[74]Craig Brian Larson, "A Weekly Dose of Compressed Dignity," in *The Art & Craft of Biblical Preaching: A Comprehensive Resource for Today's Communicators*, ed. Haddon Robinson and Craig Brian Larson (Grand Rapids, MI: Zondervan, 2005), 29.

associated with sacramental forms of worship. Rather, the preacher is like a sailor at the helm of a boat making sure the boat steers the right course. The river's flow (the Spirit) is already going in a particular direction, and the preacher's job is to make sure the boat flows in the same direction. This is similar to the biblical metaphor of a pastor "shepherding the flock" (1 Pet 5:2). The pastor knows the people of the congregation and utilizes preaching as a means to guide them toward growth and solidarity. So it is through preaching that abundance is proclaimed and mediated for the church.

TESTIMONY

Testimony in worship entails an individual sharing with the community about his or her relationship with God. Evangelical traditions typically view testimony as sharing the story of how someone became a Christian. When people testify, they share a bit about their pre-conversion life, their conversion experience, and the life they lead now that they've been saved. The conversion experience is always central in evangelical testimony. In the renewal context, however, worshipers also testify about the *continuing* work of the Spirit in their lives. Testimony recounts how a person understands his or her faith in light of significant spiritual experiences, both at conversion and after. Testimonies are conveyed by individuals and received by communities, in hopes that a person's individual story can enrich the whole community. The worshiping community, however, interprets the testimony before grafting it into[75] its larger narrative context. As Pentecostal theologian Tony Richie points out, testimony "requires interpretation, evaluation, and judgment as well as weighing against the character of the one who testifies."[76] Once this is done, the individual's story becomes part of the worshiping community's broader spiritual heritage. For instance, if a person received the baptism of the Holy Spirit during worship, the community hears the story, celebrates it, and claims it as an authentication of what God is doing in their midst. Testimonies, therefore, are significant individually and socially as they become a worshiping community's "shared confessions."[77]

---

[75]This concept is discussed in detail in chap. 3.

[76]Tony Richie, "Translating Pentecostal Testimony into Interreligious Dialogue," *Journal of Pentecostal Theology* 20 (2011): 164.

[77]Richie, "Translating Pentecostal Testimony," 164.

Not only does testimony help make connections between the experiences of individual worshipers in a community,[78] it also helps make connections between past events, offering a "'reciprocal reshaping' of history and experience."[79] This means testimony enables the powerful events of the past to inform the worshiper's present circumstances. As Pentecostal theologian May Lin Tan-Chow points out, testimony keeps memory alive and truth real.[80] Testimonies safeguard worshipers from forgetting the times God worked transformationally in their lives, and, correspondingly, they also remind and reaffirm communities of their own beliefs, values, and theological commitments.[81] The persistent memory of God's powerful work in the lives of believers may even result in a reinterpretation of the past[82] as new insights reshape the way we think about past events. After all, we often only appreciate God's provision when we see our life events in hindsight. Testimony platforms remembrance and retrospection, which contributes to a living, transformative spirituality.

Testimonies are appropriately known as acts of worship because they are, by nature, doxological. They are generally spontaneous, expressive, and demonstrative verbal ascriptions of praise to God, even if they are to some extent guided by a preacher or worship leader.[83] Like every other act of worship, testimony recenters people around God's active presence. Tony Richie really captures well the formational power of testimony as an act of renewal worship:

> Pentecostal testimonies are highly personalized and often highly dramatized versions of the biblical pattern of worship as responsive "re-presentation" or "recital of God's saving acts." This connection is especially cogent if "God's saving acts" include not only conversion/new birth but also a host of attendant divine blessings (e.g., healing and deliverance, spirit baptism, answered prayer or special strength and encouragement, etc.). In other words, Pentecostal testimonies are soteriologically based doxological narratives of historical

---

[78]Richie, "Translating Pentecostal Testimony," 166.
[79]Richie, "Translating Pentecostal Testimony," 168-69.
[80]May Lin Tan-Chow, *Pentecostal Theology for the Twenty-First Century* (Burlington, UK: Ashgate, 2007), 129.
[81]Mark Cartledge, *Testimony in the Spirit*, 69.
[82]Richie, "Translating Pentecostal Testimony," 168-69.
[83]Richie, "Translating Pentecostal Testimony," 170.

occurrences viewed through the lens of faith. Plainly put, people tell stories of what they believe God has graciously done in their lives for the express purpose of giving glory to God in the presence of their hearers.[84]

As Richie points out, Pentecostal testimonies affirm redeemed life in Christ by continually reaffirming God's abundantly bestowed blessings. If one only testifies about his or her conversion, that person will unintentionally disregard God's continual work of Spirit empowerment, sanctification, healing, and edification. Pentecostal testimony highlights the sustained blessings of the Spirit in the lives of believers, which continually provides evidence for the holistic transformation that attends salvation. In other words, a "testimony of renewal" does not merely confirm a person's initiation into the faith, but proves his or her discipleship by recounting the continued sanctioning of the Spirit. God's abundance is central in renewal testimony.

SPEAKING IN TONGUES

The spiritual gift of glossolalia,[85] or speaking in tongues, is at the same time one of the more controversial aspects of renewal spirituality, and one of its defining attributes. Renewal spirituality affirms and promotes the continuing presence of *all* the spiritual gifts mentioned in the Bible (1 Cor 12:8-10, 28-29; Eph 4:11; Rom 12:6-8), believing that they should operate harmoniously, resulting in a dynamic relationship with the Spirit. Paul often affirms all the gifts and associates them with service and good works for the benefit of others rather than selfish gains. The gifts are also significant for Jesus' ministry. As Macchia writes,

> The connection between extraordinary gifts of the Spirit and the inauguration of the kingdom of God points, according to Pentecostals, to the enduring significance of these gifts in the mainstream life of the church. These gifts are too deeply connected theologically to Jesus' inauguration of the kingdom of

---

[84]Richie, "Translating Pentecostal Testimony," 170.

[85]The New Testament distinguishes at least two different forms of tongues. *Xenolalia* or *xenoglossia* is speaking in a different human language without prior knowledge of it. This is presumably what happened at Pentecost in Acts 2. While Pentecostals affirm this sort of tongues today, what is most commonly practiced in renewal worship is *glossolalia*, which refers to a heavenly language known only to God (Rom 8:26). In this section we will be referring to *glossolalia* unless otherwise noted.

God and the early experience of the Spirit to be reduced to one type of gifting that can be disposed of in favor of other, more ordinary ones.[86]

So for the renewal Christian, the gifts are not incidental to the biblical witness, but integral, and should continue to be practiced today.

This commitment stands in stark contrast with the cessationist view that believes spiritual gifts have ceased and that the Bible informs us that this was going to happen. It should be noted that this view (popular among conservative evangelicals) is primarily concerned with what we might call "miraculous" or "extravagant" gifts (speaking in tongues, gifts of healing, prophecy, etc.). Cessationists often affirm the continuing gifts of pastoring, evangelism, helps, and administration, and they even affirm that God continues to heal. They do not believe, however, that anyone can be used by the Spirit in the specific gift of healing. The key text cessationists use to defend their view is 1 Corinthians 13:8-13, where Paul refers to the cessation of prophecy, tongues, and knowledge.

> Love never ends. But as for prophecies, they will come to an end; as for tongues, they will cease; as for knowledge, it will come to an end. For we know only in part, and we prophesy only in part; but when the complete comes, the partial will come to an end. When I was a child, I spoke like a child, I thought like a child, I reasoned like a child; when I became an adult, I put an end to childish ways. For now we see in a mirror, dimly, but then we will see face to face. Now I know only in part; then I will know fully, even as I have been fully known. And now faith, hope, and love abide, these three; and the greatest of these is love.

In this passage, it appears that such gifts *will* cease, but when? Paul concludes in 1 Corinthians 13:10-13 that love never ends, but the spiritual gifts the Corinthian churchgoers value as marks of maturity and perfection will come to an end. Essentially, what Paul points out is that the church in Corinth is mistakenly viewing these "evidences of maturity" as ends in themselves. Indeed, Paul does talk about maturity and completeness, but only when the "complete" comes (v. 10). Thus, the real issue that separates the cessationist reading of the text with the renewal reading regards when the "complete" comes.

---

[86]Frank Macchia, *Baptized in the Spirit: A Global Pentecostal Theology* (Grand Rapids, MI: Zondervan, 2006), 148-49.

Some cessationists believe the "complete" was when the canon of the Bible was completed.[87] In this view prophecy is equal to scriptural revelation, and since there is no ongoing scriptural revelation, prophecy had to have ceased. But would Paul have known anything about the completion of the canon? This also implies that the Bible is now completely clear and we see God "face to face." Another view cessationists hold is that the "complete" refers to the completion of the apostolic age (the age when the apostles were still living and spreading the gospel). In that age miracles authenticated their message, so miracles are no longer needed today.[88] Again, would Paul have even considered an apostolic age? And, again, this implies that since the apostolic age is now over we should be seeing "face to face." It appears that the book of Acts does not support the idea that the spread of the gospel was complete during the apostolic age. Renewal Christians, contrariwise, are continuationists, believing the "complete" refers to the return of Christ. The images of seeing "face to face" and being "fully known" imply the actual presence of the coming King. If Paul thought that gifts were about to cease, then why would he spend so much time instructing the Corinthians in their correct use? The implication of this view beckons a kingdom theology: the spiritual gifts are for now, the time in between the inauguration and con-summation of the kingdom of God—the time in between the first and second comings of Christ.

This is all to say that the gift of tongues is affirmed and valued as an integral aspect of renewal worship today. Tongues in worship can be seen primarily as "spontaneous, glossolalic expressions of praise and thanksgiving."[89] Glos-solalia comes to worshipers as inarticulate groans, known only to God, that express a deep communication that transcends cognitive meaning. Tongues are also commonly used for intercessory prayer when words fail to adequately express the heart's message.[90] Although tongues occur spontaneously in wor-ship, worshipers still have the ability to mediate the language. As Pentecostal theologian Keith Warrington writes,

---

[87]Merrill Unger, *New Testament Teaching on Tongues* (Grand Rapids, MI: Kregel, 1973), 97-98.

[88]John MacArthur, *Charismatic Chaos* (Grand Rapids, MI: Zondervan, 1992), 281-82.

[89]Robert Menzies, *Speaking in Tongues: Jesus and the Apostolic Church as Models for the Church Today* (Cleveland, TN: CPT Press, 2016), 146.

[90]Menzies, *Speaking in Tongues*, 146.

The gift of tongues is best understood as an extemporaneous or spontaneous manifestation in a form that is quasi-language. The speaker is in control of her/ his speech and the forming of the sounds; the Spirit does not manipulate or coerce the speaker into a particular speech pattern. It is possible that the sounds themselves already existed in the mind and experience of the speaker, being reconstituted in the form of the tongues s/he employs though it also possible that they are previously unimagined phonetic forms. Most Pentecostals have concluded that speaking in tongues is a phenomenon that has divine and human elements in that the Spirit inspires the manifestation but the person articulates the sounds.[91]

For many Pentecostals, tongues are not seen as some sort of supernatural, or dreamlike language, but a mode of communicating with God from a person's innermost depth. In other words, tongues are demystified and normalized in renewal worship.

Pentecostals typically recognize three distinct functions of tongues in renewal worship: they are a supernatural outpouring and eschatological sign to unbelievers (Acts 2:11), they are a private prayer language (Rom 8:26), and they are used for the strengthening of the church through interpretation (1 Cor 14:27). Each of these forms indicate abundance as the Spirit graces the worshiper with intercession when words cannot signify what they are truly meaning. As Romans 8:26 states, "Likewise the Spirit helps us in our weakness; for we do not know how to pray as we ought, but that very Spirit intercedes with sighs too deep for words." So tongues in worship are usually characterized devotionally as deep prayer. Like preaching and testimony, however, tongues can be proclamatory when accompanied by the spiritual gift of interpretation (1 Cor 12:10; 14:27). When interpreted, tongues function prophetically as vehicles from God to the whole church body.[92] Though this proclamatory expression of tongues does exist in many renewal worship contexts, the most frequent expression of tongues is as a devotional prayer language. The gift of tongues can also be seen as a unifying, ecumenical language that points to things to come.[93] This is a major point that deals with the

---

[91]Keith Warrington, *Pentecostal Theology: A Theology of Encounter* (London: T&T Clark, 2008), 87.
[92]Menzies, *Speaking in Tongues*, 146.
[93]Frank Macchia, "Babel and the Tongues of Pentecost: Reversal or Fulfilment?," in *Speaking in Tongues: Multi-Disciplinary Perspectives*, ed. Mark Cartledge (Eugene, OR: Wipf & Stock, 2006), 47.

social impact of tongues, which we'll flesh out in chapter six. For now, it suffices to say that speaking in tongues is an integral expression of renewal worship, and when this gift is paired with preaching and testimony, we have a powerful verbal witness of a theology of abundance. The Spirit is proclaimed, affirmed, and experienced verbally in renewal worship.

CONCLUSION

This chapter answered the question "Who is worship for?" by identifying the relational character of God and by understanding the Spirit as the abundant Gift of God. The obvious answer to the abovementioned question is simply *God*, but the more complex context of that straightforward answer conveys a theology of abundance. The theology of abundance articulated in this chapter flows naturally from the theological method of renewal worship put forward in chapter one. The universal outpour motif of Acts 2 indicates the overflow of the abundant Spirit and allows believers to see God's blessings in all things. Believers can then reciprocate this blessing to God and others through action and proclamation. As we conclude our discourse concerning the object of renewal worship, let us take some time to reflect on these concepts with another doxology:

> *Praise God who loves us so*
> *Abundantly bestowed*
> *Praise God from whom all blessings overflow.*

3

HOW RENEWAL WORSHIP WORKS

WORSHIP AS A SHAPING NARRATIVE

I appeal to you therefore, brothers and sisters, by the mercies of God, to
present your bodies as a living sacrifice, holy and acceptable to God,
which is your spiritual worship. Do not be conformed to this world, but
be transformed by the renewing of your minds, so that you may discern
what is the will of God—what is good and acceptable and perfect.

ROMANS 12:1-2

IN THE OFT-QUOTED passage above, Paul delivers a call to worship to the first century community of believers in Rome. Some scholars and pastors see this passage as a call to "rational worship" through a renewal of the mind. After all, Romans 12:2 indicates that the renewing of the mind constitutes a spiritual transformation that protects believers from yielding to worldliness. What's sometimes missed, however, is that verse 1 describes spiritual worship as presenting the *body* as a living sacrifice. If we pay attention to this, then we'll see that Paul's call to worship is not merely a call to *rational* worship. Romans 12:2 logically flows from Romans 12:1, and Paul is looking for believers to holistically offer their bodies *and* renew their minds. It is through holistic worship that believers align with God's will and discern how God wants them to live. A believer's moral obligations and life decisions are also aligned through worship. Spiritual worship, for Paul, is not merely rational, but works across the board, engaging the whole self and affecting the whole worshiping community.

Holistic realignment is a constructive consequence of worship. By attributing reverent honor to God, a worshiper's heart, mind, will, and desires conform to God's. It's like a small four-cylinder car that goes out of alignment whenever it drives off road, hits curbs, or simply travels too long without a tire rotation. Eventually the car needs an alignment so it can properly function toward its intention. Recurrent vehicle maintenance will keep the car in a proper working order. In the same way, one of the primary functions of worship is to continually realign a person so they can be in right relation with God and others. Alignment here is fundamentally relational as worshipers in a worshiping community reconcile with the triune God. As follows, worship works both individually and communally and on multiple levels. On one level it works to reconcile people individually to God, on another level it works to reconcile people to their communities, and finally it works to reconcile whole communities back to God. Worship proposes to bond people to God's story of redemption and reconciliation. It helps people envision themselves as players in God's grand narrative, and it helps facilitate both personal approbation and communal solidarity.

This chapter discusses how worship works. While worship can be defined as turning our hearts toward God as a response to God's self-revelation, it works toward complete reconciliation, shaping both individuals and communities. As discussed in the introduction, because different worshiping communities emphasize different aspects of the same Christian narrative, worship works a little differently across traditions. Every worshiping community has the same twofold aim of glorifying God and drawing people into God's presence, but how this is accomplished will differ from tradition to tradition. The questions addressed in this chapter concern specifically how renewal worship works. Why is music so prevalent in renewal worship? How does renewal worship reinforce God's story? What aspect of God's story does renewal worship emphasize and how? The thesis of this chapter is that musical worship helps form a Pentecostal's guiding narrative. We will look at how music demonstrates and reinforces the Pentecostal story aesthetically, helping people discover their own part in the narrative.

MUSIC AS SACRAMENT

When mentioning Pentecostal and charismatic worship, what is often envisaged is the worship music. We might think about ecstatic praise and expressive movement, testimony and proclamation, or of prayerful tarrying and intercession, but it's hard to imagine any of these events occurring independently from the music. From Pentecostalism's inception as a revivalist movement, music has been ubiquitous to every expression of its worship. Nevertheless, worship is more than the music. It is not something people make, but a response to who God is. But because of the importance given to music in Pentecostal worship, this chapter argues that musical worship plays a pivotal affective role in the human response.

History and experience have shown that music is perhaps the most affective liturgical element in Pentecostal worship, especially as it is utilized to draw people into deeper experiential spirituality.[1] In fact, music is so vital in Pentecostal worship that it can be viewed as sacramental when Pentecostals seek to "sing to the LORD a new song" (Ps 96:1), and invite God to inhabit their praises (Ps 22:3).[2] This idea has become so pervasive in contemporary worship that worship scholars Swee Hong Lim and Lester Ruth credit Pentecostal worship music's popularity as catalyzing this new liturgical shift. They write:

> Pentecostalism contributed contemporary worship's sacramentality, that is, both the expectation that God's presence could be encountered in worship and the normal means by which this encounter would happen. But this contribution was not about redefining the sacraments of baptism and Communion but reshaping an understanding of God's people praising and worshipping, especially as these people sang. What emerged was a sacramentality of music or corporate song expressed in biblical texts such as Psalm 22:3, where God is said to inhabit, dwell, or be enthroned upon the praises of God's people.[3]

---

[1]Mark Jennings, *Exaltation: Ecstatic Experience in Pentecostalism and Popular Music* (Bern: Peter Lang, 2014), 30.
[2]Lester Ruth and Swee Hong Lim, *A History of Contemporary Praise & Worship: Understanding the Ideas That Reshaped the Protestant Church* (Grand Rapids, MI: Baker Academic, 2021), 124; Swee Hong Lim and Lester Ruth, *Lovin' on Jesus: A Concise History of Contemporary Worship* (Nashville: Abingdon, 2017), 123; Lester Ruth, "Introduction: The Importance and History of Contemporary Praise & Worship," in *Essays on the History of Contemporary Praise and Worship*, ed. Lester Ruth (Eugene, OR: Pickwick, 2020), 6.
[3]Lim and Ruth, *Lovin' on Jesus*, 18.

Liturgically, therefore, musical worship is seen as a sort of dwelling place for God, and not only as a communal expression of love. According to worship scholar Adam Perez, this theology of worship became particularly prevalent as Integrity Hosanna! Music began releasing worship tapes for mass consumption in the early 1980s.[4] The first and most popular tape released during this time was Ron Tucker's *Behold His Majesty* (1983), which included Foursquare pastor, author, and songwriter Jack Hayford's hit praise chorus "Majesty." This album is, for Perez, an "archetypal example for understanding the theology of worship at work in musical sound."[5] This is the first major, mainstream instance where the sacramentality of music is actually encoded in the music itself.[6] A theology of music's sacramentality implies that God is literally present when worshipers gather and sing God's praises. God inhabits the praises of the worshiping community because the communal gathering conforms itself to be receptive of God's presence, which is continually already present.

Since worship *begins* with the ever-present God, worshipers do not call God down to enter their domain. Worship is not a sort of summoning or conjuring of God. Harold Best warns against the potential of idolatry by making music the object of worship rather than God:

> Whenever we assume that art mediates God's presence or causes him to be tangible, we have begun the trek into idol territory. Our present-day use of music as the major up-front device for worship is a case in point. We need to ask ourselves if we, as worship leaders, are giving the impression that we draw near to God through music or that God draws near because of it. Is music our golden calf?[7]

What Best is pointing out is that we must retain the proper place of music and not prop it up beyond its own status. Christians sometimes take good things and elevate them beyond their intended significances. Have you ever observed a Christian treat the Bible as if *it* was God? The Bible is holy, and it is vitally imperative for every Christian's life, but it is *not* the fourth person of the

---

[4]Adam Perez, "Sounding God's Enthronement in Worship: The Early History and Theology of Integrity's Hosanna! Music," in Lester Ruth, ed., *Essays on the History of Contemporary Praise and Worship* (Eugene, OR: Pickwick, 2020), 88.

[5]Perez, "Sounding God's Enthronement," 90.

[6]Perez, "Sounding God's Enthronement," 88.

[7]Harold Best, *Unceasing Worship: Biblical Perspectives on Worship and the Arts* (Downers Grove, IL: InterVarsity Press, 2003), 166.

Trinity! Yet some Christians wield the Bible as if it is more authoritative than God. Similarly, typically good things like financial prosperity, national pride, or romantic love can be propped up ahead of God. When a good thing supersedes a Christian's personal relationship with God, then that person has made an idol out of it. Musical worship too can be made into an idol.

Best's question—"Do we draw near to God through music, or does God draw near because of it?"—is crucial. If God becomes tangible *because* of music and the arts, then music and the arts are powerful mediums that we can manipulate to attempt to summon—even control—God. Music and the arts, however, *can* be vehicles where God *does become* in some way tangible to worshipers. Those statements might sound the same, but they bear a key distinction: in the first case music and the arts hold power over God and we seek to control God, whereas in the second case music and the arts are purely avenues that God uses to become present. God is in control when God chooses to be present among the praises of the worshiping community. God is not summoned in the second case, but comes to us graciously and relationally. Furthermore, God's "coming to us" does not entail God coming down from heaven to enter our midst. While God is transcendent, God is also concurrently the ever-present God who dwells in our hearts and in our communities. *We* are the temple of God (1 Cor 3:16-17).[8] Musical worship creates the scenario where worshipers align with the already present God. When worshipers vulnerably stand in the presence of God, open and ready to receive whatever it is God wants to give, then God is enthroned upon their praises. Worship must be seen as relational between God and the worshiping community or it will fall into dead ritual, or worse, it will fall into idolatry.

Biblical scholar G. K. Beale argues that throughout the Bible idolatry is depicted as people resembling or becoming the very thing they worship. God made people to be imaging beings, so they're always reflecting something.[9] People become whatever stocks their ultimate motivations, which are the things they are ultimately committed to and subsequently worship. When

---

[8]Without deviating into a long tangent, let me briefly state that this both/and aspect of God is possible because of the Trinity. Through the Trinity, God is transcendent above us (Father), with us (Son), and in and around us (Spirit). See Eph 4:4-6.

[9]G. K. Beale, *We Become What We Worship: A Biblical Theology of Idolatry* (Downers Grove, IL: IVP Academic, 2008), 16.

people worship God, they become more like God, but when they worship an idol (anything else propped up before or in place of God), they become like it. As Beale states, "We resemble what we revere, either for ruin or restoration."[10]

The scriptural passage that started Beale's investigation on idolatry is Isaiah 6:9-10 when God scolds the Israelites:

> And he said, "Go and say to this people: 'Keep listening, but do not comprehend; keep looking, but do not understand.' Make the mind of this people dull, and stop their ears, and shut their eyes, so that they may not look with their eyes, and listen with their ears, and comprehend with their minds, and turn and be healed."

God admonishes the idolatrous Israelites, making them as spiritually insensitive, inanimate, and lifeless as the idols they were worshiping.[11] God essentially abdicates the people over to their ultimate desires. They become what they worship. The golden calf of the Exodus account embodies, in a way, every idol that humanity has ever propped up. The golden calf was constructed by the Israelite's own hands and was cold and lifeless.[12] When the Israelites worshiped it instead of the living God, they became "spiritually inanimate and empty like the lifeless and vain aspect of creation to which they have committed themselves."[13] Even a good thing like music can assume the form of a golden calf. But if worshipers resemble what they worship, what does it mean to become like music?

When the Israelites became like the golden calf they worshiped, they did not physically become like the calf, but began sharing characteristics with it. Like the golden calf, the Israelites became cold and lifeless, attractive on the outside, but hollow on the inside. In the same way, when an artform like music is idolized, we begin to emulate its characteristics to the point that it ruins us. Music is a channel for cathartic, emotional expression. Music embodies and even induces emotion, giving emotions a tangible reality through vocalizations and closely associated bodily motions. Music is not merely spectator entertainment, but moves us emotionally and bodily. In fact, music historically

---

[10]Beale, *We Become What We Worship*, 49.
[11]Beale, *We Become What We Worship*, 47.
[12]Beale, *We Become What We Worship*, 77-78.
[13]Beale, *We Become What We Worship*, 284.

facilitated communal gatherings, regularly accompanying liturgical and folk dances.[14] By giving flesh to our emotions, music connects us bodily with our minds and emotions, and helps us to recognize our own presence in the context of our surroundings and communities.[15] When people worship music, however, these good characteristics become apotheosized. People begin to live for the emotional release and embodied euphoria that music produces. Ironically, therefore, people can idolize musical worship even though its intended purpose is to aid a person's worship of God. When music becomes an idol, musical worship turns into "music-worship."

When worshipers begin to live for the embodied euphoria or emotional release of music, they become people that are driven by their bodies and emotions. The telos, or end result of music-worship can thus see healthy embodiment lead to oversexualization or conversely to prudery. It can also lead to a lack of emotional regulation, which can produce debilitating consequences. Unchecked emotional release can grow into emotional volatility and anxiety or conversely to withdrawal, avoidance, shame, or depression. But this does not mean that we should not utilize music or engage emotionally and bodily in worship. Indeed, the opposite is the case. To avoid emotional and bodily engagement in worship is to *not* worship God holistically. God made us with bodies and gave us emotions, and God called this creation "very good" (Gen 1:31). To deny such a crucial aspect of our own human nature is to not fully relate to God in our humanity, and worse, to insinuate that part of God's creation is not good. As Zac Hicks helpfully points out, music "props up our emotions, preventing them from falling to the left or the right so that the source of our prayer comes not just from our lips but from our hearts."[16] In other words, music in worship helps to connect our hearts and our minds.

---

[14]According to Daniel Levitin, it was only since the Renaissance that music began to be appreciated disinterestedly in isolation. See Daniel Levitin, *This Is Your Brain on Music: The Science of a Human Obsession* (New York: Plume, 2006), 257.

[15]For a deeper look into the neurological and psychological effects on music-evoked emotion, see Hans-Eckhardt Schaefer, "Music-Evoked Emotions—Current Studies," *Frontiers in Neuroscience* 11 (2017), www.ncbi.nlm.nih.gov/pmc/articles/PMC5705548/ (accessed January 22, 2020), and Hussain-Abdulah Arjmand, Jesper Hohagen, Bryan Paton and Nikki Rickard, "Emotional Responses to Music: Shifts in Frontal Brain Asymmetry Mark Periods of Musical Change," *Frontiers in Psychology* 4 (2017), www.frontiersin.org/articles/10.3389/fpsyg.2017.02044/full (accessed January 22, 2020).

[16]Zac Hicks, *The Worship Pastor: A Call to Ministry for Worship Leaders and Teams* (Grand Rapids, MI: Zondervan, 2016), 66.

When music is worshiped, worshipers are driven by music-evoked emotion, but when music is rightly focused in worship, it helps regulate our hearts and emotions. Music is powerfully affective and helps our holistic formation. As Hicks writes,

> Worship is a place where issues of ultimate human concern are addressed—sin, guilt, death, forgiveness, freedom, eternal life. When we come before our Maker in worship, we all bring these ultimate concerns to the table. Worship devoid of emotion is a dangerous thing because it can train us into believing that these concerns really aren't concerns. This is why emotionless worship is just as toxic to our faith as haphazardly emotional worship is. If our human wiring is to feel what we are concerned about, then *not* feeling what we *should* be concerned about subconsciously trains us to believe that these ultimate concerns are either untrue or not real.[17]

Worship addresses our ultimate concerns, and we become what we are ultimately committed to. So, if we are to worship God in spirit and in truth, we must worship God holistically, addressing and feeling what we are ultimately concerned about. In kind, every aspect of our human existence (mind, body, spirit, and emotions) is transformed and conformed to the image of Christ.

When I stated at the beginning of this section that musical worship is the most affective liturgical element in Pentecostal worship, I meant that it is the element of Pentecostal worship that most capably creates space for God to shape a person's heart aesthetically. This is not unique to Pentecostalism, however. In fact, every religious tradition can look to their liturgical or ritual elements as catalysts for aesthetic spiritual formation. What interests me, however, is what exactly those elements are in renewal traditions, and how they function. In Pentecostal worship, music is both the space where new charismatic experiences frequently occur, and the space where the community's interpretations of preceding charismatic experiences are emotively reinforced. Musical worship paired with the intellectual cultivation that comes from preaching, teaching, and testimony provides the worshiper a holistic account of their own experiences in the narrative context of Pentecostalism. When musical worship also engages other art forms (visual art, drama,

---

[17]Hicks, *Worship Pastor*, 148.

spoken word, video, etc.), it creates an even more potent space for aesthetic spiritual formation.

Music is paramount in Pentecostal worship because it serves as an invitation to "enter into" God's presence. Powerful songs and sensational forms supply Pentecostal worshipers some immediacy to the presence of God.[18] Music is not a portal or means for mystical escapism, but a centering mode of aesthetic expression that encourages solidarity as worshipers sing, pray, sway, clap, dance, and shout together. It brings people together and helps put them in right relation with each other and God. As Don Saliers puts it, "Liturgical participation can heighten our sense of joy in the details of life and in the mystery of being related to God and to one another as kin."[19] This communal unanimity creates a space for worshipers to align their hearts with God's heart personally in their own prayer life, and to align their own story with that of the worshiping community's. God is already present, but music unites people and raises their awareness of the constant Spirit. David Taylor states it well: "In worship the faithful bring their whole humanity, alongside the whole people of God, in proclamation, prayer, and praise, before the presence of the whole Godhead for the sake of the whole world."[20] God inhabits our praises and musical worship helps to shape us as a people.

THE WORSHIPING COMMUNITY

Due to the modern confidence of the solitary person, one thing that sometimes gets lost in evangelical circles is the role community plays in forming a person's beliefs. People are connected to their communities in several ways. Beyond the fact that communities comprise people that live in close proximity, or share common attributes, interests, or goals, communities also help people understand themselves and the world around them. People come to know who they are and what their experiences mean through a collective, interpretative negotiation of their circumstances. These most fundamental considerations are the lived experiences of individuals that lie bare before the

---

[18]Birgit Meyer, "Aesthetics of Persuasion: Global Christianity and Pentecostalism's Sensational Forms," *South Atlantic Quarterly* 109, no. 4 (2010): 742.

[19]Don Saliers, *Worship Come to Its Senses* (Nashville: Abingdon, 1996), 37-38.

[20]W. David O. Taylor, *Glimpses of the New Creation: Worship and the Formative Power of the Arts* (Grand Rapids, MI: Eerdmans, 2019), 36.

community, and the community helps to understand what these facts mean in light of their greater context. The rituals communities produce help place "individual experience within collective identity."[21] Hence the community plays an important role in a person's self-understanding and their comprehension of their own experiences. If we are to discover how renewal worship works, we must look closely at how the renewal community interprets religious experiences and roots people into their faith narrative.

The interpreting community. Communities are formed when people share experiences. When individuals are affected by a common event, they are compelled to understand the event through their own interpretive frameworks. In fact, they can *only* grasp the event through their particular frameworks. Here we can notice some circularity: people interpret events through their own interpretive lenses, and their lenses are shaped by those very experiences. Although this is circular, this is not a self-actualizing vicious circle like that of the workaholic who buys things to make life easier, and then has to work more to pay off the debt accrued while buying those time-saving conveniences. Rather, it is a hermeneutical spiral that uncovers new meaning every time the interpretive process circles back around to the event's point of reference. Philosopher Paul Ricoeur sees it like a spiral that circles back at different heights, revealing something new about the experience with each new rotation.[22] The event doesn't interpret itself; it is interpreted by a circumferential framework that ultimately becomes its context. The interpreted facts are hereafter grafted into the framework, but there still is a progression of understanding that occurs. Past experiences inform our comprehension of new experiences, and new experiences shape our memory of past experiences. As David Tracy states,

> For every event of understanding, in order to produce a new interpretation, mediates between our past experience and the understanding embodied in our linguistic tradition and the present event of understanding embodied in our linguistic tradition and the present event of understanding occasioned by a fidelity to the logic of the question in the back-and-forth movement of

---

[21]John Rempel, *Recapturing an Enchanted World: Ritual and Sacrament in the Free Church Tradition* (Downers Grove, IL: IVP Academic, 2020), 3.

[22]Paul Ricoeur, *Interpretation Theory: Discourse and the Surplus of Meaning* (Fort Worth: Texas Christian University Press, 1976), 79.

the conversation. We constantly mediate, translate, from our past under-standing to our present one. We consistently find that understanding *happens* in precisely this deeply subjective yet intersubjective, shareable, public, indeed historical movement of authentic conversation.[23]

A person's interpretive framework, or linguistic tradition as Tracy calls it, is continually updated by new experiences, and every new event drops into the greater story of the person's interpretative framework.

For Ricoeur, a hermeneutical understanding of an experience is tied to the plot of its narrative and how the experience fits within it. We can think of an interpretive framework as a complex story—the story of *your* life. Every event that transpires gets "emplotted" into the plot of your story. As the new event is grafted in, it is understood in light of all the other events that have taken place in your life. Your story is the context of your new experience, and once your experience is emplotted into your larger narrative, it becomes part of your new, more expanded, context. The new event also sheds light on other parts of your story, revealing something new to you about yourself and the world. Emplotment is necessary for embedding new experiences into a person's interpretive framework.

Communities consist of individuals who share overlapping—at least at crucial points—interpretive frameworks. A person can be a part of a number of communities that are defined by culture, heritage, ideology, affili-ations, and so on. The community that interests us here is a person's faith community. If we were to apply Ricoeur's ideas about emplotment to religious experiences, we would say that our community of faith shares our religious interpretive framework. Not only do they share our religious story, they also help to shape the story. The dialogue we have with our religious community helps us screen out some of the possible interpretations we may have of a religious experience.[24] For instance, the experience of raising hands in wor-ship can be interpreted as reaching out to God, or surrendering to God, or taking on a posture of vulnerability before God, and so on. These are, typically, all viable ways that renewal communities have interpreted hand raising during worship. Hand raising should not mean, however, that we are

---

[23]David Tracy, *The Analogical Imagination: Christian Theology and the Culture of Pluralism* (New York: Crossroad, 1981), 101.
[24]Ricoeur, *Interpretation Theory*, 17.

summoning God from on high like a sorcerer or siphoning God's power like a Jedi channeling the Force. The community in which the individual is a part has screened out these latter possibilities as illegitimate interpretations. This process of filtration is the interpretive community making sense of the "chaos of facts" people encounter regularly.[25]

It should be noted, however, that communities do not simply grow into fixed, unalterable monoliths. Their interpretive frameworks shift and change over time. While the interpreting community makes sure that the interpretation does not veer away from the basic narrative structure that was organized through plot,[26] the *prophet* seeks to change the community's overall narrative. The prophet does not revise things wholesale, otherwise that person would not be speaking the community's vernacular. Foreign adversaries cannot affect consensual modification onto a community that already has a longstanding plot full of history. Rather, the prophet is an insider who looks to shift the narrative gradually through a natural progression. This gradual shift may seem radical to an insider, but actually only traverses the routes made possible given the community's ideology, culture, vernacular, and modes of understanding. To give just one example, Martin Luther King Jr. prophetically changed some of the American narrative of racial inequality by teasing out the implications of many of the community's already-held doctrines. Since most Americans were self-confessed Christians, King, drawing on his own Christian theological convictions and experience as a preacher, used the theological doctrine of the *imago Dei* to make a case for racial equality. In his speeches, King also compared the civil rights era to biblical narratives like the exodus account. He followed the law of the land by inculcating the necessity of peaceful protests and acted out Jesus' instruction for peacemaking (Mt 5:38-48) through nonviolent, passive resistance. King helped change the narrative of the United States as an American, not as an outsider. He spoke the common vernacular and drew out fresh inferences of the culture's religious and ideological commitments. King was an American prophet who changed the overall narrative for what it means to be an American.

---

[25]Paul Ricoeur, *Hermeneutics & the Human Sciences*, trans. and ed. John Thompson (Cambridge: Cambridge University Press, 1981), 290.

[26]Paul Ricoeur, *From Text to Action: Essays in Hermeneutics, II*, trans. Kathleen Blamey and John Thompson (Evanston, IL: Northwestern University Press, 2007), 5.

Because the worshiping community shares histories, terminologies, and traditions, it is ultimately the judge of what constitutes a suitable interpretation of an event within the narrative discourse. The prophet attempts to shift the narrative (unfortunately, it doesn't always go over well for the prophet), but both the prophet and the narrative still come from the same community. These ideas concerning worship and prophetic witness will be further fleshed out in chapter five. For now, let us plainly infer that we are part of interpreting communities, and our experiences are interpreted by us as communal people. Because each religious community carries its own theological commitments and cultural distinctives, we will next explore what characterizes a Pentecostal worshiping community.

The charismatic community. When we talk about the Pentecostal worshiping community, we are talking about a faith community that hedges its interpretive boundaries of experience within the Pentecostal tradition. Kenneth Archer states that the shared story and shared charismatic experience forms the narrative framework that encloses a Pentecostal's interpretive parameters.[27] In other words, the interpretive parameters from which a person can know how to interpret his or her experiences are set by a shared charismatic experience. This shared charismatic experience is essential to any Pentecostal spirituality.[28] Unlike other traditions that are united by common doctrines or traditions, Pentecostalism began as an ecumenical movement full of diverse people who were united by a common experience.[29] The charismatic experience is commonly associated with the intense and direct experience of Spirit baptism.[30] While there are many theological interpretations of Spirit baptism within Pentecostalism,[31] the core of the

[27] Kenneth Archer, "The Fivefold Gospel and the Mission of the Church: Ecclesiastical Implications and Opportunities," in *Toward a Pentecostal Ecclesiology: The Church and the Fivefold Gospel*, ed. John Christopher Thomas (Cleveland, TN: CPT Press, 2010), 35.

[28] See Steven Land, *Pentecostal Spirituality: A Passion for the Kingdom* (London: Sheffield Academic Press, 1993), 26; Daniel E. Albrecht, *Rites in the Spirit: A Ritual Approach to Pentecostal/Charismatic Spirituality* (Sheffield Academic Press, 1999), 10; Allan Anderson, *An Introduction to Pentecostalism: Global Charismatic Christianity* (Cambridge: Cambridge University Press, 2004), 60-62; Keith Warrington, *Pentecostal Theology: A Theology of Encounter* (London: T&T Clark, 2008), 20-27; Margaret Poloma and Ralph Hood, eds., *Blood and Fire: Godly Love in a Pentecostal Emerging Church* (New York: New York University Press, 2008), 6.

[29] Anderson, *Introduction to Pentecostalism,* 60.

[30] Simon Chan, "Evidential Glossolalia and the Doctrine of Subsequence," *Asian Journal of Pentecostal Studies* 2 (1999): 195.

[31] Frank Macchia, *Baptized in the Spirit: A Global Pentecostal Theology* (Grand Rapids, MI: Zondervan, 2006), 20.

doctrine states that Christ immerses believers in the Spirit for empowerment, renewal, and the releasing of spiritual gifts for mission.[32] The experience of Spirit baptism is, therefore, a guiding motif for understanding the charismatic experience that forms the Pentecostal narrative framework. Testimony also becomes central for a Pentecostal spirituality since it is, as discussed last chapter, the witness of God's work in the lives of the people. Pentecostals see their lives and callings as part of God's greater story.

While rational knowledge has been highly valued in our post-Enlightenment era, Pentecostals understand the legitimacy of the charismatic experience through what philosopher James K. A. Smith calls "narrative knowledge."[33] This type of knowledge entails knowing that we are part of God's story by the authority of the Bible and experience. This type of knowledge cannot be rationally deduced, but only shared and witnessed. For Archer, the latter rain narrative is the Pentecostal guiding narrative that is shared through charismatic experience and testimony. This narrative is an eschatological story that involves God's restoration of all things.

The latter rain motif is based on the weather cycle in Palestine and God's promise that rain would be provided for the harvest. The "former rain" has been interpreted as the Spirit's outpouring in Acts 2, and the "latter rain" was understood as a new outpouring in the early twentieth century, evidenced by a new emphasis on Spirit baptism. Both the former and latter rains were plentiful for the harvest, and the latter rain still empowers Pentecostals today to spread the gospel all over the world and usher in the kingdom of God. Archer believes that Pentecostals situate themselves in this latter rain narrative, reading the Luke-Acts account not merely as a historical story, but as the beginning to *their* story. As Pentecostal pastor and theologian Johnathan Alvarado states, "Pentecostal worshipers often recast themselves as the principal characters in the story. . . . These unique Pentecostal ways of understanding texts take seriously the mystical, supernatural, and enchanted worldview that people of the Spirit enjoy."[34] Harkening back to Ricoeur, a Pentecostal's

---

[32]Macchia, *Baptized in the Spirit*, 81.

[33]James K. A. Smith, *Thinking in Tongues: Pentecostal Contributions to Christian Philosophy* (Grand Rapids, MI: Eerdmans, 2010), 64.

[34]Johnathan Alvarado, "Pentecostal Worship and the Creation of Meaning," in *Toward a Pentecostal Theology of Worship*, ed. Lee Roy Martin (Cleveland, TN: CPT Press, 2016), 232.

personal charismatic experience gets emplotted into the grand plot of this guiding narrative, which stems biblically from Acts 2. Pentecostals interpret their own lives as part of God's grand story, and this all circles back to Pentecost, where the Spirit of God fell upon the church. If the latter rain narrative is the Pentecostal guiding narrative, then a Pentecostal's experiences will be understood within that framework. This leads to one final question: How does the Pentecostal worshiping community use worship music to interpret and reinforce the espoused and operant theological commitments of Pentecostalism?

REINFORCING THE STORY

Renewal worship tells and reinforces the Pentecostal story through its aesthetic presentation, and it helps a person see his or her own place in the narrative. For Macchia, it is in worship that Christian identity is fundamentally formed.[35] Worship both responds to God and to one another in response to God,[36] so together the community joins in solidarity for spiritual formation. In Pentecostalism, worship precedes and even shapes doctrine. Pentecostal ethicist Daniela Augustine calls communal worship Pentecostalism's *theologia prima* from which doctrine gets its form and content.[37] Macchia agrees, stating, "Worship brings right belief into life so that it might then nourish and support life witness. Worship is the context in which the church lives the biblical story in resistance to the world and in witness to an alternative reality."[38] So worship holistically shapes belief and guides action. This is accomplished by faithfully emphasizing the guiding Pentecostal narrative over and over again through multisensory encounters. According to Smith, "Pentecostal worship is 'experiential' because it assumes a holistic understanding of personhood and agency—that the essence of the human animal cannot be reduced to reason or intellect."[39] Renewal worship encourages visceral,

---

[35]Frank Macchia, "Signs of Grace: Towards a Charismatic Theology of Worship," in *Toward a Pentecostal Theology*, 154.

[36]Macchia, "Signs of Grace," 155.

[37]Daniela Augustine, "Liturgy, *Theosis*, and the Renewal of the World," in *Toward a Pentecostal Theology of Worship*, ed. Lee Roy Martin (Cleveland, TN: CPT Press, 2016), 154. This is done through "choreographed, enacted theology in songs and hymns, prayers and sermons, symbolic gestures and congregational movements" (154).

[38]Macchia, "Signs of Grace," 154.

[39]Smith, *Thinking in Tongues*, 72.

embodied, choreosonic acts in its liturgical setting to promote worshiping God fully and holistically as whole persons.[40] This section will briefly consider how renewal worship utilizes the arts in general for aesthetic formation before focusing on musical worship.

The arts and music in aesthetic formation. People are holistic and learn, communicate, and relate to each other in many different ways. When worship is holistic it engages every sensory aspect of our creatureliness. A worshiper's aim to know God more should include *hearing* God's creative voice echo throughout the walls of the church, *seeing* God's vision for a restored world, *touching* the wounded hands and side of the resurrected Christ, *smelling* the aroma of perfumed oil that was poured out at the feet of Christ, and *tasting* the sweetness of God's abundant Spirit. Worship is most formative when it utilizes *all* of our imaginative modes of expression, and the arts have the ability to reflect God's good creation back to God. As David Taylor states,

> In corporate worship the church takes the stuff of creation and makes an art of it: song from wind, dance from motion, architecture from stone, poetry from language, paint from pigments. The church does so not only to make sense of its life before God in praise, nor only because of its desire to remain obedient to the will and Word of God, but also because liturgical art is a way for the people of God to take pleasure in God's beloved creation.[41]

Because the arts represent our highest forms of human expression, it is imperative for the church to allow the arts to affect worshipers in their own ways.[42] What this means is that the liturgical arts should aim to engage the worshiping community's emotions and desires and should not be restricted or dictated by church leaders that lack aesthetic sensibilities. When artists speak into the aesthetic forms utilized in worship, not only will the arts be able to effectively communicate in their own ways, but the church will begin utilizing different members of the body of Christ to edify and nourish the whole worshiping community. But while the arts should speak their own languages, Taylor is

---

[40]Ashon Crawley coined the term *choreosonic* to mean the juxtaposition of movement and sound in a ritual or liturgical act. See Ashon Crawley, *Blackpentecostal Breath: The Aesthetic of Possibility* (New York: Fordham University Press, 2017), 93.

[41]Taylor, *Glimpses of the New Creation*, 59.

[42]Taylor, *Glimpses of the New Creation*, 2.

quick to point out that they should not shape worshipers on their own terms.[43] An artistic expression in the church should not be appreciated as an end in itself, rather a work of liturgical art must function as a means to another end. The liturgical arts are acts of worship that glorify God and draw people into the presence of God.

While modern worship services tend to utilize auditory and visual modes of transmission, they can leave tactile or kinesthetic learners spiritually malnourished. Pentecostalism has long ascribed to bodily, nonverbal communication to come alongside verbal proclamation. Pentecostals believe there are times words fail to adequately communicate spiritual truths, so communicating nonverbally becomes imperative. As Romans 8:26 states, "Likewise the Spirit helps us in our weaknesses; for we do not know how to pray as we ought, but that very Spirit intercedes with sighs too deep for words." Allowing expression and formation to happen in holistic ways opens people up to know God deeper and to express their humanity bodily.[44]

As discussed earlier, music is intrinsically tied to embodied action, and for Pentecostals, musical worship is one of the strongest drivers of the shared charismatic experience and opens up space for choreosonic worship to ensue. In his article "Singing, in the Body and in the Spirit," theologian Steven Guthrie argues that music is used in the sanctifying work of the Holy Spirit because it engages people holistically through their bodies and senses. Guthrie states,

> A sense-denying spirituality leaves at least half of our humanity in the darkness, alienated from God. Not only the mind, but the body and the senses are to be brought out into the light. It would seem then that the sensualist, the one who has abused body and sense, more than anyone needs to have body and sense engaged by the Spirit. In songs, hymns, and spiritual songs, the world of bodily experience is enlisted in praise, re-defined doxologically, and reoriented toward the worship of God and the benefit of the community.[45]

---

[43]Taylor, *Glimpses of the New Creation*, 2.

[44]This chapter intentionally focuses on music, and bodily movements that accompany music. However, dance and other bodily practices are vital in many Pentecostal and charismatic church communities. For more on this see chap. 3 in Steven Félix-Jäger, *Spirit of the Arts: Towards a Pneumatological Aesthetic of Renewal* (New York: Palgrave Macmillan, 2017).

[45]Steven Guthrie, "Singing, in the Body and in the Spirit," *Journal of the Evangelical Theological Society* 46, no. 4 (2003): 641.

Music helps to reorient and redefine a person's body and emotions that may have been given over to self-gratification.[46] As discussed earlier, it is the idolization of music's power that leads to our ruin, but Guthrie points out that the Spirit works through the same affective power of music to quicken our bodies and spirits and reorient them to God. The negative emotional and sensual effects of music are due to music's affective power aimed away from God. The best way to contest this is not to deny music and its power, but to aim it toward God in worship. The human capacity for music and creativity is part of God's good, created order, and it would be a mistake to deny it because of the possibility of its abuse.

Music, according to Guthrie, also allows for "sensitivity and responsiveness to the created order and to other human beings."[47] There is a strong communal component to music's formational power. Not only does music unite people as they sing, sway, and clap together in unison, it also unites people to a common theme. What is being expressed in a worship song gets sung communally, and a diverse group of people with varying experiences unite their voices for a common, storied utterance. The individual's vulnerability is met by the outstretched arms of a shared community. As the people sing together to God, there is both a vertical (up-down and down-up relation) and a lateral connection. The people are unified with one voice as they live and express the same shared experience, and then the unified people of God connect with the relational God to whom the worship is directed. It is in this communal space that God speaks to entire communities. Communities are reconciled to God when they worship together in solidarity. This is what was demonstrated to the believers in the upper room in Acts 2 and is what is available every time communities gather together in worship.

The formational power of music in context. Next let us consider some practical, contemporary examples of how renewal worship music reinforces the Pentecostal narrative. This allows us to put some flesh on the bones of our study and see how the ideas stated above work out practically in the context of renewal worship. At the start of this chapter I described Pentecostal worship as constituting resounding music; expressive, bodily movement;

---

[46]Guthrie, "Singing, in the Body and in the Spirit," 646.
[47]Guthrie, "Singing, in the Body and in the Spirit," 642.

prayerful intercession; and verbal acts of worship, such as testimony and proclamation. There are many more acts of worship that could be discussed, but just a few examples will suffice. We will look at three contemporary Pentecostal worship song performances and see how they display and reinforce the types of worship acts quoted above, and how those support a guiding Pentecostal narrative.

The narrative of Spirit empowerment is often supported by the notion of the triumphant freedom granted when one yields to the Spirit. When Jesus Culture, a world-renowned charismatic worship team based out of Redding, California, sings the song "Freedom" (2018), they model and exude ecstatic worship with lively expressive movement.[48] The music is always driving with either a full band carried by electric guitar riffs, or at a lower intensity when it is mobilized by "four on the floor"[49] from the kick drum. The music is written to encourage clapping from the start, but the song raises dynamically and encourages dancing in the musical breaks, choruses, and in the bigger parts of the bridge. The music is played loud, and the surroundings are dark, but supercharged with moving lights, encouraging congregants to shout and dance in the sort of communal solitude found in dance clubs. The lyrics portray the freedom that is found in the Spirit. This freedom helps believers overcome fear, burdens, and the scars of the past, and to live in the fullness of abundant life in Christ. The lyrics also imagine what freedom in the Spirit looks like bodily with the lyrics, "Run into wide open spaces, grace is waiting for you. Dance like the weight has been lifted, grace is waiting." These lyrics induce ecstatic praise as they portray the joys of overcoming. Some of what's being reinforced through "Freedom" is the liberative power that comes from dependence on the Holy Spirit. Also reinforced is the notion that the people of God should sing loud and dance as the Spirit of God overcomes them with joy.

Many Pentecostal worship services start with upbeat, declarative songs in order to bring the people together physically through motion and spiritually through a loud broadcast of their hopes and desires. The first song or two

---

[48]Jesus Culture, "Jesus Culture—Freedom (feat. Kim Walker-Smith) (Live)," www.youtube.com /watch?v=dKxeZsZvp7E (accessed January 12, 2020).

[49]Lexico.com cogently defines "four on the floor" as "a rhythm in 4/4 time in which the bass drum is played on every beat, characteristic of some styles of dance music."

often act as a sort of wakeup call, alarming worshipers that it's time to get together and focus on God. The songs are positive, upbeat, and anthemic. They establish a sense of excitement and gratitude among the worshipers, helping them to momentarily set aside the fears and troubles that accompanied them into the worship gathering. The first song is usually loud and exciting because it is supposed to swiftly spark the people into alignment. When the people are unified and aligned to the purposes of God, then the worship sets often slow down and get more intimate. Once aligned, the worshipers are spiritually and emotionally prepared to deal with their fears and troubles, and much of the remaining worship set, ministry time, and sermon addresses those issues.

A great example of testimony and proclamation in worship is present in gospel artist Travis Greene's song "Intentional."[50] "Intentional" is a groovy mid-tempo gospel song that features a full band and a small mixed choir. The worship leader of a gospel group, Greene in this instance, typically establishes the melody through the first verse and the first chorus, and then has the choir sing the melody in unison for the rest of the song. During this time the worship leader ad libs for the remainder of the song, singing parts of the lyrics, prayerful confessions, and giving directives to the congregation through commands and vocal runs. What results is a deeply interactive experience where the crowd feels completely involved in the making of the music, and part of the confessional witness being portrayed from the stage.

The lyrics of "Intentional" are very simple and repetitive. The song ruminates on Romans 8:28, which states, "We know that all things work together for good for those who love God, who are called according to his purpose." Greene and the choir sing a modified fragment of the verse over and over: "All things are working for my good, 'cause He's intentional." Functionally, the congregants are letting that verse sing over their circumstances and allowing the lyrics to pour over them. In gospel music, lyrics are not necessarily rational

---

[50]Travis Greene, "Travis Greene—Intentional Live," www.youtube.com/watch?v=IDv0ZCnqJME (accessed January 12, 2020). In the video, Greene ad-libs phrases like, "I think we have some witnesses here tonight," "He's been doing it for a long time," "We have joy because we know it's working," "It ain't over till it's good," etc. These phrases are only partially rehearsed with musical cues, but flow improvisationally from the stage, creating a unique experience every time the song is performed.

or didactic, but have a participatory function.[51] The congregation is composed of "those who love God," so this song acts as a means to fully embrace the promise that was given in Romans. Halfway through the song Greene rapidly calls out many instances of specific examples where God has a better vision for current circumstances. Here Greene calls out things so they may be overcome, and the people testify about God's good provision through these events.

This is one of many examples where testimony and proclamation are given powerful agency through music in the renewal worship service. Some of what's being reinforced here is that the charismatic community is God's witness on earth. The community testifies about the good things God has already done in the lives of those who love God, but also broadcasts the continual provision that comes from life in the Spirit. Renewal worship often proclaims God's abundance, reinforcing through testimony how life in the Spirit brings power and favor.

Finally, an example of prayerful intercession and tarrying through musical worship is when Bethel Music's Amanda Cook and Jeremy Riddle lead Hillsong Worship's "What a Beautiful Name" and enter into a time of spontaneous worship.[52] The slow-tempo song starts gradually and prayerfully with ambient pads droning on the root and a piano impressionistically alternating between two chords. Cook begins to extemporaneously repeat the phrase "Right in this moment, this is the moment we were born for." Gently the drums begin to swell through cymbals and toms, setting up an air of expectation before Cook begins to sing the lyrics of "What a Beautiful Name." The song poetically describes how the incarnation of Christ led to the defeat of sin and the redemption of humanity. Cook, however, uses the song as a catalyst, calling for the redemption of particular sins or spiritual bondages. After singing "What a Beautiful Name" Cook tagged a spontaneous chorus that followed the simple descending melody that the piano and guitar were playing. The lyrics proclaimed, "No more separation between earth and heaven. You have

[51] Wen Reagan, "Forerunning Contemporary Worship Music: The Afro-Pentecostal Roots of Black Gospel," in *Essays on the History of Contemporary Praise and Worship*, ed. Lester Ruth (Eugene, OR: Pickwick, 2020), 133.

[52] Bethel TV, "What a Beautiful Name + Spontaneous Worship—Amanda Cook and Jeremy Riddle," (accessed January 11, 2020). Although Bethel Music and Hillsong Worship are both world-renowned worship collectives that write influential original music, they often play each other's songs. Song sharing is characteristic of all renewal worship.

closed the distance." As the music grew, Cook began prophesying, prayerfully speaking and singing against loneliness and isolation. The music lingers on as Cook briefly ministers to the congregation and then the band shifts into a new song led by Riddle.

Charismatic worship leaders, by the prompting of the Holy Spirit, seek to find new and particular ways to minister to the congregation. The universal story of redemption becomes personalized through intercession and spontaneous worship. The Spirit knows the hearts of the people better than any person, so the worship leader seeks to be led by the Spirit for the sake of ministry. Worship leaders often receive a "word" through prayer prior to the worship service, and then incorporate this phrase into the spontaneous worship. In this way spontaneous worship, while largely improvisational, is partially scripted. It's like a lead guitarist who has a repertoire of guitar licks that have been perfected in practice. When the guitarist begins to solo in a performance, they string together the pre-rehearsed guitar licks with many other notes and runs that are played in the key extemporaneously. Musical and lyrical improvisation in spontaneous worship is commonly at least partially rehearsed. In spontaneous worship the musicians follow the leader and skillfully swell, grow, and retract at unplanned, yet pivotal moments. These musical movements emphasize the flow of the Spirit among the people and help people cathartically release their burdens onto God. Here the worship service becomes a space for prayer, intercession, release, and healing. What is reinforced is that believers must rely on the Spirit for counsel and liberation, and that God is present when worshipers purposefully create space for a divine encounter. By creating an atmosphere that is both personal and communal, music fosters a sacred space full of expectancy that is germane for prayer and intercession.

In the examples above, renewal music reinforced the message of Spirit empowerment and the theology of abundance discussed last chapter. The lyrics espoused Pentecostal theological commitments, and the performances demonstrated how those commitments were ritually encoded. Renewal worshipers enter worship with an expectation of breakthrough, freedom, empowerment, and God's favor. It is a triumphant message that is reinforced over and over again. When this message is reinforced, it takes root in the lives of the individual worshipers and transforms the culture of the community. In renewal worship God's story of Spirit empowerment, made available through the redemption and reconciliation of Christ, becomes the story of the people.

Since God is present in the people's praises, it makes sense that Pentecostals and charismatics find ways to continually praise and worship with music throughout the worship service. Liturgical elements that are partial to renewal worship like proclamation, testimony, and intercessory prayer are still present, but are now tied to musical expression. In a way, music scores these liturgical elements, accentuating their aesthetic impact and amplifying their affective potential. This blending of music with other liturgical elements creates a "whole body experience."[53] Worshipers are able to experience the liturgical elements robustly in variegated ways. Music establishes a highly emotive atmosphere for other liturgical elements to dwell in.

In his book *Spirit and Sacrament*, pastor and scholar Andrew Wilson makes a case for merging liturgical eucharistic worship with Spirit-filled charismatic worship. Wilson seeks to join the "best of both worlds" in worship by combining the theologically rich sacramental liturgies found in the historical traditions, with the exuberant spiritual abundance of charismatic traditions. To our point about music scoring liturgical elements in worship, Wilson comically shares a story: "A couple of years ago, I was asked by a church leader if I had any advice on how to get anti-liturgical charismatics to engage with the creeds. 'Use music,' I replied. 'If you have someone playing a pad sound on the keyboard in the background, charismatics will do anything.' I was joking, obviously—but only just."[54] This is especially funny because in 2014 Ben Fielding and Matt Crocker of Hillsong Worship wrote the song "This I Believe (The Creed)" in response to apologist and historian John Dickson's tweet that read: "Dear Hillsong, could your brilliant songwriters please put the Apostles' Creed to inspiring music. Do world-Christianity a massive favour."[55] Putting

---

[53] A. J. Swoboda, "God is Doing Something New: A North American Liturgical Experience," in *Scripting Pentecost: A Study of Pentecostals, Worship and Liturgy*, ed. Mark Cartledge and A. J. Swoboda (London: Routledge, 2017), 124.

[54] Andrew Wilson, *Spirit and Sacrament: An Invitation to Eucharismatic Worship* (Grand Rapids, MI: Zondervan, 2018), 132.

[55] "This I Believe (The Creed) Song Story," *Hillsong Collected* blog, July 3, 2014, www.hillsong.com /collected/blog/2014/07/this-i-believe-the-creed-song-story/#.Xlrxay2ZPBI (accessed February 29, 2020).

the creed to music gave the traditionally significant words stronger affective appeal, sanctioning it to shape Christians in new ways. Likewise, playing music softly behind spoken creeds or other liturgical elements connects those elements to the communal songs that were sung throughout the worship service. By establishing an affecting atmosphere behind liturgical elements, music unites each of these elements aesthetically to the holistic worship experience.

CONCLUSION

This chapter answered the question "How does renewal worship work?" by highlighting, in particular, how worship music helps shape the Pentecostal guiding narrative. Drawing from Paul Ricoeur and Kenneth Archer, this chapter showed how the Pentecostal story is demonstrated and reinforced aesthetically throughout the worship service. The brief case studies above helped show these ideas in action by presenting various ways a person is formed spiritually through renewal worship music. Perhaps the most positive effect of tethering every worship ritual to music and the arts is that people are treated holistically. Music and the arts help shape hearts, not just minds, and renewal worship powerfully utilizes aesthetic sensibilities to address the whole person.

This chapter closes out part one of the book. By establishing a theological method for understanding renewal worship (chap. 1), addressing the relational character of renewal worship (chap. 2), and discussing how renewal worship forms individuals and communities (chap. 3), we have answered the "what," "who," and "how" of renewal worship. The purpose of part one is to profile renewal worship, giving it an ample framework for understanding its nature and impact on the body of Christ. Part two shifts gears and seeks to hermeneutically approach particular practices within renewal worship, uncovering what these worship practices mean and how they affect renewal communities and Pentecostals worldwide. Before we move on to the next part, however, let's once again reflect on the content of this chapter with the following doxology:

> Praise God who shows us grace
> Who's present in this place
> Praise God who is enthroned upon our praise.

PART 2

RENEWAL WORSHIP IN CONTEXT

4

HOW RENEWAL WORSHIP FLOWS

BETWEEN WORD AND SPIRIT

For all who are led by the Spirit of God are children of God. For you did not receive a spirit of slavery to fall back into fear, but you have received a spirit of adoption. When we cry, "Abba! Father!" it is that very Spirit bearing witness with our spirit that we are children of God, and if children, then heirs, heirs of God and joint heirs with Christ—if, in fact, we suffer with him so that we may also be glorified with him.

ROMANS 8:14-17

AS IS TYPICAL in Pauline literature, the passage above is loaded with profound theological insight. This short passage from Romans affirms some of the salvific roles of each person of the Trinity, and it shows how Christ and the Spirit are fundamentally connected soteriologically. As believers, we are included into God's family when the Spirit bears witness to our spirit that we are children of God by adoption (Rom 8:15-16). As adopted children, we can call God "*Abba,*" the Aramaic word for father. So by adoption, believers enter into a real, familial relationship with God through Christ's sacrifice, and it is the Spirit who leads us to become joint heirs with Christ (Rom 8:17).

A significant but often ignored part of this passage is the second part of Romans 8:17, which states that being a joint heir with Christ *requires* suffering with Christ before we are glorified with Christ. In fact, Paul makes this a conditional statement: "We are joint heirs with Christ—*if, in fact,* we suffer with him." That means the Spirit indeed leads us to a life of victory (glorification), but only after we've suffered with Christ. The blessings that come with a life in Christ come from a *full* participation in the life of God in Christ through the Spirit, but since a "full participation" is required, we must also suffer with Christ as Christ suffered for us. This is what New Testament scholar Michael Gorman refers to as *cruciformity*: "Conformity to Christ, or holiness, understood as participation in the very life of God—inhabiting the cruciform God."[1] According to Paul, victory comes as a consequence of cruciformity. To better nuance what a theology of abundance entails, we must account for every aspect of the Christian life, recognizing how abundance flows from sacrifice. It is this perplexing connection of victory *and* suffering, along with the oscillation between formation and deconstruction in renewal worship, that will drive the content of this chapter.

This chapter discusses how renewal worship is navigated spiritually in a worship service. We will refer to this navigation as the "flow" of renewal worship, depicting it as oscillating between the formational power of the Word and the deconstructive power of the sanctifying Spirit. As such, this chapter presents "oscillation" metaphorically to help us understand the functions of spiritual growth and formation in renewal worship. This chapter then looks at these oscillations as they emerge practically through structured and spontaneous forms of worship, and thematically through triumphalistic expressions of worship and lament. While this chapter begins abstractly by looking at the formational powers of the "hands of God," it later vacillates to see how the Word made flesh concretely exemplifies the cruciformity that accompanies an abundant life. Finally, this chapter shifts gears to offer a prescriptive look at how the oscillation between Word and Spirit creates a charged space for spiritual growth and formation to take place. By navigating the flows of renewal worship, worship pastors discern how to address the worshiping community's spiritual needs while helping worshipers fully turn their attention toward God.

OSCILLATING BETWEEN WORD AND SPIRIT

According to Frank Macchia, Pentecostals tend to focus theologically more on the eschatological, renewing work of Christ and the Spirit than on abstract

---

[1] Michael Gorman, *Inhabiting the Cruciform God: Kenosis, Justification, and Theosis in Paul's Narrative Soteriology* (Grand Rapids, MI: Eerdmans, 2009), 2; emphasis added.

conceptions of the Father.[2] Hence, Pentecostals "generally confront the Trinitarian framework for Spirit baptism through issues surrounding the relationship between Word and Spirit. In this context, all Pentecostals recognize that the Spirit is the agent by which we are incorporated into Christ and born anew."[3] Pentecostal theology is grounded by the present-day experience of God through the Spirit, and it is the Spirit who subsumes us into the life of Christ. Although renewal worship is expressed principally through pneumatological language, it does not focus on the Spirit *in lieu of* Christ—quite the contrary! Pentecostals uphold *both* Christ *and* the Spirit as mutually essential for Christian faith and practice. In fact, the Pentecost account of Acts 2 indicates how, through a sort of role reversal, believers are able to participate in the life of Christ by the power of the Holy Spirit. Theologian Jürgen Moltmann writes, "Christ's history in the Spirit begins with his baptism and ends in his resurrection. Then things are reversed. Christ sends the Spirit upon the community of his people and is present in the Spirit. That is the history of the Spirit in Christ. The Spirit of God becomes the Spirit of Christ. The Christ sent in the Spirit becomes Christ the sender of the Spirit."[4] Christ sends the Spirit to the church, just as Jesus was sent to humanity by the Spirit. And just as the Spirit descended upon Jesus at his baptism, now Christ is the baptizer in the Spirit. For Pentecostals, it is impossible to know Christ without the Spirit, and we never would have known the Spirit without Christ.[5]

Christ and the Spirit belong together and have worked in tandem even before the incarnation, since the very beginning of time. In fact, there is scriptural evidence supporting the idea that all of creation was, in some way, fashioned by and through Christ and the Spirit. As John 1 indicates, it was

---

[2]Frank Macchia, *Baptized in the Spirit: A Global Pentecostal Theology* (Grand Rapids, MI: Zondervan, 2006), 113.

[3]Macchia, *Baptized in the Spirit*, 113.

[4]Jürgen Moltmann, *The Source of Life: The Holy Spirit and the Theology of Life* (Minneapolis: Fortress, 1997), 15.

[5]This has even led Protestant pneumatologists such as Jürgen Moltmann and Amos Yong to reject the *filioque* clause that was added to the Nicene-Constantinopolitan Creed, citing that the clause makes the Spirit subordinate to the Son, even if it was only intended to reflect salvation history. It is more appropriate to understand both the Son and the Spirit as proceeding from the Father alone as it was originally stated in the creed. Hence, Yong has reapproached the "two hands" terminology Irenaeus put forth. See Amos Yong, *Beyond the Impasse: Toward a Pneumatological Theology of Religions* (Eugene, OR: Wipf & Stock, 2014), 86-87; Jürgen Moltmann, *The Spirit of Life: A Universal Affirmation* (Minneapolis: Fortress, 2001), 71-72.

through the preincarnate Christ—the Word, or *Logos*,[6] of God—that all things were created. Consider John 1:3: "All things came into being through him, and without him not one thing came into being." John 1 also references Genesis 1 with the opening lines, "In the beginning." A renewal reading of Genesis 1 sees God "speaking" things into existence through the Word, but also recognizes the presence of the Spirit playing an active role in creation.[7] Genesis 1:2 mentions a "wind from God" or *ruakh* sweeping over the face of the waters. The term *ruakh* is the common Old Testament word for Spirit. So the Spirit was presiding over the primordial waters before, starting in Genesis 1:4, God spoke order into the formless voids. God's breath (Spirit) and voice (Word), were the powers of creation.[8] Psalm 33:6 also places Word and Spirit (breath) at creation: "By the word of the LORD the heavens were made, and all their host by the breath of his mouth." The Spirit's sweeping motion over the chaotic waters, and the Word's force for order in the subsequent days of creation, were both essential for creation, hence their inclusion in the creation account.

One of the first theologians to connect Word and Spirit at creation was second-century bishop Irenaeus. Many early Christian thinkers did not always distinguish Word from Spirit. In fact, prior to Irenaeus and long before the creedal foundations were set at Nicaea and Constantinople,

---

[6]The term *Logos* in John 1 really indicates a guiding, structural force that keeps things in motion together. This sense of the term is derived from pre-Socratic philosopher Heraclitus who posited that all things in nature are in a state of perpetual flux and are connected by a logical structure or pattern, which he termed *Logos*. In this sense, when the author of John calls Jesus the *Logos* of God, he is saying something quite significant—that Jesus is the guiding structural force, by whom all things were made. Although there is some debate on whether John intentionally used the Greek philosophical sense of the word, second-century apologist Justin Martyr seems to affirm its use, stating, "And when Socrates endeavoured, by true reason and examination, to bring these things to light, and deliver men from the demons, then the demons themselves, by means of men who rejoiced in iniquity, compassed his death, as an atheist and a profane person, on the charge that 'he was introducing new divinities'; and in our case they display a similar activity. For not only among the Greeks did reason (Logos) prevail to condemn these things through Socrates, but also among the Barbarians were they condemned by Reason (or the Word, the Logos) Himself, who took shape, and became man, and was called Jesus Christ" (*The First Apology of Justin Martyr*, chap. 5 in Philip Schaff, *Ante-Nicene Fathers* vol. 1, Christian Classics Ethereal Library).

[7]For historical work on this point, see Athanasius and Didymus, *Works on the Spirit: Athanasius's Letters to Serapion on the Holy Spirit, and Didymus's on the Holy Spirit*, trans. Mark DelCogliano, Andrew Radde-Gallwitz and Lewis Ayres (Crestwood, NY: St. Vladimir's Seminary Press, 2011), 11-15.

[8]Robert Johnston, *God's Wider Presence: Reconsidering General Revelation* (Grand Rapids, MI: Baker Academic, 2014), 184.

Christian thinkers did not often distinguish Word and Spirit from created beings, and it was left unclear if Word and Spirit were as divine as the Father.[9] Irenaeus, on the other hand, used creation to distinguish the Father, Son, and Spirit from that which was created.[10] Consider what he wrote in *Against Heresies*:

> Angels did not make us nor did they form us nor indeed could angels make an image of God nor [could] any other besides the true God nor [could] a Power far removed from the Father of all things. For God did not need these [beings] to make what he had himself beforehand determined to make, as if he himself did not have his Hands. For always present with him are the Word and Wisdom, the Son and Spirit, by whom and in whom he made all things freely and of his own will, to whom he also speaks, when he says, "Let us make man after our image and likeness."[11]

According to Irenaeus, God alone—the Father by way of the Son and Spirit—created human beings. Irenaeus used this "hands imagery" to support his argument (against his Gnostic opponents) that there is one Creator God—as the one God works through Word and Spirit.[12] The hands imagery precedes Irenaeus, however. There is quite a bit of biblical reference to the hands of God, especially the right hand of God,[13] and there is apocryphal writing[14] and early Christian apologetic writing (*To Autolycus*) that supports the idea as well. But with Irenaeus, we get the sense that Word and Spirit work in tandem through a symbiotic creative relationship.

[9]Anthony Briggman, "Irenaeus: Creation & the Father's Two Hands," *Sapientia* April 19, 2017, https://henrycenter.tiu.edu/2017/04/irenaeus-creation-the-fathers-two-hands/ (accessed September 19, 2020).
[10]Briggman, "Irenaeus."
[11]Irenaeus of Lyons, *Against Heresies*, 4.20.1, in Andrew Raddee-Gallwitz, ed., *The Cambridge Edition of Early Christian Writing*, vol. 1, *God* (Cambridge: Cambridge University Press, 2017), 34.
[12]Anthony Briggman, *Irenaeus of Lyons and the Theology of the Holy Spirit* (Oxford: Oxford University Press, 2012), 121.
[13]The right hand symbolizes strength for both God and humans in Scripture (Ps 139:10; Ex 15:6). It also has come to symbolize God's power, particularly in reference to the creation and God's acts of deliverance (Ps 60:5; Is 48:13) and is said to be auspicious (Ps 16:11; 48:10). Christ's sitting at the right hand of the Father symbolizes that he too is significant for bringing deliverance (Heb 1:3; Eph 1:20-21). The left hand, however, is not explicitly discussed in Scripture like the right hand, but it is mentioned in a few different ways. It is discussed in contrast to the right hand (Prov 3:16), as a negative direction (Mt 25:33; Eccles 10:2), as an honored place in conjunction with the right (Mk 10:35-45). For more on this see "Left Hand, Right Hand," in *A Dictionary of Biblical Tradition in English Literature*, ed. David Lyle Jeffrey (Grand Rapids, MI: Eerdmans, 1992), 442.
[14]2 Esdras 8:7-8; Shepherd of Hermas, parable 9; Wisdom 8–9.

Creation, for Irenaeus, was seen as a trinitarian act, as God used "his Hands" to fashion all of creation. In *Against Heresies* 2.30.9, Irenaeus sees the Word as conferring existence to creation, and Wisdom (the Spirit) as arranging and forming what was brought into existence. According to historian Anthony Briggman, Irenaeus sees the Spirit as rendering what was created into "a harmonious whole."[15] The Spirit is thus the creative force behind creation. Not only does Irenaeus associate Word and Spirit as important agents of creation, but through the hands imagery he also affirms the Spirit's full divinity and the "the distinction and equality of the Spirit in relation to the Son,"[16] which was a significant step in early Christian theological reflection. The "two hands metaphor" makes for a robust trinitarianism that shows the Spirit and Word constantly and inseparably working together.[17] Amos Yong points out that when Word and Spirit are viewed together, our religious experience, which shapes our theological method, is "both concrete—of Christ—and dynamic—of the Spirit—even while ultimately being of God (Christ as the representation of the Father and the Spirit as the presence of the Father)."[18] They are so intertwined, we can think of the Spirit as universalizing the Word, and the Word as particularizing the Spirit.[19] This is even true for us today: Christ gave us the Spirit, and the Spirit makes Christ known to us.

Although Irenaeus saw the Spirit as a creative arranger, I wonder if there is a more appropriate way to think of the Spirit's creative power than merely as one who arranges or organizes. After all, considering the creation account of Genesis, the Spirit's presence in the formless, chaotic void better associates the Spirit with unbridled, uncontrolled power, not necessarily as a power that arranges things.[20] In fact, the Spirit is associated with spontaneity and unbridled power in other parts of Scripture as well. John 3:8 states, "The wind blows where it wishes, and you hear its sound, but you do not know where it comes from or where it goes. So it is with everyone who is born of

---

[15]Briggman, *Irenaeus of Lyons*, 146.

[16]Briggman, *Irenaeus of Lyons*, 146.

[17]Yong, *Beyond the Impasse*, 43.

[18]Yong, *Beyond the Impasse*, 44.

[19]Yong, *Beyond the Impasse*, 43.

[20]Steven Guthrie, *Creator Spirit: The Holy Spirit and the Art of Becoming Human* (Grand Rapids, MI: Baker Academic, 2011), xvii.

the Spirit."[21] And of course the Acts 2 account of Pentecost sees the Spirit come suddenly like "the blowing of a violent wind" (Acts 2:2). Finally, and perhaps most significantly, it is by the power of the Spirit that believers are sanctified (Rom 15:16; 1 Pet 1:2; 2 Thess 2:13). Sanctification is the process of purification or consecration; it is the Spirit burning away the sins and iniquities of believers so that they would be made holy in the sight of God. This sort of power is different from the formational power of the Word—it is a deconstructing power. At creation, the Spirit's deconstructing power entails setting apart and making "good," but as sin has affected creation, it also now means a deconstruction of evil (sanctification) that incites activities such as lament, confession, and repentance. Perhaps, therefore, we can see the Word as the structured, formational power that creatively orders things, and the Spirit as the spontaneous, deconstructing power that creatively breaks things down. Each person of the Trinity participates in the act of creation even while there are distinct ways in which the creative act plays out in the life of the believer. The Father creates through the Son and Spirit, the Son bringing a creative order and the Spirit bringing a creative deconstruction.

But while there are distinct ways in which the creative acts of God play out in the life of the believer, there still is unity in the Trinity. The Word and Spirit are not doing two different actions but are involved differently in the same action. Since every act is a trinitarian act, we can see the Word as the formational power *of* the Spirit, and the Spirit as the deconstructing power *of* the Word. They are unified in action, so when we are convicted by the Spirit, it is not wrong or unfair to say the Word or the Father has convicted us. In fact, later during the fourth century, mature pro-Nicene theologies affirm what has been described as a doctrine or principle of inseparable operations, in which every act of the divine person entails the presence of the other divine persons. For instance, Gregory of Nyssa says,

> But in the case of the Divine nature we do not similarly learn that the Father does anything by Himself in which the Son does not work conjointly, or again that the Son has any special operation apart from the Holy Spirit; but every

---

[21]It should be noted that the word "wind" in the Greek is πνεῦμα (*pneuma*) and "Spirit" is Πνεύματος (*pneumatos*). So, by using essentially the same word, Jesus is intentionally linking the concepts and connotations of wind and Spirit.

operation which extends from God to the Creation, and is named according to our variable conceptions of it, has its origin from the Father, and proceeds through the Son, and is perfected in the Holy Spirit.[22]

As long as we recognize God's creative action ultimately as unified trinitarian acts, I think it is helpful to appreciate the Word's and the Spirit's distinct roles in these actions because it helps us understand how renewal worship guides spiritual formation. Both the formational and deconstructing forces are powerful and necessary for believers to be truly conformed to the image of Christ.

Believers must die to their old, sinful realities (Gal 2:20-21; 1 Cor 15:31; Jn 3:30) and be built up as new creations in Christ (Eph 4:22-24; Col 3:10; 2 Cor 5:17). God works holistically in the lives of believers to bring about this total transformation, and just as the Hands of God were at work at creation, so are they at work in us when we are made into new creations. The work of sanctification and spiritual growth is a lifelong work in the believer, so there will be times when the formational power of the Word takes center stage, and other times when the deconstructing power of the Spirit leads the charge. The main point here, and of this chapter, is that an important characteristic of renewal worship is its ability to oscillate between formation and deconstruction. Often in renewal worship the liturgical elements like songs, preaching, and testimonies demonstrate victory and proclamation, but at other times they call for repentance, lament, and intercessory prayer. The renewal-worship pastor's role is to discern the leading of the Spirit and guide the people into whichever approach to spiritual formation is needed. As renewal worship oscillates between Word and Spirit, it does so practically between structure and spontaneity, and thematically between triumph and lament; we will look at these two themes respectively.

Between structure and spontaneity. One of the hallmarks of renewal worship is its propensity toward spontaneity. Spontaneous worship typically refers to unplanned musical worship that comes straight from the heart of the worshiper without prior preparation. A commonly cited Scripture passage that purportedly deals with spontaneous worship is Ephesians 5:18-20: "Be

---

[22]Gregory of Nyssa, *On "Not Three Gods,"* in *Readings in the History of Christian Theology*, rev. ed., ed. William Placher and Derek Nelson (Louisville, KY: Westminster John Knox, 2015), 1:49.

filled with the Spirit, as you sing psalms and hymns and spiritual songs among yourselves, singing and making melody to the Lord in your hearts, giving thanks to God the Father at all times and for everything in the name of our Lord Jesus Christ." Paul's term "spiritual song" is often thought to mean "spontaneous song."[23] For instance, in their worship blog Worship U, Bethel Music defines a spiritual song as "something that comes straight from your heart and your history with God—expressing to Him in your own words what He means to you."[24] It's a song that comes directly from a worshiper's spirit which connects to God's Spirit. Spontaneous worship is, therefore, a deep communion with God from spirit to Spirit.

Although Bethel Music encourages utilizing spontaneous worship, they do not disregard the importance of worship planning. Their blog post states, "While there is power in singing and declaring a song already written for our Sunday setlist, God also wants to meet us where we are in a specific moment in time."[25] Renewal worship promotes a both/and logic between structure and spontaneity, although renewal worship services don't always leave much room for spontaneity. Lim and Ruth point out that a great irony in contemporary worship is its value for extemporaneity, but in reality worship services often follow a closely managed order of service.[26] There is a desire for the Spirit to move spontaneously, but the structure is so established that it is sometimes difficult to break away from it. Nevertheless, the heart of renewal worship is less about categorically choosing one form of worship over the other, and more about discerning when God is seeking structure, spontaneity, or even "planned spontaneity" in worship.

Planned spontaneity is when space for improvisation is left open in a prearranged service or song. Here Pentecostal worship takes its cue

---

[23]Edward Foley, ed., *Worship Music: A Concise Dictionary* (Collegeville, MN: The Liturgical Press, 2000), 287. This argument is also made by practitioners: see Bob Sorge, *Exploring Worship: A Practical Guide to Praise & Worship*, 3rd ed. (Grandview, MO: Oasis House, 2018); Terry Law and Jim Gilbert, *The Power of Praise & Worship* (Shippensburg, PA: Destiny Image, 2008); and Tom Kraeuter, *Times of Refreshing: A Worship Ministry Devotional* (Lynnwood, WA: Emerald Books, 2002).

[24]"What is Spontaneous Worship," Worship U, 2019 (accessed September 26, 2020).

[25]"What is Spontaneous Worship."

[26]Swee Hong Lim and Lester Ruth, *Lovin' on Jesus: A Concise History of Contemporary Worship* (Nashville: Abingdon, 2017), 36.

historically from an "amalgamation" of sounds that have blended Black spirituals, Protestant hymnody, and the rhythm and emotions of blues and jazz.[27] Early twentieth-century Afro-Pentecostal churches, for instance, utilized this notion of planned spontaneity to promote freedom in the Spirit. Historian Grant Wacker states that through planned spontaneity, "Pentecostal worship oscillated between antistructural and structural impulses."[28] They did this to serve both the expression of uninhibited emotion, and the pragmatic aspects of leading an ordered service.[29] As we've discussed above, the key for planned spontaneity is to follow God's lead as worshipers oscillate between structure and spontaneity. Like jazz improvisation, there are still musical parameters that soloists work within in planned spontaneity. Wen Reagan writes,

> The spontaneity came from the lack of rehearsal, lyrics, or set list. This pattern created an atmosphere where the Spirit could move as the Spirit saw fit. But the planning was also there, and it came in the form of the repertoire, which was small enough to memorize. In other words, there was a scripted "book of common song," a generous and flexible structure—but structure nonetheless—that was rehearsed (in that it was repeated every Sunday) and pre-meditated (in that it was a bounded set list) body of musical common knowledge that ordered the service. This repertoire provided room for improvisation within a planned structure.[30]

This "common repertoire" becomes the bedrock from which spontaneous improvisations can emerge.

Discernment becomes the vehicle where worship pastors lead congregants through "the emotional landscape of worship"[31] by navigating between the push and pull of structure and spontaneity. Sometimes what is needed is the structural force of the Word that builds worshipers up. This is frequently the case in Black gospel music as new identities of adoption are bestowed

---

[27]Wen Reagan, "Forerunning Contemporary Worship Music: The Afro-Pentecostal Roots of Black Gospel," in *Essays on the History of Contemporary Praise and Worship*, ed. Lester Ruth (Eugene, OR: Pickwick, 2020), 117-18.

[28]Grant Wacker, *Heaven Below: Early Pentecostals and American Culture* (Cambridge, MA: Harvard University Press, 2001), 99.

[29]Wacker, *Heaven Below*, 99-100.

[30]Reagan, "Forerunning Contemporary Worship Music," 137-38.

[31]Reagan, "Forerunning Contemporary Worship Music," 135.

upon people that have endured oppression. Sometimes the deconstructing force of the sanctifying Spirit is needed to break down people that have a false sense of security due to affluence. Both of these impulses are needed at different times in the lives of Christians, and both impulses work toward spiritual growth. Because worship is active and relational, there is an expectation in renewal worship for the worship pastor to lead worshipers to a direct engagement with God.[32] The Spirit reveals what sort of engagement (structural or deconstructing) is needed, so the worship pastor discerns where the congregants are at and where the Spirit is leading. In this way, worship planning is deeply pastoral by nature.[33]

As we've seen throughout every expression of renewal worship, there is also an eschatological component to spontaneous worship. A. J. Swoboda reflects on his own church's practice of spontaneous worship, stating that the congregants often see the dynamic, spontaneous experience as an eschatological inbreaking of the Spirit.[34] When a new song is sung, congregants catch a glimpse of the kingdom that is yet fulfilled. In his church, Swoboda established a liturgical rhythm that bridges the gap of historical worship practices with fresh spontaneity. Like the common repertoire that's used for improvisation, these historical foundations give the church an established framework from which to be spontaneous.[35] In this way spontaneity creates a "trans-historical" understanding of the work of the Spirit.[36] While worshipers wait in expectation for a fresh outpouring of the Spirit, they remember what the Spirit has already done in their community. All in all, we see through these instances a practical oscillation between structure and spontaneity that supports an alternation between image building and breaking down, and between history and the eschaton. Next we will look at renewal worship oscillating between triumph and lament, showing how both are demonstrated in the life of Christ.

---

[32]Andy Lord, "A Theology of Sung Worship," in *Scripting Pentecost: A Study of Pentecostals, Worship and Liturgy*, ed. Mark Cartledge and A. J. Swoboda (London: Routledge, 2017), 85.

[33]Matt Mason, "The Worship Leader and Singing," in *Doxology & Theology: How the Gospel Forms the Worship Leader*, ed. Matt Boswell (Nashville: B&H, 2013), 182.

[34]A. J. Swoboda, "God is Doing Something New: A North American Liturgical Experience," in *Scripting Pentecost: A Study of Pentecostals, Worship and Liturgy*, ed. Mark Cartledge and A. J. Swoboda (London: Routledge, 2017), 127.

[35]Swoboda, "God is Doing Something New," 128.

[36]Swoboda, "God is Doing Something New," 128-29.

Between triumph and lament. Even though Pentecostals have a high view of the Bible, and Scripture frequently addresses suffering doxologically through lament, Pentecostals can struggle at times to adequately come to terms critically with matters of suffering.[37] This section looks at the importance of lament in worship, and how it too demonstrates an oscillation between Word and Spirit. I submit that Pentecostal triumphalism can both be corrected and rearticulated through lament.

When circumstances are difficult, sometimes the best response is to call out and reflect on the hardships head-on. For instance, consider the context from which I am writing this section. I am at my southern California home on September 6, 2020, and wildfires are torching areas near Fresno and Madera counties. We are experiencing record heat (121°F in Woodland Hills), and more than 2,094,955 acres have burned down across the state of California this year.[38] And that's not even the main story broadcasting in our national news today! The year 2020 will undoubtedly go down in history as one of the most difficult of late modernity. Some of the tumultuous highlights of this year include the drone strike and subsequent killing of Iranian general Qasem Soleimani; the impeachment trial and acquittal of US president Donald Trump; the ravishing effects of a global pandemic that has claimed countless lives, forced quarantines, and caused economic shutdowns across the globe; protests and counterprotests concerning government health mandates and control; protests and counterprotests that arose from racial crises following the circulation of video footage of police brutality and vigilante force used at a disproportionate rate against African Americans; and a contentious American election year. There is a litany of other hardships we've all endured in 2020, but these are just a few of the most consequential.

During this time, physical church gatherings have been limited or prohibited and pastors and worship leaders have had to innovate and use remote means for gathering in worship. With new charges to adequately address what is happening around the world, church leaders seek to innovate and usher in

---

[37]Stephen Torr, *A Dramatic Pentecostal/Charismatic Anti-Theodicy: Improvising on a Divine Performance of Lament* (Eugene, OR: Pickwick, 2013), 2.

[38]Holly Yan, Cheri Mossburg, Artemis Moshtaghian, and Paul Vercammen, "California Sets New Record for Land Torched by Wildfires as 224 People Escape by Air from a 'Hellish' inferno," CNN, www.cnn.com/2020/09/05/us/california-mammoth-pool-reservoir-camp-fire/index.html (accessed September 6, 2020).

new ways of ministering in a current and postpandemic reality. As we approach these times of hardship, many churches have recognized the necessity for grieving before instilling new hope for the days to come. Grieving through our present circumstances is healthy, and there is a form of biblical worship that generates hope from despair: lament.

Not only does the notion that renewal worship oscillates between Word and Spirit highlight the christological underpinnings of Pentecostal theology, it also gives adherents a theological response to a common critique of Pentecostal spirituality expressed through renewal worship: it is too triumphalistic. Triumphalism signifies the excessive celebration of one's achievements, and usually portrays an attitude of superiority. Applied to Christian spirituality, triumphalism implores believers to live the victorious Christian life, one that declares victory over sin, strongholds, scarcity, and anything that hinders God's desire for us to live life abundantly. This impulse is widespread in Pentecostal spirituality. As Pentecostal theologian David Courey states,

> The common posture of Pentecostal spirituality provides a ready example of Pentecostal triumphalism. Reality, for the faithful, is a black-and-white affair. . . . This tendency to oversimplification and reductionism characterizes Pentecostal spirituality, and indeed all triumphalism, and leads to an assertion of ultimacy for its vision, and a rejection of all that negates its claims.[39]

This posture retunes a person's perspective on life circumstances, bringing forth new expectations of what's possible when in God's favor. Eventually, however, this Pentecostal spirit of victory and optimism can lead to a denial of the facts of life. Often in the face of tragedy or crisis, Pentecostals are forced to either reinterpret their circumstances to fit a narrative of triumph, or suspend judgment on an issue, admitting that some things sit outside their realm of understanding.[40] This is an important critique, which Courey resolves by urging Pentecostals to develop a stronger theology of the cross that sees victory through sacrifice.

The key for Pentecostals is not to displace the universal outpour of the Spirit as the guiding motif of renewal worship, but to understand the cross's

---

[39]David Courey, *What Has Wittenberg to Do with Azusa? Luther's Theology of the Cross and Pentecostal Triumphalism* (London: Bloomsbury, 2015), 6.

[40]Courey, *What Has Wittenberg to Do with Azusa?*, 6.

indispensable role in the narrative. When Spirit baptism is known as the connection between the cross and the eschaton, then Pentecostals can retain a notion of victory because we have an assurance of the coming kingdom, while coming to terms with a cruciform reality that fully engages "the struggle against brokenness and injustice" in our present state of already and not yet.[41] As we've discussed above and in chapter one, the church lives in the state between Christ's inauguration of the kingdom of God at his first coming, and the consummation of the kingdom at his second coming. We oscillate between Word and Spirit *because* we are in the liminal space between the cross and the eschaton. This means that we are perpetually negotiating hope and grief—we attain hope when the Spirit breaks into our present, often dire, circumstances. Theologian Stephen Torr states it well:

> The gap between the Kingdom breaking in and the consummation—the "now/ not yet" tension—characterizes the current act in the drama. We are to imple- ment the victory in our own lives and also in the world around us but, we will inevitably come up against suffering in the midst of that. As we look to Jesus to help us perform our parts fittingly, we can begin to notice that he moves from a place of orientation, through the suffering and disorientation, to a place of resurrection or new creation.[42]

True triumph entails responsively following Christ's lead through suffering. We can stand in victory in the midst of suffering as we cling to God's covenantal faithfulness. Our hope is reassured when we remember how God moved in past periods of suffering, but we must be open for God to move in new and unexpected ways as we are led through our present circumstances.[43]

While hope looks forward to the other side of suffering, it also equips us to walk *through* our hardships. We can choose to live in the promise of abun- dance made possible by the cross only after we bear the cross of iniquities (and inequities) with Christ. Suffering must be addressed and redressed head-on, but even then, we cannot lose sight of the coming kingdom. Just as the hope of total reconciliation helped Christ endure the cross, our hope will

---

[41]Courey, *What Has Wittenberg to Do with Azusa?*, 213.
[42]Torr, *A Dramatic Pentecostal/Charismatic Anti-Theodicy*, 185.
[43]Torr, *A Dramatic Pentecostal/Charismatic Anti-Theodicy*, 154.

help us persevere through crisis. Uncritical triumphalism ignores or disregards the hardships of life, whereas a cruciform perspective *chooses* hope in
the face of despair. Oscillating between Word and Spirit allows worshipers
to appreciate the related, flipside notions of death and resurrection that are
essential for spiritual growth. In order to resurrect in glory, one must first
experience the grief of crucifixion. Thus, the antidote of triumphalism is the
hope of renewal that comes from cruciform living.

Another related critique concerning Pentecostal triumphalism addresses
its inability to adequately worship through lament. In his book *Prophetic
Lament*, practical theologian Soong-Chan Rah describes biblical lament as
"a liturgical response to the reality of suffering (that) engages God in the
context of pain and trouble."[44] Lament is a sung or poetic expression of sorrow
or grief to God.[45] Biblically, the lament often occurs as a "candid, even if
unwilling, embrace of a new situation of chaos, now devoid of the coherence
that marks God's good creation."[46] Those who lament know something is
wrong in the world, and cry out to God in anguish as they adjust to their new
circumstances of pain and subjugation. As Walter Brueggemann points out,
lament is experienced as a "personal end of the world."[47] Lament is the impassioned cry for God's intervention while in the midst of suffering.

The hope of lament is that God would hear the suffering cries of the people
and respond favorably toward them. If hope is the affective inbreaking of the
Spirit in our present circumstances, lament is necessary to adequately appreciate what personal, communal, or societal changes need to occur. Through
grief and mourning, lament calls out the sins and injustices that bring about
suffering. Brueggemann believes that the poetic language of lament is the
ultimate form of public criticism.[48] Lament is the critical act that precedes
the prophetic task of energizing new hope that redefines a person or

---

[44]Soong-Chan Rah, *Prophetic Lament: A Call for Justice in Troubled Times* (Downers Grove, IL:
InterVarsity Press, 2015), 21.

[45]Lament is a common theme in the Bible and can easily be found in the wisdom and prophetic
literature of the Old Testament, wherever grieving takes place throughout both Testaments. In
fact, the book of Lamentations is a collection of laments that follows the suffering and despair of
the Jews following the destruction of Jerusalem in 587 BCE.

[46]Walter Brueggemann, *The Message of the Psalms: A Theological Commentary* (Minneapolis: Augsburg, 1984), 20.

[47]Brueggemann, *Message of the Psalms*, 20.

[48]Brueggemann, *The Prophetic Imagination*, 2nd ed. (Minneapolis: Fortress, 2001), 46.

community's situation.[49] Without true lament, people will remain unwittingly oppressed as society continues to disregard the roots of injustice. Rah argues that the absence of lament in contemporary worship is indicative of the success-driven triumphalism embodied by American evangelicalism. Rah's critique covers all of American evangelical Christianity, of which he includes Pentecostalism.[50] Because lament is a form of prayerful worship that arises out of need, it is difficult for someone to truly lament and maintain a triumphalistic interpretation of his or her circumstances.

According to Rah, American triumphalism broadens the privilege of dominant culture. Lament occurs when people need deliverance from something, not when they have everything and are living in celebration. Those who live in celebration seek "constancy and sustainability,"[51] they are concerned with praising God for the blessings they already have. Thanking God for being blessed is not the issue, mind you—gratitude *is* the appropriate response to gift-reception. The problem is when the privileged are blind to the injustices that surround them. As the parable of the Good Samaritan has shown us (Lk 10:25-37), being a true neighbor entails caring for and helping those who are in need, not turning a blind eye. And as the story of Jesus mourning the death of Lazarus shows us (Jn 11:1-45), being a true brother entails empathy, lamenting with those who suffer.

Because the privileged are not (apparently) directly accountable for the plight of the underprivileged, they can easily recuse themselves from meaningful engagement. But no one in dominant society is totally innocent when injustice is systemic. The threads of injustice are woven throughout the fabric of our shared histories. The triumphalist imagination ignores the nation's sins of the past because the inequalities do not directly affect them. As Rah states, "We fail to acknowledge the reality of sins committed by the church and fail to offer a moral witness to the world."[52] This indicates the church's incompetence to deal with the dark parts of historical reality. The inability of the American church to move beyond triumphalism arises out of a failure to "hear the voices outside the dominant white male

---

[49]Brueggemann, *Prophetic Imagination*, 67.
[50]Rah, *Prophetic Lament*, 108.
[51]Rah, *Prophetic Lament*, 23.
[52]Rah, *Prophetic Lament*, 47.

narrative."[53] One of the ways out of this, argues Rah, is for the contemporary church to relearn how to lament.

When worshiping bodies lament, they call out for God's mercy, acknowledging the need for justice. The worshiping body takes on a posture of vulnerability as it realizes that it does not have enough strength or aptitude to solve these matters of injustice without God.[54] Instead of adopting a triumphalistic narrative, in lament the church truly acknowledges the experience of those who suffer. Lament needs to fully run its course before the church can properly respond to injustice,[55] otherwise those in power disregard the voices of the marginalized, "fixing the problem" before truly understanding the root of the issue. It allows dominant voices to write and recount the sequence of events that led to injustice instead of the disenfranchised who have suffered the injustices. When major issues are not properly dealt with, they will return again and again, like the parable of the exorcized demon that returns to an empty house with seven worse demons (Mt 12:43-45). Lament allows for a full, unexpurgated engagement of the roots of sin.

The problem in much of evangelical worship, according to Rah, is that there is no balance between praise and lament like there is in Scripture, and "any theological reflection that emerges from the suffering 'have-nots' can be minimized in the onslaught of the triumphalism of the 'haves.'"[56] While Rah certainly posits a strong and needed critique against the materialistic, triumphalistic evangelicalism that ignores the plight of the disenfranchised, there is an omission from his argument that should be noted. Rah's main attack is against the complacency of the privileged and how that feeds into a life of celebration, but the categorization that equates celebration with privilege is too reductionistic. There are expressions of celebratory worship that arise out of a theology of abundance and not in spite of it. I am referring here to the declarative triumphalism of Black gospel music.

In their article "A House Divided? Christian Music in Black and White," Banjo and Williams conducted a study comparing Black gospel music and

---

[53]Rah, *Prophetic Lament*, 60.
[54]Rah, *Prophetic Lament*, 68.
[55]Rah, *Prophetic Lament*, 174.
[56]Rah, *Prophetic Lament*, 23.

contemporary Christian music (CCM), a predominantly White genre.
While CCM grew out of the Jesus Movement of the late 1960s and 1970s,
Black gospel music has roots that stretch all the way back to the Black spirituals of the antebellum South. Black gospel worship utilizes expressive forms
of celebration that were "present in the jubilees and ring shouts of the
enslaved African in America."[57] Joyful utterances of praise, in both present
and historical gospel music, can be viewed as exclamations indicating a will
"to conquer or overcome past and present-day issues of oppression."[58] There
is a critical, social quality of gospel music that tends to underscore the notion
of liberation from oppression. Indeed, religious studies scholar Ashon
Crawley sees the "joyful noise" that is uttered in Black Pentecostal worship
as a critique of the theology and social structures of dominant culture that
play a part in subjugating Black communities.[59] The very act of exuberant
worship in Black communities has an implicit, prophetic function. So if
lament occurs when people need deliverance from something, then the
socially conscious, celebratory worship that comes from Black worshiping
communities must be understood in this light. In other words, the joyful
declaration of victory in the face of oppression *is* a prophetic form of lament,
even if it appears triumphalistic.

As discussed in chapter two, the language of abundance in gospel worship may indicate a triumph over oppression. In gospel music, even notions
of prosperity are underscored by the fact that the performers' ancestors
were once enslaved. As mentioned above, the hope of prosperity, in this
sense, carries an image-making function—they are not slaves, but children
of a king who has given them an inheritance. While the world has told
them they are worthless, God has told them they are worthy. A great
espoused example of this sentiment can be found in the lyrics of Jekalyn
Carr's "Changing Your Story." The central message of this song is that God
will change the destructive and oppressive narratives that were fixed on
subjugated believers. This change occurs *as* a work of deliverance, and

[57]Omotayo Banjo and Kesha Morant Williams, "A House Divided? Christian Music in Black and
White," *Journal of Media and Religion* 10 (2011): 131.

[58]Banjo and Williams, "A House Divided?," 131.

[59]Ashon Crawley, *Blackpentecostal Breath: The Aesthetics of Possibility* (New York: Fordham University Press, 2017), 144.

what's needed is for believers to truly accept what it means to be transformed into the image of Christ as coheirs to the kingdom. Consider some of the lyrics:

He's changing your story
From failure to success
From bound to freedom, hey
From lack to the abundance, hey
From defeated to winning, hey [60]

This new narrative of triumph is not one of easy comfort, but a narrative of overcoming systems that cause and inscribe labels of failure, boundedness, lack, and defeat. This song was released in 2020 during the Covid-19 pandemic, and although it bears the image of triumph, it does so fully aware of the circumstances surrounding our global struggles. In an interview, Carr reflected on "Changing Your Story" and how the song relates to the hardships of 2020. She said, "God is always taking care of you my brothers and sisters, so if He did it then, He won't fall short now. . . . Don't lose your praise. Every time you magnify God over your struggle, you're getting closer and closer to your breakthrough. Remember this, we're all coming out of this with our heads up."[61] The hope offered here is one of perseverance through struggles, not of an escapism that ignores hardships.

This sort of hope takes what Paul said in Romans 8:16-17 at face value: "It is that very Spirit bearing witness with our spirit that we are children of God, and if children, then heirs, heirs of God and joint heirs with Christ—if, in fact, we suffer with him so that we may also be glorified with him." Taking a cruciform approach to abundance means we suffer with Christ as the Spirit leads us through our iniquities, and on the other side of the struggle is the blessing of glorification. Glory and abundance do not come in spite of the weakness of suffering, but because of it. As Gorman writes,

Because God's majesty and God's relationality cannot be separated, we must understand God's majesty in light of God's revealed relationality. We do not simply hold the majesty and relationality of God in *tension*; with Paul, we must

---

[60]"Changing Your Story," words and music by Jekalyn Carr © 2020 The Orchard Music (administrated by Lunjeal Music Group).

[61]Jekalyn Carr, interview by Erica Campbell (2020), in "Changing Your Story: Jekalyn Carr Previews New Powerful Song!," https://getuperica.com/149991/jekalyn-carr-changing-your-story/ (accessed September 6, 2020).

see them in *concert*, a unison revealed in the power of the cross. God is not a
god of power *and* weakness but the God of power *in* weakness.[62]

The Spirit accompanies Christ in suffering, "whose strength will be proved
in Jesus' weakness."[63] In Christ, therefore, the systems of glory through power
are flipped, and true power comes as one, by the Spirit, endures and overcomes
suffering. The full acknowledgment of struggle and the declarative hope of
deliverance in Black gospel music are akin to the biblical notion of lament. It
is power through struggle, and it is abundance through cruciformity. This is
yet another way that renewal worship oscillates between Word and Spirit—as
it navigates between triumph and lament by leaning into the hope of true
lament. As we've discussed several ways that renewal worship reflects an
oscillation between Word and Spirit, let us finish this chapter practically,
discussing how this notion of oscillation affects worship planning and design.

DESIGNING RENEWAL WORSHIP

When we think about renewal worship as oscillating between Word and Spirit,
we can get a sense of how renewal worship "flows" and how worship pastors,
through discernment, traverse the spiritual landscape of the worshiping
community. Sociologist Gerardo Martí sees renewal worship as instituting a
"power-surrender" dynamic where worshipers ready themselves to receive
the gift of the Spirit for empowerment to carry on the kingdom of God's global
ministry of witness and reconciliation. Martí writes, "Worship involves the
hopeful anticipation of the Pentecostal ego motivated to participate in an
event-dependent effort (the gathering of worshipers) to surrender to God
(setting aside distractions, letting go) that leads the believer to deploy spiritual
power. Empowerment is mobilized to achieve what become sacredly charged
tasks in everyday life."[64] The worship gathering is, therefore, a space where
one takes on a posture of surrender in order to uninhibitedly receive spiritual
empowerment. Key to the power-surrender dynamic is the worshiper's *expec-*
tation of a relational encounter with God.[65] This expectation for encounter

---

[62]Gorman, *Inhabiting the Cruciform God*, 33.
[63]Moltmann, *Spirit of Life*, 62.
[64]Gerardo Martí, "Maranatha (O Lord, Come): The Power-Surrender Dynamic of Pentecostal Worship," *Liturgy* 33, no. 3 (2018): 21.
[65]Martí, "Maranatha (O Lord, Come)," 23.

cultivates a disposition of spiritual renewal that's repetitively reenacted through worship.[66]

Because the worshiping community comes ready and expectant for divine encounter, the worship pastor truly needs spiritual sensitivity when it comes to faithfully navigating the space between Word and Spirit. Although the worship pastor plays an important role in leading people into the presence of God in worship, the Spirit is ultimately the guide that decides where to take the worshiping community spiritually. Since God is relational, the worship pastor must be willing and ready to work in a relational collaboration with God as the whole worshiping community follows the Spirit's lead. In this final section we will discuss the role "flow" takes in renewal worship, and how this shapes the way renewal worship is planned.

The flow and form of renewal worship. Theologian Lexi Eikelboom defines "flow" as "a perfect state of concentration without struggle. In flow, one is working on something with such absorption that one's sense of time disappears."[67] Worshipers are spiritually formed as they oscillate between the constructive power of the Word and the deconstructing power of the Spirit in a state of flow. This state of flow is different from the overflow of the Spirit discussed in chapters one and two. The universal outpour of the Spirit is a kenotic gesture, a self-emptying of God onto humanity, whereas the flow we are discussing here is a human state of presence. Flow, here, is a sort of hyperfocus that allows one to be absorbed into the workings of God through worship. Pentecostal theologian Peter Althouse states that Pentecostals enter a liminal state of ritual play in renewal worship. Worship becomes the "space for liminal play" that allows the pneumatological and eschatological imaginations of worshipers to recall and enter into God's story of redemption and renewal.[68] Althouse's "space for liminal play" is in line with Eikelboom's concept of "flow," as flow admits us into the liminal space. Taking these concepts together, we can picture renewal worship as the charged, liminal space where worshipers flow between Word and Spirit, envisioning new realities as they take form in the present. As Althouse writes, "In the interplay

---

[66]Martí, "Maranatha (O Lord, Come)," 26.

[67]Lexi Eikelboom, "Flow and the Christian Experience of Time," The Rhythmic Theology Project, https://rhythmictheologyproject.com/2016/10/08/flow/ (accessed September 12, 2020).

[68]Peter Althouse, "Betwixt and Between the Cross and the Eschaton: Pentecostal Worship in the Context of Ritual Play," in *Toward a Pentecostal Theology of Worship*, ed. Lee Roy Martin (Cleveland, TN: CPT Press, 2016), 266-67.

between the rules and boundaries of ritual play (Word) and the unlimited and open possibilities of the kingdom coming (Spirit), the imagination is inspired to glimpse and grasp the realities of the future kingdom."[69] Flow makes space for the push and pull between structure and spontaneity as we encounter the Spirit in worship and are continually subsumed into the life of Christ.

It should be noted that the concept of flow in worship is not new. In the edited volume *Flow: The Ancient Way to Do Contemporary Worship*, Lester Ruth contends that contemporary renewal worship has recovered some historical elements of worship that traditional modern worship has missed, namely, "an open-endedness of time, extemporaneity, and the order as a flowing sequence of essential activity."[70] These themes derived from a description of worship by the second-century apologist Justin Martyr,[71] and have regained prominence in contemporary worship. In particular, the third element, the flow of essential actions in worship, has become a central concern for contemporary worship.[72] As was mentioned last chapter, music in renewal worship typically underscores the other elements of the worship service. This is done to create "an atmosphere and environment that is conducive to awareness of God's presence."[73] It helps foster the charged, liminal space where spiritual encounters occur. Flow allows worshipers to remain and linger in a moment and to be gradually and purposefully led into another phase of communal worship. In this way, the enrapturing power of flow functions as the crucial antidote to a busy society driven by time and productivity.[74]

Although music is essential for renewal worship, Pentecostals do not merely look to create musical flow for aesthetic pleasure but to embark on a journey toward divine encounters.[75] A pastor friend of mine regularly jokes that the Spirit's anointing stops when the keyboardist stops playing. Although he's

---

[69]Althouse, "Betwixt and Between the Cross," 267.

[70]Lester Ruth, "An Ancient Way to Do Contemporary Worship," in *Flow: The Ancient Way to Do Contemporary Worship*, ed. Lester Ruth (Nashville: Abingdon, 2020), 11. It should be noted that Ruth does not use the term "renewal worship" but refers specifically to Pentecostal, charismatic, and nondenominational traditions in this citation.

[71]Ruth, "Ancient Way," 4.

[72]Zachary Barnes, "How Flow Became the Thing," in *Flow: The Ancient Way to Do Contemporary Worship*, ed. Lester Ruth (Nashville: Abingdon, 2020) 13.

[73]Barnes, "How Flow Became the Thing," 20.

[74]Barnes, "How Flow Became the Thing," 21.

[75]Glenn Packiam, *Worship and the World to Come: Exploring Christian Hope in Contemporary Worship* (Downers Grove, IL: IVP Academic, 2020), 45.

saying this in jest, he is demonstrating the importance music plays for establishing a continuous flow between elements of worship. Flow is not a way to manipulate the congregation into certain emotions, but a means to unify and connect the elements of worship for a cohesive experience. As Zac Hicks states,

> Flow . . . comes down to transitions and an intuitive sense of timing about the way one element moves into another. Too much pause feels like a lull. Too quick a shift feels like a jolt. Silence, which is important in worship, should always be intentional. Developing sensibilities for these things comes from experience and processing a host of factors, including the types of technologies and entertainment our congregations are accustomed to.[76]

Renewal worship pastors should be skilled at both establishing flow and sensing the leading of the Spirit.

Although worship pastors know their congregations and can prayerfully and purposefully lead them, the Holy Spirit may at any moment intervene on the journey and lead people elsewhere. Here the worship pastor must utilize discernment to faithfully follow where the Spirit is headed. Biblically, the spiritual gift of discernment refers to a "discernment between spirits" (1 Cor 12:10), which allows believers to clearly differentiate the work, influence, or presence of God against that of fleshly or demonic powers. The concept of discernment fundamentally involves judging whether something is of God or not, and it requires decisive leadership once a conclusion has been found. Discernment in renewal worship can certainly involve discerning the hand of God in worship against outside forces, but there's also a discernment that takes place *within* worship. Here the judgment is not one of ethical deliberation, but a judgment for what is most appropriate for the time, place, and context of worship. This sense of discernment in worship, according to Cornelius Plantinga and Sue Rozeboom, is meant to judge what's fitting for the context of worship.[77] "Fittingness" is better understood as an aesthetic judgment within a liturgical context.[78]

---

[76]Zac Hicks, *The Worship Pastor: A Call to Ministry for Worship Leaders and Teams* (Grand Rapids, MI: Zondervan, 2016), 186.

[77]Cornelius Plantinga Jr. and Sue Rozeboom, *Discerning the Spirits: A Guide to Thinking About Christian Worship Today* (Grand Rapids, MI: Eerdmans, 2003), 51.

[78]Philosopher Nicholas Wolterstorff uses the term *fittingness* as an aesthetic category to describe how closely the qualities and complexes of something align. See Nicholas Wolterstorff, *Art in Action: Toward a Christian Aesthetic* (Grand Rapids, MI: Eerdmans, 1980), 98.

As worship pastors lead congregants to experiential encounters of God, they must be in tune with flow and pay attention to the direction the Spirit is leading the people to oscillate. No one knows the hearts of worshipers better than the Spirit, so it is of utmost importance that worship pastors be sensitive to the prompting of the Spirit and be willing to let the Spirit wreck their service plans at any time. In an age of run sheets, personal in-ear monitors, backing tracks with cues and clicks, and programmed-to-the-second lighting cues, it is sometimes difficult for renewal worship pastors to abandon service plans on a whim. Nevertheless, renewal worship leaders must be, above all else, obedient to the Spirit's prompting. They should be guided by the Spirit when they create the service structure, but must also be willing to abandon it all if the Spirit leads them to. This can, however, be practiced. Just as a musician can practice improvising by regularly playing over a vamping progression, worship teams can learn to modulate quickly in key parts of worship services. Worship pastors or music directors (MDs) can, for instance, feel the Spirit's prompting and stay on a progression longer. Perhaps during a bridge, the MD can turn the track off so the rest of the song can be improvised. Worship teams can practice changing progressions quickly by having the worship pastor or MD call out or signal scale degrees utilizing the Nashville Number System.[79] The point is, renewal worship pastors must take a both/and approach that values structure *and* spontaneity, and they must be skilled and spiritually sensitive enough to lead their teams and their congregations through these flows.

Planning renewal worship. Having a willingness to deconstruct plans when the Holy Spirit prompts does not mean renewal worship should avoid worship planning. As we've pointed out above, renewal worship oscillates between structure and spontaneity, so even when there is an openness to quickly adapt, worship is always rooted in some kind of form. The question is not if renewal worship should have form, but what sort of form flows from the *overflow* of the Spirit. Chapter one argued that renewal worship should be rooted in the Pentecost narrative of Acts 2 and understood through the lens of the continuous outpour of the Spirit and as an inbreaking of what is

---

[79]The Nashville Number System is a system used for quickly transposing music by looking at the scale degrees of the key signature. It is also a method for writing transposable chord charts.

to come. Then chapter two fleshed out the notion that God's self-impartation of Godself came to us as the abundant Spirit of the relational God, and renewal worship is our response to God's gift of the Spirit. Whatever style or structural design renewal worship takes in its myriad global expressions, it should always follow a form of relationality that begins with the Spirit being poured out on all flesh, and continues with worshipers responding relationally and in reverence. Constance Cherry defines form as an intentional ordering of the acts of worship. All worship services have form; the question is whether the form is effective or ineffective, if it flows out of the nature and function of worship or not.[80] For our purposes, chapters one and two focused on the nature of renewal worship, and chapter three and the above sections of this chapter discussed its function. So our task is to see what sort of form can flow out of these portrayals of renewal worship.

Just as we've deemed the object of renewal worship as the relational God in chapter two, Cherry sees worship as fundamentally relational. Accordingly, worship design must follow a relational form. She advocates for a "dialogical approach" that utilizes discernment for navigating the "dialogue" of worship. Cherry writes, "In its most basic form, corporate worship is a real meeting between God and God's people. Like any meeting, this one takes place through dialogue. God speaks and listens to the gathered community; we speak and listen to God. In the course of a guided conversation (the worship order), the encounter happens."[81] Scripturally we see God relating to people dialogically in a pattern that starts with God initiating a conversation, the person responding (in amazement, confession, denial, etc.), God speaking, the person responding, and God sending.[82] This pattern of revelation and response fits well with our definition of renewal worship laid out in the introduction: turning our hearts toward God as a response to God's self-revelation.

Cherry sees the ancient course of the fourfold order of worship as drawn from early Christian church orders such as the *Didache* and the *Apostolic Tradition* as a great example of form that adheres to God's relationality. The

---

[80]Constance Cherry, *The Worship Architect: A Blueprint for Designing Culturally Relevant and Biblically Faithful Services* (Grand Rapids, MI: Baker Academic, 2010), 39.

[81]Cherry, *Worship Architect*, 45.

[82]Cherry, *Worship Architect*, 45. Cherry cites several scriptural examples of this pattern (Ex 3:1-12; Is 6:1-13; Lk 1:26-38, 24:13-35).

four parts of the sequence include the gathering, the Word, the table, and the sending. Here worshipers enter a journey into God's presence through the gathering, they hear from God through the Word,[83] they respond to God through the table, and they are commissioned to go out through the sending.[84] This form can be practiced formally with doxologies, liturgical prayers, responsive readings, preaching, the Eucharist, and benedictions, or informally with communal singing and prayer, preaching, testimonies, altar calls, and blessings. The style of worship can be contextualized to the worshiping community, but what's important is that the relational pattern of revelation and response is upheld. Not every tradition, for instance, will serve a weekly Communion, but as long as some form of communal response follows the sermon, the people will still respond to whatever God has revealed through the sermon.[85] We can understand renewal worship as taking a relational form of worship, and pairing it with a relational flow between Word and Spirit. Thus, renewal worship pastors must utilize discernment to follow the Spirit's guidance through the form and function of the worship service.

Renewal worship tends to take an informal approach to the fourfold order, and each aspect of the order is essential to renewal worship. Recall in previous chapters we discussed the nature and significance of various elements of renewal worship, including preaching, prayer, testimony, Communion, and altar calls, and how music underscores the majority of these elements. Although some adherents tend to equate worship with the music portion of the service, we've

---

[83] At this point you may have noticed a bit of slippage with my usage of the term *Word* throughout this chapter. As mentioned, "Word" (*logos*) refers to Jesus, according to John 1, but is also used to identify Scripture in popular evangelical parlance. Pentecostal sermons that relate Word and Spirit typically contrast Scripture and Spirit rather than Son and Spirit. But throughout this chapter, I have been contrasting Son and Spirit, using John 1 as my base. To bridge these ideas, however, I'd like to follow Karl Barth and recognize Scripture as *participating in* the Word since it is the divinely inspired record of the Word, and preaching as also participating in the Word since it is the proclamation of the Word (see Karl Barth, *The Göttingen Dogmatics: Instruction in the Christian Religion*, trans. Geoffrey Bromiley [Grand Rapids, MI: Eerdmans, 1991], 1:15.). This creates a threefold account of God's self-disclosure to humanity that's rooted, fundamentally, in the revelation of Jesus Christ as Word of God. Barth calls this the "three addresses of God"—Jesus is God's revelation, Scripture is *from* revelation, and preaching is *from both* revelation *and* Scripture. This polyvalent understanding of "Word" helps us understand the place of Word in the fourfold order of worship—it encapsulates the reading of Scripture and the proclamation of the Word through creeds, preaching, prayers, and anything else that asserts the revelation of God.

[84] Cherry, *Worship Architect*, 47.

[85] Ruth Duck, *Worship for the Whole People of God: Vital Worship for the 21st Century* (Louisville, KY: Westminster John Knox, 2013), 74.

come to understand that music is not synonymous with worship; worship is deeper and more encompassing than mere music. Each worship element cited above plays a significant role in relating and responding to God. Each is essential for a holistic experience of worship. Nevertheless, music *does* play a unifying and connecting role in the flow of renewal worship. The musical part of the worship service is often extended in the gathering of the fourfold order, and typically integrates prayer, testimonies, and responsive ministry times.

After discussing the form of renewal worship, the next aspect of worship design that should be discussed is song selection. Because music in renewal worship is so integrative, the songs that are sung can make connections between the gospel and the lives of the congregants. To keep the gospel message at the heart of worship, worship pastor Ken Boer applies a simple method of biblical application to the song selection part of worship planning. He sees three corresponding layers of connection that reinforce the gospel message: the first layer is "the gospel" itself. This is the gospel message of Christ's redemption and, I would add, the Spirit's reconciliation, in its most abstracted and primary form. The second layer comprises the "implications" of the message. Here one is looking for the ensuing consequences of the gospel story. One might ask, *What does this good news then lead to?* Finally, Boer calls the third layer "our lives," which refers to practical application of these principles to the life of the worshiper.[86] Boer recounts Galatians 4:4-7 (a passage thematically related to Rom 8:14-17) as an excellent, scriptural example of these principles in practice:

> But when the fullness of time had come, God sent his Son, born of a woman, born under the law, in order to redeem those who were under the law, so that we might receive adoption as children. And because you are children, God has sent the Spirit of his Son into our hearts, crying, "Abba! Father!" So you are no longer a slave but a child, and if a child then also an heir, through God.

The first "gospel" layer here is God sending Jesus to redeem those under the law, the second "implications" layer is that we are no longer slaves but children of God, and the third "our lives" layer is that we can cry out to God and find the help we need.[87]

---

[86]Ken Boer, "The Worship Leader and the Gospel," in *Doxology & Theology: How the Gospel Forms the Worship Leader*, ed. Matt Boswell (Nashville: B&H, 2013), 196-97.

[87]Boer, "Worship Leader," 197.

It's important to note that each individual song does not have to establish a full spectrum of gospel-implication-application. Individual songs can focus on different aspects of this range of spiritual formation, but the gospel-implication-application spectrum can be teased out throughout the whole worship set. Some songs like, for instance, Hillsong UNITED's "Scandal of Grace" (2013) clearly portrays the gospel message of redemption, whereas Hillsong's "Who You Say I Am" (2018) focuses on the implications of redemption. Finally, the worship set can end, perhaps, with Elevation Worship's "Overcome" (2017) as a triumphant song that practically applies the gospel message and its implications. If we think about the whole set as spiritually formative, then we can understand each song as parts of a greater whole. The parts themselves do not have to bring you all the way from Genesis to Revelation, but taken together, the songs can express a spiritual sojourn through the gospel message.

Different aspects of the gospel can be emphasized in each worship set too. Maybe the worship set surrounds the theme of the Creator God creating us anew, or maybe it's eschatological in nature, about the hope of the coming King breaking in today. The point is, worship pastors are shepherding a flock that they will continually walk alongside. There is no need to force the whole Bible into one song, but it is important to recognize how worship works to form people week in and week out. As we've been discussing this whole chapter, what's important is discernment. The shepherd must know his or her flock, and it will take spiritual discernment to know how to practically lead them through the gospel message. Renewal worship pastors should be skilled in their craft and obedient to the Spirit—they should be trained in all of the planning methods discussed above, but must also be trained to be spiritually sensitive to go wherever the Spirit is leading. When worship pastors do that, then they truly can be the shepherds God has called them to be—shepherds that, working alongside the pastor, help navigate the space between Word and Spirit, aesthetically connecting the Spirit's work in the hearts and minds of the congregants so the gospel message can take root and bring transformation.

CONCLUSION

This chapter answered the question "How does renewal worship flow?" by examining the way renewal worship oscillates between Word and Spirit. We utilized the term "oscillation" to exhibit the several ways renewal worship goes between the formational, structural power of the Word, and the deconstructive power of the sanctifying Spirit in order to promote spiritual growth and formation. We recognized the oscillation between Word and Spirit practically as renewal worship navigates between structure and spontaneity, and thematically as it navigates between triumph and lament, before discussing the ways in which the flow of renewal worship is planned, implemented, and sometimes abandoned by the prompting of the Spirit. It is the task of the renewal worship pastor to skillfully navigate these oscillations and to follow the Spirit's prompting in the worship service. Before discussing the role of the prophetic in renewal worship in the next chapter, let's reflect on the contents of this chapter, once again, with the following doxology:

Praise God who sanctifies
Who burns away our lies
Praise God who sees us when we're glorified.

5

WHAT RENEWAL WORSHIP SAYS

THE PROPHETIC FUNCTIONS OF RENEWAL

Then afterward
I will pour out my spirit on all flesh;
your sons and your daughters shall prophesy,
your old men shall dream dreams,
and your young men shall see visions.
Even on the male and female slaves,
in those days, I will pour out my spirit.

JOEL 2:28-29

THE PASSAGE ABOVE is not Acts 2:17-18, but Joel 2:28-29. This is the Old Testament passage that Peter quoted at Pentecost, which indicates a prophetic fulfillment was taking place in first century Jerusalem. But what exactly was being fulfilled and how? According to biblical scholar Craig Keener, many Jewish people believed the Spirit of prophecy departed Israel since prophecies became so rare from the time of Malachi and on.[1] In consequence, they also believed that in the future God would pour the Spirit out on all people in such a full way that the Spirit of prophecy would be restored to usher in the kingdom of God. Peter quoting Joel 2 suggests that he understood the cross and postcrucifixion events as fulfilling, at least partially, Joel's prophecy. Joel prophesied about the great Day of the Lord, which pictured the establishment of God's reign in a restored, just society, where the Davidic

---

[1]Craig Keener, *Gift Giver: The Holy Spirit for Today* (Grand Rapids, MI: Baker Academic, 2001), 22.

line is reestablished and God's Spirit is poured out. While the Old Testament sees the Day of the Lord as a cataclysmic event that would usher in the kingdom of God (Is 2:19; Amos 5:18-20; Zeph 1:2-18; Mal 4:1; Joel 2), Peter pictures the death and resurrection of Christ along with the subsequent outpouring of the Spirit and birth of the church as fulfilling these prophecies. This fulfillment is partial, however, as the church waits for the consummation of the kingdom of God at the eschaton, but Pentecost is, nevertheless, the pivotal event that saw the Spirit's outpour finally take place.

As a method for our theology of renewal worship, we have rooted our concept of worship biblically in the Acts 2 account of Pentecost, utilizing the universal outpour motif as our guiding theme. We have noted how Acts 2:17 bears an eschatological component ("In the last days")[2] while recognizing the pneumatological significance of the universal outpour ("I will pour out my Spirit on all people"). We have not yet discussed, however, how the second part of Acts 2:17 and Acts 2:18 (along with Joel 2:28-29) recognizes prophecy as an appropriate consequence of the universal outpour: "And your sons and your daughters shall prophesy, and your young men shall see visions, and your old men shall dream dreams. Even upon my slaves, both men and women, in those days I will pour out my Spirit; and they shall prophesy" (Acts 2:17-18). As we will see throughout this chapter, this has significant ramifications for a theology of renewal worship. Focusing on this part of Joel's prophecy and the Pentecost account helps us understand how renewal worship functions prophetically in both the local and global church today.

While chapter three discusses Pentecostalism's shaping narrative and shows how prophets shift the narrative as cultural insiders, this chapter expands that conversation showing how spiritual alignment through worship helps the worshiping community to understand the Spirit's activity in their community and around the world. Prophecy occurs in worship when worshipers are led by the Spirit to speak into the community's shared, social contexts. When a society perpetuates things that oppose God and God's ministry, the prophet dissents and energizes the worshiping community to stand against

---

[2]Luke Timothy Johnson points out that Peter changing "Then afterword" from Joel to "In the last days" is significant because it shows Peter establishing Pentecost as an eschatological event (Luke Timothy Johnson, *Prophetic Jesus, Prophetic Church: The Challenge of Luke-Acts to Contemporary Christians* [Grand Rapids, MI: Eerdmans, 2011], 32).

the dominant society's vision. Worship is essential for establishing solidarity around a unified prophetic message, so worship pastors must be aware of the prophetic functions of worship. To make this case, this chapter distinguishes two renewal connotations of the prophetic: prophecy as a spiritual gift, and prophecy as a social function. While the ecclesial gift of prophecy may differ from that of the Old Testament prophets, prophecy still plays a significant role in the life of the church today. Finally, this chapter discusses how worship is used prophetically for broadcasting communal, regional, and global messages. In this way, prophecy, as a consequence of the universal outpour, extends God's ministerial message to the ends of the earth.

RENEWAL WORSHIP AND THE RENEWED IMAGINATION

In his book *Prophetic Jesus, Prophetic Church,* New Testament scholar Luke Timothy Johnson sees the Luke-Acts narrative as establishing a prophetic vision of the kingdom of God that began with Jesus in Luke's Gospel and is carried over by the early church in the book of Acts. Johnson points out that the Spirit who is poured out on all flesh *is* the Spirit of prophecy that is manifested by dreams and visions (Acts 2:17) and signs and wonders (Acts 2:19).[3] And because these are all characteristic of Jesus' prophetic ministry, Peter indirectly identifies Jesus as a prophet: "You that are Israelites, listen to what I have to say: Jesus of Nazareth, a man attested to you by God with deeds of power, wonders, and signs that God did through him among you, as you yourselves know" (Acts 2:22). It was the manifestation of the Spirit surrounding Jesus that ultimately proved Jesus was not only a prophet, but also the promised deliverer. As Keener states, "By appealing to their continual experience with the Spirit, the Christians not only appealed to a supernatural empowerment their opponents did not even claim. They also declared that the time of promise had arrived in Jesus of Nazareth!"[4] As prophet and deliverer, Jesus is at once the bearer *and* giver of the Spirit of prophecy. Johnson sees Pentecost as the pivotal event that transferred Christ's prophetic ministry to the church.[5] Jesus is the giver of the Spirit of prophecy when his prophetic ministry is transferred to the church. As Johnson writes, "The one who in his

---

[3]Johnson, *Prophetic Jesus,* 32.
[4]Keener, *Gift Giver,* 22.
[5]Johnson, *Prophetic Jesus,* 37.

life was a prophet is the source of the prophetic spirit that is now manifested in signs and wonders ('as you see and hear')."[6] It is Jesus as the Spirit baptizer who pours forth the Spirit of prophecy.

What's significant about Johnson's connection of Pentecost with the Spirit of prophecy is that the Spirit is, just as with the Old Testament prophets, the effective cause of prophecy. This connects Old Testament prophecy with the prophecy of the church even as prophecy then and now function differently. Johnson draws out some significant implications of prophecy if the Spirit is indeed always the cause of prophecy. First, the Spirit is the force that expresses the presence of the living God through physical beings. Second, God uses prophets to discern and identify how God is at work in the world. Third, prophecy is, therefore, not a human endeavor but an act that originates with God. Fourth, inspiration is best understood as the way the Spirit makes God's vision available to prophets. Fifth and finally, inspiration fails when it is distorted by evil spirits or selfish desires.[7] These five implications are consistent in both the Old Testament and in prophecy today, and we can see these points manifest in the worship of the church. In renewal worship specifically, there are at least two connotations of the prophetic: prophecy as the outworking of a spiritual gift, and prophecy as a critical, social function. Both rely on the Spirit's inspiration and focus on the renewing of the imagination, but one works on a particular, communal level, whereas the other works on a more general, societal level. We will look at each of these connotations in turn.

The prophetic as a spiritual gift. In the New Testament, Paul catalogs spiritual gifts in at least three places: Romans 12 counts the gifts of encouragement, giving, leadership, mercy, prophecy, service, and teaching, and 1 Corinthians 12 lists administration, discernment, healing, interpretation, tongues, prophecy, wisdom, apostleship, faith, helps, knowledge, miracles, and teaching. Ephesians 4 lists five ministerial roles that are gifted by the Spirit to an individual: apostle, pastor, teacher, evangelist, and prophet. The differences in these passages indicate the lists are not comprehensive, but Paul uses them as examples of spiritual gifts when he is advising different church communities. There are commonalities, however, that indicate the importance of

---

[6]Johnson, *Prophetic Jesus*, 32.
[7]Johnson, *Prophetic Jesus*, 43-44.

gifts in the early church. A gift that's consistent in all of these lists and discussed in several other places in both the Old and New Testaments is the gift of prophecy.

There is a noted difference between Old and New Testament prophecy, however, which is implied in Matthew 11:11-14 when Jesus calls John the Baptist the last and greatest of the old prophets:

> Truly I tell you, among those born of women no one has arisen greater than John the Baptist; yet the least in the kingdom of heaven is greater than he. From the days of John the Baptist until now the kingdom of heaven has suffered violence, and the violent take it by force. For all the prophets and the law prophesied until John came; and if you are willing to accept it, he is Elijah who is to come. Let anyone with ears listen!

While John the Baptist is the greatest prophet of those "born of women"—that is, among all of humanity in former ages—those in the kingdom of heaven are greater than he. This in no way devalues John's ministry, but it shows that there is a superior sense of prophecy that occurs in the kingdom. During his ministry, Jesus inaugurated the kingdom of God on earth (Mt 3:2; 4:17; Mk 1:15). Through his sacrifice, Jesus transferred the temple of God where the Spirit dwells from Jerusalem to the hearts of believers (1 Cor 3:16-17; 2 Cor 6:14-18; Eph 2:19-22). It seems, therefore, that the activity of the Spirit before and after Christ indicates a major shift for the gift of prophecy.

Prophets in the Old Testament were mouthpieces of God (Ex 4:12; Deut 18:18; Jer 1:9; Ezek 2:7), that would recite exactly what God revealed to them. Over and over again God admonishes the prophets to "speak my words to them." Prophets were held to an austere standard of judgment, and if a prophecy didn't come to pass, the prophet was subjected to severe punishments, even death (Deut 18:20). In the Old Testament, God came upon and spoke through the prophet, so the prophet's duty was to recount faithfully what God had revealed. Often those revelations anticipated something that would occur in the future, so it was easy to see if a prophecy came to pass or not. The Spirit's role in prophecy shifts fundamentally in the New Testament because of Christ's work of redemption on the cross, and the church's subsequent indwelling of the Spirit. In the Old Testament the Spirit came upon prophets and spoke through them, but in the New Testament the

Spirit already indwells all believers, and communicates to them directly. The mediatory characteristic of prophecy between God and the people is now located in Christ through the Spirit. In other words, believers have immediate access to God through Christ the Spirit baptizer, as the Spirit now indwells the church. In the Old Testament, communication with God was predicated upon mediators. The prophet spoke on behalf of God to the people, and the priest spoke on behalf of the people to God. Jesus' sacrifice removed our need for any external mediators. Christ is now both the prophet (Mt 21:11; Lk 4:24) and the priest (Heb 7:25; 9:12), and in Christ we have immediate access to God by the Spirit.

The gift of prophecy in the New Testament carries the same purpose as the other gifts: for the equipping, edification, and maturation of the body of Christ (Eph 4:11-15). Peter indicates that the gifts are to be used in service to others (1 Pet 4:10), not as a means to prop up our own spiritual authority. Prophecy, and all the spiritual gifts in general, are never about us as individuals. New Testament prophecy is, essentially, a gift that encourages and edifies the church. Consider what Paul said about prophecy in 1 Corinthians 14:3-5 (NIV):

> But the one who prophesies speaks to people for their strengthening, encouraging and comfort. Anyone who speaks in a tongue edifies themselves, but the one who prophesies edifies the church. I would like every one of you to speak in tongues, but I would rather have you prophesy. The one who prophesies is greater than the one who speaks in tongues, unless someone interprets, so that the church may be edified.

The reason Paul sees prophecy as a greater gift than tongues is because of its effects. Paul is measuring greatness by how much the gifts benefit others; he's not citing any intrinsic qualities that make the gifts great. In other words, the reason prophecy is greater is because it is communal and helps to fulfill the purpose of spiritual gifts (equipping, edification, and maturation) better than tongues, which fulfills those purposes on a personal level. While in the New Testament there are no clear qualifications listed for the office of the prophet, those who are called prophets seem to function in ways that encourage and edify the church. As mentioned, in the Old Testament the office of the prophet was primarily an intermediary position between God and the people, and later after the times of the judges, the office was also an advisory role to the king. But the one thing that is consistent in the Old Testament and New Testament is that the Spirit inspires the words of the prophet.

Keith Warrington states that in general, "Most Pentecostals identify prophecies as those occasions when an individual, inspired by God, speaks spontaneously and extemporaneously with an emphasis on edification or exhortation."[8] Pentecostals follow the New Testament model that emphasizes prophecy's purpose of edification, but they also acknowledge the Old Testament notion that prophecy exhorts. Prophetic exhortation in the New Testament isn't exactly like that of the Old Testament because the Spirit also indwells the recipients of prophetic exhortation. Now the words of the prophet can be verified directly by the Spirit, hence the gift of discernment is also listed among the spiritual gifts in 1 Corinthians 12. To illustrate this sense of prophecy, imagine a scenario during a renewal worship service where a person receives a word of prophecy for someone else. The person who received the prophetic word then moves toward the subject (the final recipient of the prophetic word) and delivers the message, stating something like, "I believe God wants me to say this to you." Upon receiving the message, the ideal result would be that the recipient was blessed by the word as it conveyed a response to something that the person was struggling with or it expressed something the recipient just needed to hear. While this scenario seems straightforward enough, there are some important distinctions and concepts to unpack here.

First, let's define terms. A *prophetic word* is when a person receives a strong feeling or impression concerning someone or something that communicates God's thoughts or intentions toward the subject. Prophetic words are often distinguished, in charismatic circles, as "words of knowledge" or "words of wisdom." A word of knowledge is a "divinely given fragment of knowledge,"[9] whereas words of wisdom concern the inspired application of knowledge.[10] While the former speaks toward some sort of revelation a person receives about a person or a thing, the latter refers to the "wisely spoken application of knowledge, the wisdom of which would not have been known

---

[8]Keith Warrington, *Pentecostal Theology: A Theology of Encounter* (London: T&T Clark, 2008), 82.
[9]Mark Cartledge, "Charismatic Prophecy: A Definition and Description," *Journal of Pentecostal Theology* 5 (1994): 93.
[10]Cartledge, "Charismatic Prophecy," 91.

except for the revelation."[11] These are the connotations typically associated with the concept of prophetic words.

Second, let's recognize the instinctive nature of prophetic words. Beginning a prophetic word with "I believe" conveys a level of subjectivity, which leaves room for fallibility. The prophetic word would not be intentionally, or deviously false, but liable to misunderstanding. A nonabsolute starting point makes room for the possibility that the person may be equating a mere strong feeling with a prophetic word. Without this caveat, the prophet may claim a spiritual authority that's even on par with Scripture, making the prophecy some sort of spiritual rule or standard that is to be respected uncritically. In these cases, the prophetic word interlopes the ministerial purposes of encouragement or edification. And as Keener reminds us, "There is nothing more dangerous than someone acting with the assurance that the Spirit has spoken to him or her when in fact he has not. . . . The charismatic early Christians recognized that all claims concerning revelations must be tested (1 Cor 14:29; 1 Thess 5:20-22), and they continued in the apostles' teachings (Acts 2:42)."[12] This instinctive component of prophecy today is one of the biggest contrasts to that of Old Testament prophecy, where prophets aimed to be infallible delegates of God.

Third and finally, let's understand the importance of discernment when receiving prophecy. The final recipient must discern or test the validity of the prophecy. As Keener points out, while the gift of discernment is important for distinguishing between true and false prophets, it is also important for discerning the voice of God for ourselves.[13] We use discernment when we judge the accuracy of a prophecy, and when we test the spirits to see whether they're from God (1 Jn 4:1). And, as stated above, discerning prophecies today is possible because both parties already have the Spirit indwelling them.

The New Testament pictures prophecy as an immediate form of inspiration by the Spirit that is portrayed as a *charism* of the Spirit.[14] A charism is a spiritual gift, but particularly an endowment of extraordinary power from God.

---

[11]Cartledge, "Charismatic Prophecy," 91.

[12]Keener, *Gift Giver*, 195.

[13]Keener, *Gift Giver*, 189.

[14]Samuel Muindi, *Pentecostal-Charismatic Prophecy: Empirical-Theological Analysis* (Oxford: Peter Lang, 2017), 109.

Prophecy is, therefore, a special, empowering gift of the Spirit for the benefit of the church. According to Pentecostal theologian Samuel Muindi, the Pentecostal-charismatic congregational-liturgical setting sees this New Testament notion of "prophecy as *charism*" as the standard way of understanding prophecy in renewal worship today.[15] Like Johnson, Muindi also ties Spirit baptism to prophecy:

> In Pentecostal-charismatic experiences, the notion of Spirit Baptism, as an experience of spiritual initiation and empowerment ("anointing"), is viewed as the onset of an enhanced openness and sensitivity to the realm of the divine Spirit. The charismatic-prophecy experience can therefore be visualized as an intense moment of interface between the Holy Spirit and the human spirit (or the deep unconscious human dimension) which overwhelms the human spirit with revelatory impulses.[16]

Accordingly, because Pentecostal worshipers believe they have experienced the outpour of the Spirit, they perpetually carry an openness and expectation for the Spirit to manifest in many ways, including prophecy.[17] Acts 2 indicates that Pentecostals view prophecy as originating in the Spirit.[18] Worship creates the context for Spirit-led prophetic utterance.[19] Muindi sees prophecy as an "intuitive divine-human intermediatory phenomena,"[20] which means prophecy is a response from divine-human interaction. In particular, prophecy begins with God revealing something to a person who then shares the revelatory message even before that person has attempted to rationalize its meaning. Because the final recipient of the prophecy is someone else, the initial recipient of the prophecy needs to merely be a faithful messenger of the revelation. The gift of prophecy is, therefore, the transferal of a divinely inspired message for another's benefit. The communal point of this gift is to edify the final recipient, which thereby builds up the church. In this sense, the gift of prophecy can be seen as blessing the church on a specific, communal level.

---

[15] Muindi, *Pentecostal-Charismatic Prophecy*, 109.

[16] Muindi, *Pentecostal-Charismatic Prophecy*, 117.

[17] Muindi, *Pentecostal-Charismatic Prophecy*, 178.

[18] Melissa Archer, *"I Was in the Spirit on the Lord's Day": A Pentecostal Engagement with Worship in the Apocalypse* (Cleveland, TN: CPT Press, 2015), 303.

[19] Archer, *"I Was in the Spirit on the Lord's Day,"* 302.

[20] Muindi, *Pentecostal-Charismatic Prophecy*, 2.

The prophetic as a social function. Seeing prophecy as a charism is biblical and accounts for the communal function of the gift of prophecy in worship, but there is another, also biblical, concept of prophecy that sees its critical function on broader, societal levels. In this societal sense of prophecy, the final recipient of the prophetic word is not an individual, rather the prophetic message is aimed at the social consciousness of the society at large. We discussed in chapter three that prophets have the ability to shift a society's narrative ever so slightly into new directions. To push adherents toward the new yet reachable terrains of the community's narrative trajectories, prophets must be cultural insiders that travel across the society's possible ideological modes of understanding. The prophet does not enter the discourse with an entirely alien set of cultural ideals or principles, but confronts the border of an ideological zone and pushes it out a few steps. In this way, prophecy bears a social function as it challenges and fundamentally alters the community's overarching socioreligious narrative.

We can look at the prophetic actions of Jesus to get a sense of how prophecy has a socioreligious function in the New Testament. The account of Jesus' demonstrative act of turning over the tables of the money changers and letting out the doves in the temple (Mt 21:12-13; Mk 11:15-19; Jn 2:13-22) was a deliberate prophetic performance, and a needed response to an outmoded order of atonement. Jesus rebelled against the sacrificial system of the temple, as it was no longer bearing any fruit.[21] Jesus' act momentarily rendered the temple inoperable, symbolically showing how the social institution was culturally bankrupt as it was both corrupt and out of season. In John's account of the story, Jesus said he would destroy the temple and rebuild it in three days (Jn 2:19), which locates the temple's new system of atonement in Christ, particularly because his death would satisfy all atoning sacrifices. Through this prophetic act Jesus pushed the Israelites past the bounds of what was acceptable as atoning acts of worship. While Jesus spoke the narrative's

---

[21]This is especially evident in the Markan account of the story. Here the story of Jesus turning over the tables at the temple is interposed between the story of the cursed fig tree. This "Markan sandwich" indicates that the temple no longer bears fruit because it, like the cursed fig tree, is out of season. The passage ends with Jesus exclaiming that forgiveness now comes through him (Mk 11:24-25). For a longer exegesis of this passage see Robby Waddell, "Prophecy Then and Now: The Role of Prophecy in the Pentecostal Church," in *Transformational Leadership: A Tribute to Dr. Mark Rutland* (Lakeland, FL: Small Dogma Publishing, 2008), 129-44.

language and fully engaged in its customs, his act was loaded with symbolic and intentional gestures that aroused shock and intrigue in everyone in the temple. Prophets, like Jesus in this instance, can seem rebellious because they are opposing a prevalent social institution, but if the institution is corrupt, then that critical energizing voice is needed. This critical stance is dangerous for the prophet, however, since the system's authoritative constituents are culturally, and often financially, invested in the social institution. As Johnson states, "When the witness is public and political and the prophetic word issues a challenge to the values and systems of society, then the suffering of the prophet who speaks, embodies, and enacts this word is going to be commensurate to the degree of resistance generated by the stakeholders in the society's dominant values."[22] Indeed the case can be made that it was Jesus' prophetic act in the temple that ultimately cost him his life. Nevertheless, Jesus' rebellious gestures show us how the prophetic also can bear a critical social function.

Perhaps the best chronicler of the critical social function of prophecy is Walter Brueggemann. Although he's written on the topic in many places, Brueggemann's classic text concerning biblical prophecy is *The Prophetic Imagination*. For Brueggemann, the prophet is "a child of the tradition" who thoroughly comprehends his or her tradition's cultural atmosphere and linguistic system. The prophet is "at home in that memory that the points of contact and incongruity with the situation of the church in culture can be discerned and articulated with proper urgency."[23] In other words, the prophet, as a cultural insider, declares a culturally transformative message with urgency. This socially critical prophetic ministry is, according to Brueggemann, entirely applicable for the church today.[24] The global church today exercises this prophetic ministry whenever it opposes a dominant societal consciousness that is in any way unjust. Whenever the church offers a community a new vision of a just society under the lordship of Christ, it functions prophetically.

The main ministerial task of the prophet is to offer an alternative vision of a more just cultural consciousness to a society that is dominated by unjust

---

[22]Johnson, *Prophetic Jesus*, 169.
[23]Walter Brueggemann, *The Prophetic Imagination*, 2nd ed. (Minneapolis: Fortress, 2001), 2.
[24]Brueggemann, *Prophetic Imagination*, 19.

precepts.[25] This alternative is rooted in God's justice, which is marked by compassion. Brueggemann sees Moses as the first and quintessential prophet. As exemplified by his encounter of God in the burning bush (Ex 3:1-17), and the reception of the Ten Commandments (Ex 20:1-17), Moses was the first to hear messages directly from God that were to be transmitted to the liberated people of God. Accordingly, Moses established the precedents of prophetic ministry, and his tactics became normative for the prophet. The laws were communicated to help the people of God remain holy as they worshiped a holy God. Moses' intention was that a new community's holiness would be formed around the precepts of freedom, justice, and compassion.[26] Moses sought to establish a new social reality that was diametrically opposed to the oppressive and exploitative society characterized by Egypt. Just as Moses' actions became normative for the Old Testament prophets, Pharaoh's actions became normative for establishing what Brueggemann calls the "royal consciousness."

The royal consciousness is a social perception that identifies entirely with the present regime that is in power. This political regime forms the cultural status quo of the society, often promoting policies that oppress and subjugate many of its citizens. An oppressive royal consciousness was displayed by the Egyptians in the book of Exodus, and Moses established an alternative prophetic consciousness in Israel once the Hebrews were liberated. In order to avoid top-down subjugation, Israel did not have a king at all. Their only sovereign was God. Israel maintained a semblance of a judicial system, however, as litigations were arbitrated by judges, and a legislative system through priestly lawmakers. But after some time, the people clamored for a king so they could have comparative might to other nations. Samuel, the last judge, gave them a strong warning reminding them what was at stake—a king would hold power over them and bring them right back into the sort of subjugation they left when they fled Egypt. Samuel stated,

> So Samuel reported all the words of the LORD to the people who were asking him for a king. He said, "These will be the ways of the king who will reign over you: he will take your sons and appoint them to his chariots and to be his horsemen, and to run before his chariots; and he will appoint for himself commanders

---

[25]Brueggemann, *Prophetic Imagination*, 3.
[26]Brueggemann, *Prophetic Imagination*, 6-7.

of thousands and commanders of fifties, and some to plow his ground and to reap his harvest, and to make his implements of war and the equipment of his chariots. He will take your daughters to be perfumers and cooks and bakers. He will take the best of your fields and vineyards and olive orchards and give them to his courtiers. He will take one-tenth of your grain and of your vineyards and give it to his officers and his courtiers. He will take your male and female slaves, and the best of your cattle and donkeys, and put them to his work. He will take one-tenth of your flocks, and you shall be his slaves. And in that day you will cry out because of your king, whom you have chosen for yourselves; but the LORD will not answer you in that day." (1 Sam 8:10-18)

Eventually, Samuel cautioned, the Israelites would once again be enslaved. While the Israelites might remain unconquered from foreign adversaries, their internal political system would force them into compliance through oppressive policies. Samuel's warning proved prophetic as it came to pass during Solomon's administration. Brueggemann sees Solomon's reign as reestablishing the royal consciousness that Moses fought so hard against. He writes, "The tension between a criticized present and an energizing future is overcome. There is only an uncriticized and unenergizing present. It follows, of course, that the Mosaic vision of reality nearly disappeared."[27] Put differently, Solomon's reign silenced the prophetic imagination and forced cultural compliance on the people.

Solomon's royal consciousness was marked by three major characteristics: (1) The nation was marked by *affluence*, which led society's focus away from a covenant of justice and toward a state of consumption that commodified people, (2) it established *oppressive social policies* that marked the expansion and economic progress of the state to maintain levels of consumption, eroding the interest of justice and freedom, and (3) it promoted a *static religion* where both God and freedom became subordinated to the purpose of the king and became controlled by the empire through the royal court.[28] This royal consciousness was so overbearing that it numbed people to their dire circumstances.[29] It instilled a dominant imagination that sustained feelings of complacency, self-sufficiency, anxiety, autonomy, and restlessness.[30] The

[27]Brueggemann, *Prophetic Imagination*, 25.
[28]Brueggemann, *Prophetic Imagination*, 26-28.
[29]Brueggemann, *Prophetic Imagination*, 41.
[30]Walter Brueggemann, *The Practice of Prophetic Imagination: Preaching an Emancipating Word* (Minneapolis: Fortress, 2012), 42.

task of prophetic ministry was to inspire and reignite an alternative vision of reality. Its charge was to reopen new possibilities and reject the dominant notions of closure and absolutism.[31] Just as Moses inspired a new vision of a just society to the Hebrews, the prophet shows oppressed people that there is a better way.

The prophet critiques the royal consciousness and energizes new hope in the people by naming a new reality and providing a new narrative.[32] This new hope is energized in the midst of a context of loss and grief.[33] As discussed last chapter, grief and dire circumstances must be named, and the people must be made sensitive enough again so they can fully come to terms with their experiences of suffering. The prophet must show the people that their suffering is real and theologically meaningful.[34] This is where the worship form of lament is important—the prophetic task must take seriously the bad realities of existence in order to counter the governing ideology that sustains it,[35] and lament is the act of worship that engages God in response to a reality of suffering.[36] Ruth Duck points out that the Bible actually shows us how to incorporate lament into worship, "by naming lamentable situations honestly and poignantly, asking for God's help, evoking trust in the God of healing and justice, and complaining if God seems to be silent or unconcerned."[37] Naming the reality of suffering in worship helps the worshiping community become spiritually sensitive and expectant before energizing a new hopeful vision of restoration and renewal. By establishing a progression of awareness, grief, and hope, the prophet works poetically and creatively to "re-experience the present world under a different set of metaphors."[38] The prophet speaks abstractly about hope, which instills a novel vision for the whole society, but the prophet

---

[31]Brueggemann, *Practice of Prophetic Imagination*, 32.

[32]Brueggemann, *Prophetic Imagination*, 59-60.

[33]Brueggemann, *Practice of Prophetic Imagination*, 110.

[34]Brueggemann, *Practice of Prophetic Imagination*, 60.

[35]Walter Brueggemann, *Reality, Grief, Hope: Three Urgent Prophetic Tasks* (Grand Rapids, MI: Eerdmans, 2014), 33.

[36]Soong-Chan Rah, *Prophetic Lament: A Call for Justice in Troubled Times* (Downers Grove, IL: InterVarsity Press, 2015), 21.

[37]Ruth Duck, *Worship for the Whole People of God: Vital Worship for the 21st Century* (Louisville, KY: Westminster John Knox, 2013), 251.

[38]Walter Brueggemann, *Hopeful Imagination: Prophetic Voices in Exile* (Philadelphia: Fortress, 1986), 24.

also offers concrete steps for bringing about a real newness that redefines the current situation.[39]

One of Brueggemann's major convictions is that this sort of prophetic ministry is still relevant in the church today.[40] Consider Brueggemann's depiction of our current Western context:

> The urgent news is that our society is on the way to our common death, by greed, by lust, by indifference, by cynicism, by despair, by a thousand forms of violence and brutality. That is the main story. And in the midst of all that, Jesus has put this little community that may make a difference. Reverse the process. Break the cycles. Practice our God-given humanness and gather the power and love and the self-discipline to do it.[41]

Our society is headed toward ruin as we grasp onto our own versions of the royal consciousness. As the church engages in the prophetic ministry of "reversing the process" of subjugation and commodification, we are called to participate in the healing of the world and to be a blessing through prophetic utterances. Brueggemann writes, "To cause blessing is to transmit God's power for life that God gives us to others, because we are channels for that power and not reservoirs, the force of blessing given that flows through our lives and out beyond us to others. All the others!"[42] Although our prophetic acts may not always appear as blessings, they are done to bring about God's vision of transformation for the world. Prophetic ministry requires us to be attuned to the things God cares about, to have "a heart that breaks with the things that break God's heart," which includes having a passion for justice and the courage to speak out as the Spirit prompts, even if the message is discommoding.[43] According to Zac Hicks, worship can become offensive to people when it is prophetic. He writes, "Worship prophesies to the world, 'You will be made new, but you first must die.' . . . Worship, centered on the earth-altering events of the death and resurrection of Christ, inherently points to the consummation of those events—the return of Christ—when the world

---

[39]Brueggemann, *Prophetic Imagination*, 67.

[40]Brueggemann, *Prophetic Imagination*, 1.

[41]Walter Brueggemann, *A Gospel of Hope*, comp. Richard Floyd (Louisville, KY: Westminster John Knox, 2018), 122.

[42]Brueggemann, *Gospel of Hope*, 122-23.

[43]Leonora Tubbs Tisdale, *Prophetic Preaching: A Pastoral Approach* (Louisville, KY: Westminster John Knox, 2010), 10.

will see full justice and full salvation. Worship assaults the world by proclaiming its death."[44] Worship is prophetic when it reinforces a message of hope that's rooted in the death and resurrection of Christ. Likewise, the social function of renewal worship is prophetic when it reinforces a message that destabilizes a society's corrupt social constraints and proclaims a new hope that is rooted in God's vision of renewal. Having considered the ways in which worship can be prophetic, the final section of this chapter considers, in particular, how the prophetic ministry of renewal worship manifests practically.

THE PROPHETIC MINISTRY OF RENEWAL WORSHIP

Every expression of prophetic ministry in the context of renewal worship is united by the basic notion that prophets act as intermediaries, communicating messages from God to others. These messages are intended to edify individuals, the community, or society at large. The central prophetic task is to communicate God's message faithfully, because these narrations indicate where and how the Spirit is leading in every social context. Prophecy, therefore, seeks to understand the interworkings of the Spirit's ministry in the world by communicating God's trajectories for people and communities, and by instilling visions of what a renewed reality looks like. As discussed in chapter one, spiritual alignment through worship helps worshiping communities understand the Spirit's activity in both the local community and around the world. To conclude this chapter, we will consider two more things: how local worshiping communities align themselves to God's ministry through worship, and how God even sends *global* messages through renewal worship.

Being led by the Spirit entails sensitivity from the worshiping community as constituents discern the Spirit's work. Theologian Craig Van Gelder points out that the Spirit's universal outpour in Acts 2 makes God's power and activity knowable. He writes, "The scriptural framework presents the Spirit as being *poured out* to become active within the particularities of specific communities of faith and their contexts."[45] Not only did the Spirit's outpour form the church,

---

[44]Zac Hicks, *The Worship Pastor: A Call to Ministry for Worship Leaders and Teams* (Grand Rapids, MI: Zondervan, 2016), 82-83.

[45]Craig Van Gelder, *The Ministry of the Missional Church: A Community Led by the Spirit* (Grand Rapids, MI: Baker Books, 2007), 27.

but because the Spirit now indwells the church, we can discern the Spirit's plans and actions for the world. The worshiping community must therefore seek to understand the Spirit's ministry in the world. The goal is not to push what *we* think will make the world better, but to submit to what God is already doing in the world since only God truly knows how universal reconciliation comes about.

Because communities all have distinctive contexts and needs, the Spirit is at work in various communities in different ways. But the Spirit is *always* at work, so the worshiping community must be sensitive to the Spirit's activity. The stream is already flowing; we just need to make sure we're sailing with the current, not against it. The question is not *if* the Spirit is working in the community, but *how*. The Spirit has operated in many different ways throughout the Bible, depending on the context of the particular biblical narrative. For instance, the Spirit's guidance looks very different to a community that needs encouragement than it does for a community that needs liberation, or for a community that needs correction. Each situation carries a different set of circumstances that requires different actions from the Spirit. Accordingly, Van Gelder has pointed out several ways the Spirit has ministered throughout the Bible: by demonstrating God's creative power (Gen 1:2; Jn 1:1-3), by affirming God's intention for creation so all might flourish (Gen 9:1-17; Jn 10:10), by confronting the principalities and powers and restraining evil (Gen 3:15; Eph 6:10-12), by reconnecting people and restoring communities (Gen 6–8; 1 Pet 2:9-10), by empowering leadership to guide faith communities into redemptive action (1 Sam 17:41-47; Acts 19:11-20), by extending mercy and establishing justice (Is 58:6-14; Acts 6:1-6), and by engaging the world through witness (Is 42:1-9; Acts 1:8).[46] Because God's grand narrative spans across the globe and throughout time, the key is to know where the particular narrative of the worshiping community sits within the larger narrative and how the Spirit is leading us to minister within this context.

Van Gelder's list is not exhaustive, but we can use it as a starting point to ask in what ways the Spirit is at work in our particular community, and how the Spirit intends to work through us to affect societal change. Is our society in need of human flourishing or the restraint of evil? Does our society need

---

[46]Van Gelder, *Ministry of the Missional Church*, 28.

empowered leadership or an elevated sense of justice? Does our society need healing and restoration? Our communities will likely engage simultaneously with several of these issues and others that we haven't even mentioned. The point is that the Spirit's work will vary according to the worshiping community's circumstances. It is important, therefore, to know the community's context by creating something like a community profile that identifies the social, economic, and cultural trends and characteristics of the broader community. This can help ministers understand the social parameters that have been set by the community.

When I was hired to chair the Worship Arts and Media program at my current academic institution, for instance, the administrators and student representatives who interviewed me made it clear that fostering diversity in worship was a top priority for the school. In the past ten years, the institution has undergone a tremendous amount of demographic change, going from a predominantly White school to a minority-majority school. Today, more than half of the student body is non-White, and the largest demographic is Hispanic. In fact, the school is considered a "Hispanic-Serving Institution" under the Higher Education Act, and many students are "first generation" students. By doing a community profile, it was clear that the worship of the school needed to better represent the community. This means that as a Foursquare institution the worship should be charismatic, and as a demographically diverse community, it should be stylistically diverse, reflective of the community. To achieve this, we developed three distinct chapel teams that express worship uniquely. One of our teams is proclamatory, leans stylistically into gospel, and calls people to change their identities to what God has envisioned for them. Another team is declarative, leans stylistically into the charismatic worship of Spanish-speaking Latin America, and fosters empowerment through the binding of sin by the power of the Spirit. Finally, one team is oriented around intercession, leans stylistically into the ambient rock of Contemporary Worship Music (CWM), and prays for personal healing and communal reconciliation. Each team begins with the thematic, stylistic, and narrative conventions of the genre, but moves freely thereabout to follow wherever God is leading them, even if it moves beyond the genre's conventions. We also mix the teams up for a few weeks midsemester to promote unity and extemporaneity. Like three distinct tones making a chord instead of a monophonic sound, we want to foster an air of unity through diversity that engages the whole student body while retaining the ability to move freely within, and adjacent to, a narrative framework. The Spirit will always meet us where we're at in our cultural and social contexts.

When the Spirit pushes a community past society's social parameters, the ministry becomes prophetic. As mentioned in chapter three, Martin Luther King Jr.'s work of racial reconciliation was prophetic because it began within the social structures of the American South, and King, by the guidance of the Spirit, used biblically rich rhetoric and nonviolent resistance to prophetically call out, publicly grieve, and energize a new vision of peace and reconciliation. In so doing, King was able to push past and eventually expand the social parameters of American society at large. Although there still is a long way to go on this front, King, by the power of the Spirit, was able to establish more justice in the United States for African Americans than was previously the case. But these *American* issues of racial reconciliation are regional and not global. The Spirit does different work in areas where these sorts of injustices exist through different guises. But God is constant, and *all* the work the Spirit does around the world is always to finally reconcile all of creation back to God. And as we will see next, the chief aim of this prophetic work is ultimately to create a space for worship by removing and displacing any hindrance to worship.

The simple task of worship ministry is to lead people into the presence of the relational God, but when a major part of this task requires a critical or liberating component, then worship *must* function prophetically. While we've already noted that Moses is the archetype of the biblical prophet, and the exodus involved God's people rising against the royal consciousness of Egypt, Pentecostal pastor and hymn writer Jack Hayford points out that the ultimate issue driving the exodus was worship.[47] By sending Moses to deliver the Hebrews out of bondage, God sent a leader to liberate his people *so that* they may know and worship God freely.[48] Pharaoh knew that people who are free to worship God can't be bound by earthly powers, so he subjugated the Hebrews and propped himself up above God. As Hayford writes, "Because

---

[47]Jack Hayford, *Worship His Majesty: How Praising the King of Kings Will Change Your Life, Revised and Expanded* (Ventura, CA: Regal, 2000), 86.

[48]Hayford, *Worship His Majesty*, 78.

the spirit of the world will always seek to retain oppressive power over God's own, worship is at the core of God's message."[49] Considering this, worship functions prophetically in at least two ways: first, worship is prophetic when communities worship *through* suffering and subjugation because they are proclaiming a new reality in the face of dire circumstances, and second, the life of worship is the "destiny" of God's people[50]—it is the end goal of any prophetic utterance. To this Hayford writes, "Worship is our means of deliverance—the key to throwing off our chains and unshackling our future."[51] As discussed in chapter three, the incident of the golden calf flew in the face of Moses' prophetic ministry, and it did so by displacing the means and goal of liberation: worship.

Another way renewal worshiping communities align themselves to the Spirit's ministry is by what charismatic groups have broadly, if not ambiguously, termed "prophetic worship." The charismatic sense of prophetic worship is less about societal engagement and more focused on an openness to hear God individually while dwelling in the spiritually charged space of God's presence. Author and practitioner Vivien Hibbert defines prophetic worship as "presence worship," a form of worship that expresses one's communion with God.[52] She writes, "Prophetic worship is filled with God's voice and manifest presence as he responds to us. Whenever we recognize and make way for God's voice in our worship, we have prophetic worship. His participation in our worship is the 'prophetic' component."[53] Hibbert's definition supplements our relational characterization of "worship as response" by calling the worshiper to be attentive to God's reply. Prophetic worship necessitates, accordingly, a state of openness to God's communication. This same notion is echoed by author and prophetic minister Helen Calder: "Prophetic worship could be seen as a Divine conversation. On our part, we are honouring and adoring God, while He in turn is breathing His purposes into our hearts and lives, and the life of our church."[54] Since worship is our response

---

[49]Hayford, *Worship His Majesty*, 78.

[50]Hayford, *Worship His Majesty*, 88-89.

[51]Hayford, *Worship His Majesty*, 91.

[52]Vivien Hibbert, *Prophetic Worship* (Texarkana, AR: Judah Books, 2020) loc. 298, Kindle.

[53]Hibbert, *Prophetic Worship*, loc. 298, Kindle.

[54]Helen Calder, *Prophetic Worship: Develop Your Ministry of Encounter* (Melbourne, FL: Enliven Ministries, 2017) loc. 60, Kindle.

to God's self-revelation (see chaps. 1 and 2), this sense of prophetic worship is the next step of an ongoing dialogue. It is God's response to our response.

As discussed last chapter, a hallmark of renewal worship is for worshipers to come ready and expectant for divine encounters. Through flow, the push and pull between structure and spontaneity is navigated by the worshiping community, and the Spirit guides where the people are led. What creates this charged space of expectancy among charismatics is a spiritual posture of openness and surrender. This is propelled by a charismatic ritual dynamic that encourages appropriate ways of "behaving, believing and feeling in relation to sacred space."[55] As sociologist Michael Wilkinson and theologian Peter Althouse point out, "The ritual activity that occurs in charismatic worship and the way in which people are changed is primarily one of 'surrender' or 'letting go' of performance and the embrace of spontaneous flow and intimacy that is produced in prayer."[56] Thus, the ritual dynamic of prophetic worship creates the possibility to prayerfully extend the conversation between God and the worshiper.

The charismatic sense of prophetic worship begins with the individual and extends out to the community, causing communal transformation to occur when the Spirit aligns individuals to a common narrative. In other words, the communal movement of the Spirit occurs when particular, individual alignments correspond with a broader vision for the people. By establishing an in-out track for spiritual alignment, the charismatic sense of prophetic worship seems to go against the out-in sense of alignment that occurs when communities reinforce shaping narratives (see chap. 3). Rather than seeing these two pathways as conflicting, it's more accurate to view the in-out and out-in senses of alignment as cooperative: the worshiping community sets the spiritual parameters through a preestablished ritual space, but it is the agreement between individual alignments that creates the broader movement. Perhaps it is best to see this relationship as *out-in-out*. The narrative parameters are set by the worshiping community (out), the individual aligns with God's vision (in), and the individual alignments come to agreement and create a communal move of God (out). It is in this way that local

---

[55]Michael Wilkinson and Peter Althouse, *Catch the Fire: Soaking Prayer and Charismatic Renewal* (DeKalb, IL: NIU Press, 2014), 71.

[56]Wilkinson and Althouse, *Catch the Fire*, 91.

communities function prophetically, hearing God's voice and following the Spirit's leading.

As we've already discussed, renewal worship also works prophetically on societal levels when it identifies and calls out social injustices that contradict the Spirit's work of reconciliation and renewal. Here the ministry of renewal worship extends beyond the community and speaks to broader social structures that affect multiple networks of communities. While this is certainly true, the prophetic ministry of renewal worship does not end at the societal level. I'd like to submit that God even sends *global* prophetic messages through renewal worship. The Spirit communicates messages to individuals, communities, and societies, but what if there is a message that God wants to broadcast globally? When a singular message is transported globally through a song that is sung by thousands of local churches around the world, renewal worship becomes a global prophetic voice.

In our age of technological innovation, varying global civilizations easily interact due to continual advances in information technologies and telecommunications.[57] Consequently, all forms of entertainment, including music, are shared and communicated globally. Because music has such strong mimetic qualities and offers nonverbal means of relating, it is both memorable and has the ability to unite disparate people groups through emotional appeals.[58] Likewise, worship music bears strong mimetic qualities that can easily travel and unite worshiping communities around the world. In recent years renewal worship music has helped propagate the Pentecostal message of abundance throughout the globe and in many different church denominations and traditions. Monique Ingalls maintains that media networks and technology allow Pentecostal music and worship practices to easily travel from context to context.[59] Conferences, distribution, song licensing, radio play, and television help promote the sonic appeal of Pentecostal worship,

---

[57]David Lyon, *Jesus in Disneyland: Religion in Postmodern Times* (Cambridge, UK: Polity, 2000), 64.

[58]Jeremy Begbie, "Faithful Feelings: Music and Emotion in Worship," in *Resonant Witness: Conversations Between Music and Theology*, ed. Jeremy Begbie and Stephen Guthrie (Grand Rapids, MI: Eerdmans, 2011), 325-26.

[59]Monique Ingalls, "Introduction: Interconnection, Interface, and Identification in Pentecostal-Charismatic Music and Worship," in *The Spirit of Praise: Music and Worship in Global Pentecostal-Charismatic Christianity*, ed. Monique Ingalls and Amos Yong (University Park: Pennsylvania State University Press, 2015), 5.

along with its style of embodied spirituality. Among the most popular, internationally known worship collectives are Hillsong UNITED, Jesus Culture, and Bethel Music. Each of these groups fit squarely in the realm of renewal worship and have universalized the Pentecostal message, making it more accessible to global and broadly evangelical audiences.

Consider, for instance, the massive global appeal of Hillsong UNITED's "Oceans (Where Feet May Fail)." The song was released in 2013 by Hillsong UNITED on their album titled *Zion*. When it came out, "Oceans" quickly became a global hit, peaking at number one on the Billboard Hot Christian Songs chart in November of 2013. The song kept tremendous staying power as well as being named the number one Christian song of the 2010s by Billboard. The song spent sixty-one nonconsecutive weeks as number one in the three years following its release, and has spent 191 weeks on the list overall.[60] The song's immense popularity means the message behind "Oceans" was also globally distributed, and this message, I would add, extends Pentecostal and charismatic theological commitments, especially since Hillsong UNITED is one of the worship ministries that came out of Australian Pentecostal megachurch Hillsong Church. David Taylor remarks that the song's textual elements align perfectly with Pentecostal and charismatic sensibilities, making it "*the* perfect charismatic-pentecostal song."[61] The lyrics call worshipers to a dynamic and resilient faith, they portray an intimacy with God, and refer to God's uncontainable power and mystery.[62] Ultimately the worshiper surrenders to God's call to move out in faith. This concept is evident in the bridge lyrics: "Spirit lead me where my trust is without borders."[63] If Taylor is right about the song's Pentecostal and charismatic sensibilities, then these theological commitments have been reinforced millions of times as thousands of

---

[60]Hallels News, "Hillsong United's 'Oceans (Where Feet May Fail)' is the #1 Song on Billboard Hot Christian Songs for the 2010s," JubileeCast (2019), https://jubileecast.com/articles/22607/20191120/hillsong-uniteds-oceans-where-feet-may-fail-is-the-1-song-on-billboard-hot-christian-songs-for-the-2010s.htm (accessed November 21, 2020).

[61]W. David O. Taylor, "What Makes Hillsong's 'Oceans (Where Feet May Fail)' So Popular?," *Diary of an Arts Pastor*, June 10, 2015, https://artspastor.blogspot.com/2015/06/what-makes-hillsongs-ocean-where-feet.html.

[62]Taylor, "What Makes Hillsong's 'Oceans (Where Feet May Fail)' So Popular?"

[63]"Oceans (Where Feet May Fail)," words and music by Joel Houston, Matt Crocker, and Salomon Ligthelm, CCLI 6428767 © 2012 Hillsong Music Publishing Australia (administered by Capitol CMG Publishing).

worship gatherings around the world have repeatedly sung this song in worship. Could it be that God desired to distribute a global message of encouragement for believers to have unbridled faith and trust in God? Perhaps this is a prophetic message God wanted to circulate around the world throughout the 2010s, and the song "Oceans" became God's medium of transmission. As the songwriters of "Oceans" sought to follow the Spirit's leading (into the great unknown?) when writing this song, perhaps the Spirit led them to make a prophetic proclamation for a global audience.

Cory Asbury of Bethel Music's song "Reckless Love" followed a similar trajectory. "Reckless Love" was released in 2017 as the lead single off of Asbury's album of the same name. It reached #1 on the Billboard Hot Christian Songs chart by March of 2018. Along with gaining global distribution and instant popularity, it was also critically acclaimed, winning both "Song of the Year" and "Worship Song of the Year" at the GMA Dove Awards in 2018, and was nominated for the 2019 Grammy Award for "Best Contemporary Christian Music Performance/Song."[64] While Asbury's original recording of the song was already a huge hit, the song has also been performed by, or in conjunction with, major artists such as Israel Houghton, Steffany Gretzinger, Justin Bieber, and Tori Kelly. Like "Oceans," this song has a general Christian message but also implies some Pentecostal theological commitments. We've already discussed the main theme of abundant, sacrificial love in the song's lyrics in chapter two, but here I would like to highlight the implicit language of prevenient grace—the enabling grace that precedes a human decision—in the lyrics. As mentioned in chapter two, verse two has the line "When I was Your foe still Your love fought for me," which portrays God seeking after the lost as an act of lovingkindness. Then later in the same verse, the lyrics state, "When I felt no worth You paid it all for me."[65] This seems to demonstrate a commitment to the Wesleyan-Arminian notion of prevenient grace held widely by Pentecostals. The song's global popularity helped to spread and

---

[64]Deborah Evans Price, "Tori Kelly Teams Up With Cory Asbury on 'Reckless Love': Exclusive," Billboard (2020), www.billboard.com/articles/columns/pop/8547607/tori-kelly-cory-asbury -reckless-love-exclusive (accessed November 21, 2020).

[65]"Reckless Love," words and music by Caleb Culver, Cory Asbury, and Ran Jackson, CCLI 7089641 © 2017 Cory Asbury Publishing, Richmond Park Publishing, Watershed Worship Publishing, Bethel Music Publishing (administrated by Bethel Music Publishing, Essential Music Publishing LLC, Watershed Music Publishing).

normalize the concepts of prevenient grace, God's sacrificial love, and the
notion that a relentless pursuit of the lost consumes God's desires. These
theological commitments are not exclusively Pentecostal, but they did come
from an ecclesial context of renewal via Bethel Music. By referencing the
parable of the lost sheep (Mt 18:12-14; Lk 15:3-7), perhaps the global message
that God wanted to send through this song was that God's loving pursuit of
the lost is relentless.

An important aspect of this song's documented rise in popularity is the
controversy that surrounded the adjective "reckless" in the chorus, used to
describe God's love. The main contention here is that the word "reckless"
improperly qualifies the notion of God's love to the point that it distorts the
orthodox understanding of divine love. Some have even gone so far as to say
this expression of God's love is heretical.[66] Even Pentecostal theologian
Andrew Gabriel believes this is not an accurate way to describe God's love.
Gabriel writes,

> I searched for the meaning of "reckless," and Almighty Google tells me that
> "reckless" describes someone who acts "without thinking or caring about the
> consequences of an action." I tried the more respectable Merriam-Webster's
> Dictionary, and, similarly, it defines reckless as "marked by lack of proper
> caution: careless of consequences" and even as "irresponsible." I don't think
> too many Christians would like to say that God is "careless" or that God's love
> doesn't "care about consequences."[67]

Gabriel's contention is that God's love should not be seen as thoughtless or
careless, and the word "reckless" connotes that. It should be noted that Gabriel
does not believe Asbury's song is heretical, as its intentions and overall theological message are sound. Gabriel recommends we continue singing the song,
but only after swapping out the word "reckless" with "perfect."[68]

---

[66]For an example, see John Piper's interview at "Should We Sing of God's 'Reckless Love'?" Desiring God (2018), www.desiringgod.org/interviews/should-we-sing-of-gods-reckless-love (accessed November 21, 2020). Here Piper also contends that the song has Calvinistic overtones of irresist-ible grace with the lyric "Before I took a breath, you breathed your life into me." I would submit that this is a reference to the Genesis account of creation, and not meant to imply any soterio-logical concept of predestination.

[67]Andrew Gabriel, "God's Love Is Not Reckless, Contrary to What You Might Sing: An Evaluation of 'Reckless Love' from Bethel Music," Andrew K. Gabriel, www.andrewkgabriel.com/2018/02/06/gods-love-reckless-bethel/ (accessed November 21, 2020).

[68]Gabriel, "God's Love Is Not Reckless."

The problem with Gabriel's argument is that he is looking at the word "reckless" as a literal, rather than metaphorical qualifier of God's love. Song lyrics fit best under the literary category of poetry. Poetry is a literary form that uses aesthetic and rhythmic qualities of language to artistically convey meaning. It is aestheticized language. Metaphors are figures of speech applied to objects or actions that are *not literally applicable* in order to convey deeper meanings. In the case of "Reckless Love," the word "reckless" is a qualifying metaphor. They are juxtaposed *precisely because* they are not literally applicable. As Pat Pattison, songwriting professor at Berklee College of Music, states, "A qualifying metaphor uses adjectives to qualify nouns, and adverbs to qualify verbs. Friction within these relationships creates a metaphor."[69] The reason metaphors are effective is because they cause friction between two concepts, and this variance creates new connotations to a phrase's meaning. The word "love" is a theological concept full of dignity and power, so using a typically negative word like "reckless" to qualify it designedly causes friction. This combination of words makes the listener stop and wonder what it means and why it was stated—a common effect of good poetry. The metaphor works powerfully when one sees the commonality between two seemingly conflicting words. What sort of connotations does the term "reckless" share with God's love? The definition Gabriel used to define "reckless" states, "Without thinking or caring about the consequences of an action." Asbury cites the shepherd who would leave the ninety-nine behind to recover the lost sheep, which connotes recklessness in at least a metaphorical sense. Asbury said as much:

> When I use the phrase, "the reckless love of God," I'm not saying that God Himself is reckless. I am, however, saying that the way He loves, is in many regards, quite so. What I mean is this: He is utterly unconcerned with the consequences of His actions with regards to His own safety, comfort, and well-being. . . . His love isn't selfish or self-serving. He doesn't wonder what He'll gain or lose by putting Himself out there. He simply gives Himself away on the off-chance that one of us might look back at Him and offer ourselves in return. His love leaves the ninety-nine to find the one every time.[70]

---

[69]Pat Pattison, *Writing Better Lyrics: The Essential Guide to Powerful Songwriting*, 2nd ed. (Cincinnati: Writer's Digest Books, 2009), 24.

[70]Cory Asbury, "The Power of Love—God's Reckless Love," Good News Fellowship, https://gnf.ca /blog/2019/04/17/the-power-of-love-gods-reckless-love-liturgy-service/ (accessed November 21, 2020).

Recklessness disregards the consequences of an action, which could lead to injury or even death. So, on an even deeper theological level, what if we consider God's love as reckless in *this* sense? Wouldn't this perfectly speak toward the incarnation that led to the death of Christ?

"Reckless Love" is not an academic treatise, but a song. When songs express theological insight, they do so aesthetically *as* works of poetry. As Duck points out, "In concise poetry congregational song can teach towering themes of theology with an economy of words that help us experience, and not merely explain, new creation."[71] Poetic renderings of God are often necessary and at times superior to lucidly informative lyrics because they point us theologically toward God's ineffability. Metaphors are important literary tools that help readers and listeners come to *know* realities about God that can't be merely explained. To this point Duck is once again insightful: "Metaphorical terms serve well to speak about God, since the tension of the terms (the ways they are like and unlike) provokes insight while leaving room for humility about what we can say or know about God."[72] So, poetically juxtaposing words like "reckless" and "love" actually helps us better grasp the mysteries of God's divine love. Gabriel's problem was that he saw the adjective "reckless" literally through an academic lens instead of metaphorically through a poetic lens. "Reckless Love" is a work of art—a combination of music and poetry—so the lyrics should be understood as such.

As we've discussed the prophetic function of renewal worship throughout this chapter, I'd like to submit here that perhaps God even uses controversies like this to catapult a song's global popularity. In fact, Brueggemann saw a similar precedence in the Old Testament prophets, who he called ancient poets: "Poetry that invites and transforms and shocks and offends may sometimes be the work of the Spirit."[73] Perhaps God allowed the controversy surrounding the lyrics of "Reckless Love" to happen so that more people would pay attention to the song's message and begin to address and confront the nature of God's love, especially as it pertains to the lost. Perhaps similar controversies were allowed to propel the messages of "How He Loves" by John

---

[71]Duck, *Worship for the Whole People of God*, 80.
[72]Duck, *Worship for the Whole People of God*, 100.
[73]Brueggemann, *Reality, Grief, Hope*, 43.

Mark McMillan and popularized by Jesus Culture, or "So Will I (100 Billion X)" by Hillsong Worship, both of which display incredible feats of poetic lyric writing. Perhaps these songs demonstrate and perpetuate global moves of the Spirit. If this is indeed the case, then these are examples of God speaking to the whole world prophetically through renewal worship.

CONCLUSION

This chapter answered the question "What is said in renewal worship?" by exploring the various ways renewal worship engages the gift of prophecy. Noticing that the Spirit of prophecy was given to the church at Pentecost, we discussed two important connotations for prophecy in renewal worship; there is the communal meaning that sees prophecy as a spiritual gift, and the broader, societal sense that sees prophecy as carrying a critical function. Both of these connotations bear biblical precedence and are utilized in renewal worship today. Next we discussed the various prophetic ministries of renewal worship, citing different ways prophecy is utilized in local, societal, and global levels. We ended by discussing how renewal worship is used to broadcast prophetic messages globally, and how some popular worship songs helped to transmit Pentecostal theological commitments to a global audience. Although we've covered a lot of ground, this chapter only begins to discuss the many creative ways the Spirit speaks through renewal worship. Nevertheless, my hope is that by recognizing the Spirit's work in renewal worship, non-Pentecostals can come to celebrate what God is doing through Pentecostalism, as we in the renewal tradition celebrate what God is doing outside of Pentecostalism.

The next chapter will wrap up our discussion concerning "Renewal Worship in Context" and conclude part two of this book. The last topic we'll need to discuss concerns who renewal worshipers are. We will look at the global community of renewal worship and discuss inroads for interdenominational reconciliation and solidarity. But first, let's once again reflect on the contents of this chapter with a summarizing doxology:

> *Praise God who makes us see*
> *Inspires us to speak*
> *Praise God who gives us words of prophecy.*

6

WHO RENEWAL WORSHIPERS ARE

THE RENEWED GLOBAL COMMUNITY

So if anyone is in Christ, there is a new creation:
everything old has passed away; see, everything has become new!
All this is from God, who reconciled us to himself through Christ,
and has given us the ministry of reconciliation; that is, in Christ God
was reconciling the world to himself, not counting their trespasses
against them, and entrusting the message of reconciliation to us.

2 CORINTHIANS 5:17-19

IN THE PASSAGE above, Paul casts a vision for the church that has eschatological implications. People are *new creations* when they reconcile back to
God through Christ. In Christ forgiveness and reconciliation are possible,
and the church takes on Christ's "ministry of reconciliation" by the power of
the Holy Spirit. Not only are we reconciled with God and each other, but, as
the passage above indicates, we are called to help others reconcile with God
and each other too. We are to forgive others as God has forgiven us (Col 3:13),
and to live peaceably with one another (Rom 12:18; Mt 5:23-24). The *new
humanity* in Christ was reconciled and made into one unified body (Eph
2:14-16). This is our task as Christians—to help bring about a reality where
redemption is full-grown and we, as the new humanity, walk humbly together
in the glory of God (Rev 21:22-27). This is our ultimate state of continual,
unfettered relation to God—a state of eternal worship. Our worship today is
a foretaste of this coming reality and contributes significantly to our ministry

of reconciliation. As we reconcile in worship, walls of prejudice and exclusion are torn down.

According to Ruth Duck, reconciliation "addresses human need for release from guilt, self-hatred, and destructive relationships through witnessing to and demonstrating the love and compassion of God."[1] In other words, reconciliation is the crucial action of relational restoration. Such a restoration can only come about through forgiveness, and this includes both God's forgiveness of our iniquities, and our forgiveness of others' sins. And as forgiveness is a healing and renewing act of the Spirit,[2] the end goal of reconciliation is a healed and unified universal church. The universal outpour has implications of reconciliation that are more than just hinted at in Acts 1–3. The Spirit was poured out indiscriminately on *all* flesh. This means the Spirit's blessing is intended for everybody, and the call to reciprocate God's love is universal. As Frank Macchia points out, not only were the Gentiles brought into the same experience of the Spirit that the Jewish Christians had, but the Spirit empowered them to bear witness even further to the ends of the earth (Acts 1:8).[3] Thus the witness of the universal outpour invites *all people* from *all over the world* to enter God's embrace. Through the Spirit, Christ unifies and reconciles all of us who were previously interspersed.[4]

This chapter seeks to identify who renewal worshipers are, not by merely describing worshipers from Pentecostal and charismatic traditions, but by understanding the global ministry of reconciliation in which renewal worshipers are called to participate. It should be noted, however, that renewal worshipers are not unique in their ministry of reconciliation. God desires for all to be saved (1 Tim 2:4), and the whole church has been empowered by the Holy Spirit to go into all nations (Mt 28:18-20). Thus, renewal worship's ministry of reconciliation is only part of a general commission for all Christians. However, we will explore how renewal worship carries this mission out in its

---

[1]Ruth Duck, *Worship for the Whole People of God: Vital Worship for the 21st Century* (Louisville, KY: Westminster John Knox, 2013), 245.

[2]Daniela Augustine, *The Spirit and the Common Good: Shared Flourishing in the Image of God* (Grand Rapids, MI: Eerdmans, 2019), 165.

[3]Frank Macchia, "Babel and the Tongues of Pentecost: Reversal or Fulfilment?," in *Speaking in Tongues: Multi-Disciplinary Perspectives*, ed. Mark Cartledge (Eugene, OR: Wipf & Stock, 2006), 35.

[4]Leopoldo Sánchez, *Sculptor Spirit: Models of Sanctification from Spirit Christology* (Downers Grove, IL: IVP Academic, 2019), 235.

own way through its own espoused and operant theological commitments. First this chapter looks at reconciliation through the lens of renewal worship by examining the witnesses of Pentecost and Azusa Street, demonstrating how in each of these cases renewal worship proliferated a message of reconciliation. This chapter then looks at the global engagements of renewal worship, tracing how it fosters global solidarity while maintaining particularity in cultures around the world. There are various methods God has used to spread the message of spiritual renewal around the world, and, to put it succinctly, this chapter looks at how God unifies people globally through renewal worship.

THE RECONCILING SPIRIT OF RENEWAL WORSHIP

Worship is unifying. When we gather in renewal worship we sing together, we raise hands together, we dance together, we pray together, we break bread together, we testify about the mighty works of God to each other, and in lament we mourn together. Not only are we united personally as we holistically worship God, but we're united with our worshiping communities as we come together with a shared experience (chap. 3). Preaching lays a foundation for communal reconciliation as it proclaims the gospel message of hope, salvation, and reconciliation. Prayers of confession are occasioned by the call to make things right with God and others, which is evidenced by Christ's own instructions to his disciples on how to pray: "And forgive us our debts, as we also have forgiven our debtors" (Mt 6:12). Prayers of healing and of thanksgiving, along with prayers of intercession, all work toward personal and communal reconciliation. Baptism speaks toward forgiveness, grace, and communal acceptance. And perhaps the greatest act of reconciliation is Communion as it marks a time of repentance, forgiveness, sanctification, and sharing the table with others in solidarity with Christ and others.[5] While the majority of these reconciling practices are shared with every Christian

---

[5]Duck, *Worship for the Whole People of God*, 251-52. There are other reconciling traditions that are not formally recognized in renewal worship. A common tradition of note is the "passing of the peace." This act of reconciliation is like a greeting where the minister gestures toward congregants and says something like "The peace of the Lord be with you always," and the congregation responds with "And also with you." Sometimes congregants are instructed to share this greeting with each other. This is an excellent sign of reconciliation as the worshipers greet each other with peace despite whatever preceded the moment.

worshiping tradition, renewal worship is distinct by its pneumatological understanding of these practices. As discussed throughout this entire book, renewal worship ties its worship practices theologically to the universal out-pour of the Spirit. All of these acts testify to the reconciling Spirit of Pentecost that was poured out on all flesh, is continually being poured out, and brings forth new global, charismatic renewals.

Worship also unites us globally with other worshiping communities as the Spirit draws all of us into a single family—a global church. Because of their unifying experience of the Spirit, Pentecostals maintain an inherent theological impulse toward unity.[6] Part of this chapter, therefore, discusses how Pentecostals are simultaneously distinct but also globally unified through renewal worship. As we think globally about worship, however, we should begin by discussing how every Christian around the world is reconciled and united in Christ by the Spirit. As you might've guessed, the quintessential biblical witness of God's reconciling work through the Spirit can once again be found at Pentecost. Daniela Augustine writes, "The Spirit's kenosis upon the broken world primes it for reconciliation with God and neighbor, stirring up the human conscience . . . toward imaging the Trinitarian protocommunal life."[7] In other words, the universal outpour of the Spirit produces fertile ground for reconciliation, and mediates our embrace of the other. It is the Spirit poured out on all flesh that enables global reconciliation and paves the way for Christian unity. Moreover, there is a direct, unifying correlation of reconciliation between Pentecost and the Azusa Street Revival that birthed the global Pentecostal movement that has captivated global Christianity in the twenty-first century.[8] In both of these pivotal moments, God's work of reconciliation was consequentially tied to an outpour of the Spirit.

The reconciling witness of Pentecost. Throughout the Bible, unity and wholeness come from dependence on God. God is the source of life and love,

---

[6]Tony Richie, "Translating Pentecostal Testimony into Interreligious Dialogue," *Journal of Pentecostal Theology* 20 (2011): 163.

[7]Augustine, *Spirit and the Common Good*, 165.

[8]Although more will be said about this below, it should be mentioned that the claim of Azusa Street as Pentecostalism's birthplace is contested. See Allan Anderson, *To the Ends of the Earth: Pentecostalism and the Transformation of World Christianity* (Oxford: Oxford University Press, 2013). However, Gaston Espinosa in his *William Seymour and the Origins of Global Pentecostalism* (Durham, NC: Duke University Press, 2014) makes an important argument for the primacy of the Azusa Street Revival for Pentecostalism, and the contribution of William Seymour.

so when people are dependent on any other thing they are led away from life and led toward death, away from love and toward exclusion. They choose to eat from the tree of the knowledge of good and evil rather than the tree of life. Independence from God leads inevitably to destruction. The archetypal biblical story of defiant human independence is that of the tower of Babel (Gen 11:1-9). This ancient story takes place when all the people of the world spoke the same language. When they settled into a new land, the people sought to build a city centered around a tower that would reach to the heavens (Gen 11:4). This was a human attempt at control and independence. They sought to "make a name for themselves" by having God in their grasps. God responded by confusing the people's languages and scattering them all over the earth: "So the LORD scattered them from there over all the earth, and they stopped building the city. That is why it was called Babel—because there the LORD confused the language of the whole world. From there the LORD scattered them over the face of the whole earth" (Gen 11:8-9 NIV). The unified language of the Babylonians led to idolatrous intentions that would inevitably enslave them to iniquity as they sought freedom *from* God.[9]

For Macchia, Babel represents a judgment that Pentecost reverses.[10] God's will for people is not one of uniformity, but to "disperse and diversify, to fill the earth (Gen 1:28), and to be blessed through the blessing given to Abram as symbolized by the name that *God* gave him (Abraham). This promise of new life was to result in the blessing of many families everywhere."[11] So for Macchia, the judgment laid out for the Babylonians was really a blessing. God's scattering of the people was *a grace* that condemned the people's idolatry and put them back on the path of "filling the earth with the proliferation of life."[12] The Christians at Pentecost took the same mandate to scatter (to the ends of the earth) as a blessed commission rather than a retributive judgment. Diversity in language was key to fulfilling this commission. As Miroslav Volf writes,

> Before Babel the whole of humanity spoke *one* language; in Jerusalem the new community speaks *many* languages. As the tongues of fire are divided and rest

---

[9]Macchia, "Babel and the Tongues of Pentecost," 41.
[10]Macchia, "Babel and the Tongues of Pentecost," 39.
[11]Macchia, "Babel and the Tongues of Pentecost," 41.
[12]Macchia, "Babel and the Tongues of Pentecost," 42.

on each of the disciples, "each one" of the Jews from "every nation under heaven" representing the global community hears them "speaking in the native language of each" (2:3-7). A theological (rather than simply historical) reading of the Pentecost account suggests that when the Spirit comes, all understand each other, not because one language is restored or a new all-encompassing meta-language is designed, but because each hears his or her own language spoken. Pentecost overcomes the "confusion" and the resulting false "scattering," but it does so not by reverting to the unity of cultural uniformity but by advancing toward the harmony of cultural diversity.[13]

Thus the Christian unity of Pentecost emerges from a universal intelligibility of diverse tongues, not from forced uniformity. Because diversity was strategic for the expansion of the gospel, it was to be upheld and even celebrated. But through the universal outpour of the Spirit, there was also unity under the banner of Christ. Pentecost was not the melding of all voices into one mono-phonic tone, but it was the bringing together of different tones that create rich and satisfying harmonies. There is only so much that can be done with a single melody, but when we are able to combine notes and rhythms, the possibilities for composition are endless.

Furthermore, the witness of Pentecost is also one of equity because repre-sentatives from varying backgrounds spoke in varied tongues to invariably share the gospel. This means that by the power of the Holy Spirit the otherwise voiceless are now given a voice, and the otherwise overlooked are now able to hear.[14] As Paul has shown us, in Christ there is no longer Jew or Greek, slave or free, male or female (Gal 3:28). This does not mean Christ has wiped away our differentiations, making us into raceless, genderless automatons. It means that Christ has wiped away our manmade[15] *divisions of power* between race, class, and gender. The divisions Paul mentions are intentionally relationally specific, so through the universal outpour *everyone*—regardless of their earthly status—is granted access to God. Any distinction that is used to create hierarchies and divisions is washed away once we're drenched in the Holy

---

[13]Miroslav Volf, *Exclusion and Embrace, Revised and Updated: A Theological Exploration of Identity, Otherness, and Reconciliation* (Nashville: Abingdon, 2019), 215-16.

[14]Volf, *Exclusion and Embrace*, 216.

[15]I am intentionally using the gender-specific term *manmade* here as a reference to history's bent toward patriarchy.

Spirit. As Macchia writes, "Barriers are crossed and reconciliation occurs in the communion of God through Spirit baptism."[16] Through indiscriminate relationality, which is another way to say "communion," Pentecost creates a radical openness to the other because the Spirit renders us reconciled and unified. To this point Daniela Augustine writes,

> Pentecost reveals that God has opened his future for the other, and the Spirit (who enfleshes that future in the human *socium*) demands the same from all flesh. The Spirit of Pentecost condemns the spirits of racism, sexism, tribalism/ ethnocentrism, and nationalism as manifestations of sin's fracturing and antagonizing of the human community. Pentecost announces God's judgment upon these social pathologies and upon all attempts for their religious justification: they have no future, for in the divinely ordained relational sacramentality of the cosmos there is no future/no eschaton without the other.[17]

This renewed sense of equity comes about as a signpost of the fully reconciled reality that is to come.[18]

Pentecost instills in us a vision of a world that promotes human flourishing and condemns powers of inequity, but this sort of reconciliation only comes about when there is genuine forgiveness. For Volf, true reconciliation happens when we sincerely seek to embrace the other. This sentiment animates his "theology of embrace," a social theology that sees sin as oppression of the marginalized and liberation as embrace of the other.[19] Mere liberation, however, is not enough. The projects of postcolonialism and postmodernity have sought to liberate oppressed people, but if "liberation" is ever achieved, someone else will eagerly move into the role of power and a new cycle of oppression will ensue.[20] That's not to say we shouldn't strive for social liberation and reconciliation; good public policies *can* move us toward a more just society. But we must recognize that our human efforts toward reconciliation are always "nonfinal."[21]

---

[16]Frank Macchia, *Baptized in the Spirit: A Global Pentecostal Theology* (Grand Rapids, MI: Zondervan, 2006), 177.

[17]Augustine, *Spirit and the Common Good*, 9.

[18]Glenn Packiam, *Worship and the World to Come: Exploring Christian Hope in Contemporary Worship* (Downers Grove, IL: IVP Academic, 2020), 2.

[19]Miroslav Volf, "Exclusion and Embrace: Theological Reflections in the Wake of 'Ethnic Cleansing,'" *Communio Viatorum* 35, no. 3 (1993): 269.

[20]Volf, *Exclusion and Embrace*, 108.

[21]Volf, *Exclusion and Embrace*, 109.

Volf casts three abnegations to support this notion: "First, the final reconcilia-tion is not a work of human beings but of the triune God. Second, it is not an apocalyptic end of the world but the eschatological new beginning of this world. Third, the final reconciliation is not a self-enclosed 'totality' because it rests on a God who is perfect love."[22] The Christian hope for reconciliation is not a rigid totalitarianism, but is rooted in God's love—the only sort of gracious and self-giving love that can lead to final reconciliation.

True Christian embrace resists the colonizing impulse of forced uniformity, but entails freeing the other from oppression and then giving them "space to be themselves"[23] even as they are encouraged to reject their "tribal deities." Casting off tribal deities means directing worship only to God. A tribal deity can refer to anything that is idolized, not just another religion's gods or god-desses. For many people the tribal deity is themselves, money, sexuality, or status. It is anything that inhabits their devotion and ultimate concern. A Christian embrace of the other means accepting them and celebrating them in their difference, but leading them to worship only God. The hard work of final reconciliation requires two-way forgiveness. Forgiveness is what poten-tially closes the gap between exclusion and embrace. As Volf writes,

> Forgiveness is the boundary between exclusion and embrace. It heals the wounds that the power-acts of exclusion have inflicted and breaks down the dividing wall of hostility. Yet it leaves a distance between people, an empty space of neutrality, that allows them either to go their separate ways in what is sometimes called "peace" or to fall into each other's arms and restore broken communion.[24]

Even if two parties leave in "peace" rather than "embrace," forgiveness is still the necessary Christian action for reconciliation.

Final reconciliation leads to embrace where communion is restored with God and others. This type of reconciliation is extremely difficult, however, because not only do the perpetrators need forgiveness, but so do the victims. For victims to repent means they no longer allow the perpetrator to define them or dictate their actions. The oppressors can no longer "determine the

---

[22]Volf, *Exclusion and Embrace*, 109.
[23]Volf, "Exclusion and Embrace," 269.
[24]Volf, *Exclusion and Embrace*, 126.

terms under which social conflicts [are] carried out."[25] Repentance thus protects victims from mirroring or dehumanizing their oppressors. This is one of Volf's more sobering points, but it corroborates Jesus' call for us to love our enemies (Mt 5:44), and follows Christ's lead for reconciliation. As Volf writes, "Instead of aping the enemy's act of violence and rejection, Christ, the victim who refuses to be defined by the perpetrator, forgives and makes space in himself for the enemy. Hence precisely as a victim Christ is the true judge: by offering to embrace the offenders, he judges both the initial wrongdoing of the perpetrators and the reactive wrongdoing of many victims."[26] Christ's judgment flows from his forgiving, outstretched arms on the cross. His outstretched arms simultaneously display his victimization as a crucified person, and his forgiveness as one who gestures toward embrace. If renewal worship reciprocates the love of God, as we've established in chapter two, then this sort of communal reconciliation should come as a result of experiencing God's reconciling presence in worship. It is through embrace that worshiping communities are healed and made whole, and Christ's example coupled with the universal outpour of the Spirit gives *everyone* the means and mandate to truly reconcile. Such witness was powerfully demonstrated at the Azusa Street Revival.

The reconciling witness of Azusa Street. Although it is more appropriate to view the genesis of Pentecostalism as encompassing a series of early twentieth-century movements and revivals that were united by common formative experiences,[27] the Azusa Street Revival has come to symbolize the birth of the Pentecostal movement. By emphasizing Spirit baptism, experiential spirituality, and an egalitarian distribution of spiritual gifts, the Azusa Street Revival demonstrated a visible outworking of what would form many of Pentecostalism's chief ecclesial characteristics. As we will see, this revival demonstrates a fresh outpouring of the Spirit, causing many to view it narratively as part of the "latter rain" of the Spirit (see chap. 3).

The leader of the Azusa Street Revival was Louisiana-born William Seymour, the son of former slaves. Early on Seymour felt a call to ministry and quickly joined the Wesleyan-Holiness movement. After spending some

---

[25]Volf, *Exclusion and Embrace*, 116.
[26]Volf, *Exclusion and Embrace*, 127.
[27]Anderson, *To the Ends of the Earth*, 47.

time in Indianapolis and Cincinnati, Seymour went to Houston, where he would come under the teaching of Charles Parham, the founder of the Apostolic Faith movement and the progenitor of the Pentecostal doctrine of tongues as initial evidence of Spirit baptism.[28] In due course, Seymour was invited to Los Angeles to pastor a small holiness church, but the church's leadership ultimately thought he was not a good fit for the pastorate due to doctrinal differences over the nature of Spirit baptism and initial evidence, so they locked him out of the church. Despite this setback, Seymour stayed in Los Angeles and began hosting prayer meetings that emphasized Spirit baptism and speaking in tongues. These meetings grew so rapidly that Seymour and company quickly needed to move to a meeting place big enough to accommodate their meetings. They found an abandoned African Methodist Episcopal Church at 312 Azusa Street, which became the location that would host the Azusa Street Mission. From 1906 to 1909 thousands of people from all over the world came to visit the Azusa Street Mission to experience revival.[29]

The Azusa Street Revival was remarkable in many ways, but for our purposes here I'd like to focus on its worship and egalitarian nature. Not only was this revival led by an African American man during the Jim Crow era, it hosted totally interracial gatherings, encouraging women and minorities to preach, teach, lead worship, and pursue leadership. These egalitarian efforts together with new Pentecostal doctrinal positions caused the revival to be ridiculed by other denominations and many news outlets. Nevertheless, this revival genuinely embodied Paul's declaration that in Christ there is no longer Jew or Greek, slave or free, male or female (Gal 3:28). Evidently, the revivalists were keenly aware of how important their egalitarian position was for the global church as Frank Bartleman, participant and chronicler of the Azusa Street Revival, wrote, "the 'color line' was washed away in the blood of Christ."[30] At the Azusa Street Revival, the Spirit was given to any believer without preconditions.[31]

---

[28] As is famously recounted, because of segregation laws, Seymour had to listen to Parham's teachings from just outside the classroom.

[29] Cecil Robeck Jr., *The Azusa Street Mission and Revival: The Birth of the Global Pentecostal Movement* (Nashville: Thomas Nelson, 2006), 4-6.

[30] Frank Bartleman, *Azusa Street* (New Kensington, PA: Whitaker House, 1982), 51.

[31] Allan Anderson, *An Introduction to Pentecostalism: Global Charismatic Christianity* (Cambridge: Cambridge University Press, 2004), 208.

The early Pentecostals thought their "apostolic mission" was to return to the power of the Spirit that was lost throughout the Middle Ages.[32] According to Anderson, the charismatic gifts stopped being regularly used in the Western church after the time of Origen (c. 184–254 CE), and only the Orthodox Church and Western mystics recognized and practiced the charismata throughout medieval and modern church history.[33] Pentecostals saw themselves as recovering the charismata for the Western tradition. Anderson writes,

> The early Pentecostals believed that something had gone wrong with the church after the "original fire from heaven" on the Day of Pentecost, and that Christianity had degenerated or had "lapsed into writing meticulous creeds and inventing lifeless rituals." The Pentecostal revival was believed to be the "latter rain" promised by God through the prophet Joel, and would be characterized by a "worldwide resurgence of faith," and "healings and miracles" that were "a prelude to the second coming of Jesus Christ."[34]

Events such as the Azusa Street Revival and concurrent revivals around the world perfectly demonstrate this latter rain teaching. Early adherents held to an eschatological understanding that the latter rain of the Spirit would empower the church and precede the second coming of Christ. The once forgotten extravagant spiritual gifts would bear witness to the coming kingdom of God. To illustrate this, one can view the event of Pentecost as turning on a tap for the first time. The running flow that occurred at Pentecost was the universal outpour of the Spirit—a discharge that made manifest the gifts of the Spirit. The Spirit was not entirely quenched during the Middle Ages, but the once gushing spout slowed to a drip, and the extravagant gifts were all but forgotten. The latter rain represents a once-again flowing tap, which was characterized by the global revivals of the early twentieth century. As Anderson writes, "Fundamental to the expansion of these revivalist movements was a conviction that the Holy Spirit had been poured out upon the earth to enable witness in every nation to spread the good news to the ends of the earth."[35] Pentecostalism grew rapidly after the Azusa Street Revival due

---

[32] Anderson, *To the Ends of the Earth*, 13.
[33] Anderson, *Introduction to Pentecostalism*, 21-22.
[34] Anderson, *Introduction to Pentecostalism*, 44.
[35] Anderson, *To the Ends of the Earth*, 145.

to a *flood* of missionary activity, which was understood, practically and theo-logically, as yet another outworking of the universal outpour.

Notably, there was a peaceful air of forgiveness and reconciliation at Azusa Street as revival leaders and participants would not retaliate negatively to detrac-tors. Bartleman wrote, "Divine love was wonderfully manifest in the meetings. The people would not even allow an unkind word said against their opposers or the churches. The message was the love of God. It was a sort of 'first love' (Rev 2:4) of the early church returned."[36] The primacy of divine love was an important aspect of Azusa Street's message of equality. For Seymour, perfect love was essential to racial reconciliation and unity. It is only through perfect love that the church could be reconciled and become the worthy bride of Christ, the imminent bridegroom.[37] In fact, in his publication *The Apostolic Faith*,[38] Sey-mour wrote that the initial evidence of Spirit baptism is "divine love, which is charity. Charity is the Spirit of Jesus."[39] While this passage does not necessarily negate Parham's doctrine of tongues as initial evidence,[40] it at least identifies the root of tongues (and every spiritual gift) as divine love, which Paul seems to indicate in 1 Corinthians 13. True reconciliation was possible at Azusa Street because divine love was displayed indiscriminately and abundantly. Seymour connected this love to the universal outpour of the Spirit, which harkens us back to chapter two's argument that the object of renewal worship is the rela-tional God who has given us the abundant Spirit. The witness of reconciliation at the Azusa Street Revival has come as a consequence of the universal outpour, which is the very substance of renewal worship.

---

[36]Bartleman, *Azusa Street*, 51.

[37]Steven Land, "William Seymour: The Father of the Holiness-Pentecostal Movement," in *From Aldersgate to Azusa Street: Wesleyan, Holiness, and Pentecostal Visions of the New Creation*, ed. Henry Knight III (Eugene, OR: Pickwick, 2010), 225.

[38]*The Apostolic Faith* was the Azusa Street Mission's periodical that was distributed at no cost to its readers. This publication was crucial for expanding Seymour's messages beyond the confines of Los Angeles (Adam Stewart, "Azusa Street Mission and Revival," in *Handbook of Pentecostal Chris-tianity*, ed. Adam Stewart [DeKalb, IL: NIU Press, 2012], 46.).

[39]William Seymour, "Questions Answered," *Apostolic Faith* 1, no. 9 (June-September 1907): 2.1.

[40]Cecil Robeck has argued that Seymour had doubts and eventually rejected the doctrine of tongues as initial evidence (see Cecil Robeck Jr., "William J. Seymour and the 'Biblical Evidence,'" in *Initial Evidence: Historical and Biblical Perspectives on the Pentecostal Doctrine of Spirit Baptism*, ed. Gary McGee [Peabody, MA: Hendrickson, 1991]), but Renea Brathwaite has argued to the contrary that Seymour did not entirely reject the doctrine, but modified it to display pastoral concerns of main-taining a godly lifestyle (see Renea Brathwaite, "Tongues and Ethics: William J. Seymour and the 'Bible Evidence': A Response to Cecil M. Robeck, Jr.," *Pneuma* 32 [2010]: 203-22).

Worship at the Azusa Street Revival is a prime example, and perhaps the first modern instance, of renewal worship. There was an incredible reliance on the Spirit's immediacy, healings and miracles regularly occurred, and anyone, regardless of race, status, or age, was able to worship and minister in the Spirit. Thousands of people from all over the world came to experience what God was doing in Los Angeles. Services ran seven days a week, multiple times a day, and they were so seamless that they often ran together.[41] The meetings practiced baptism, Communion, footwashing, public prayer, testimony, preaching, and teaching. Participants spent countless hours praying intercessory prayers in the rooms upstairs and engaged in evangelistic opportunities throughout the week.[42] Worship was vital at Azusa Street, and vibrant worship practices were interwoven throughout every aspect of the revival.

Worship at Azusa Street was characteristically dynamic. Not only was the worship primal, passionate, exuberant, and filled with emotion, but at times it was quiet and reverent when a "holy hush" fell upon the congregation.[43] A full range of human emotion was present at Azusa Street, demonstrating the revival's holistic nature. The revival also valued spontaneity. In fact, the adherents opposed planned song selection for services, opting instead for a "Spirit-led approach for worship music."[44] Participants sang spontaneous songs from memory instead of reading from hymnbooks and practiced singing in tongues.[45] Singing in tongues was understood as the Spirit singing through a Spirit-baptized person, which also authenticated the Spirit's immediacy at the revival's worship.[46] The Spirit did not respect social differences at Azusa Street. Everyone was affected by the Spirit, and anyone, regardless of race, gender, class, or age, could function in the spiritual gifts. It was this egalitarian characteristic of the revival that both set it apart from any other Christian movement, and gave it global appeal. Los Angeles became a melting pot of intercultural dialogue and communion as people from all over the world

---

[41]Robeck, *Azusa Street Mission*, 135-36.

[42]Robeck, *Azusa Street Mission*, 136.

[43]Robeck, *Azusa Street Mission*, 133. This is when the whole congregation was simultaneously moved to silence.

[44]Josh P. S. Samuel, *The Holy Spirit in Worship Music, Preaching, and the Altar: Renewing Pentecostal Corporate Worship* (Cleveland, TN: CPT Press, 2018), 31.

[45]Samuel, *Holy Spirit in Worship Music*, 33-34.

[46]Samuel, *Holy Spirit in Worship Music*, 35-36.

gathered to worship. The charismatic African American style of worship brought in by Seymour and others embraced myriad expressions of worship from all over the globe. As Robeck writes,

> When expressions from this variety of cultures were brought together in one place, something new transpired that traditional Christians in Los Angeles—indeed, the city as a whole—was ill prepared to embrace. . . . This certainly seemed a new phenomenon—this seemingly uninhibited mixture of African Americans, Latinos, Armenians, Russians, Swedes, Germans, Italians, Chinese, Japanese, Native Americans, and other ethnic groups who found space among them for the bountiful presence of ecstatic manifestations such as speaking in tongues, prophesying, claims of dreams and visions, trances, healings, exorcism, and falling "in the Spirit."[47]

The Azusa Street Revival established a community where all sorts of people gathered in worship; embraced one another; shared witness, dreams, and visions; and grasped on to a shared story of renewal.[48] This was a true display of hospitality, and the reconciling Spirit was made manifest by the perfect love exhibited to one another. Both Pentecost and Azusa Street demonstrated reconciliation on the communal and transnational scale, which paved the way for far-reaching global engagement.

GLOBAL ENGAGEMENT THROUGH RENEWAL WORSHIP

The reconciling Spirit of renewal worship is also a missionary Spirit. As indicated at the start of this chapter, the whole church was commissioned to go out to the ends of the earth and make disciples. Reconciliation and mission are intertwined because it is only through a sense of Spirit-filled unity that one can hospitably respect another culture's uniqueness while demonstrating the transformative love of God. There is a tension between the particularity of a local culture and the universality of the global church that can only be relieved through hospitable, empathetic lovingkindness, which happens to be the modus operandi of reconciliation. The rest of this chapter focuses on global engagement through renewal worship, and does so first by addressing the crosscultural dynamic of respecting cultural particularity while fostering

---

[47]Robeck, *Azusa Street Mission*, 138.
[48]Land, "William Seymour," 222.

universality in the Spirit, which is significant for understanding diversity in worship. Finally, this chapter ends by discussing various ways Pentecostalism has participated in global engagement through renewal worship.

The particular and the universal in diverse worship. Paradoxically, in Christ we keep and celebrate our own particularity *while* we are adopted into a universal family. Galatians 3:26-27 shows how being baptized into one body unites us, making us all offspring of Abraham:

> For in Christ Jesus you are all children of God through faith. As many of you as were baptized into Christ have clothed yourselves with Christ. There is no longer Jew or Greek, there is no longer slave or free, there is no longer male and female; for all of you are one in Christ Jesus. And if you belong to Christ, then you are Abraham's offspring, heirs according to the promise.[49]

Paul here shows that faith in Christ bonds us to the promise of Abraham. Volf sees in Paul a clever response to the tension between universality and particularity. He traces Paul's logic:

> The oneness of God requires God's universality; God's universality entails human equality; human equality implies equal access by all to the blessings of the one God; equal access is incompatible with ascription of religious significance to genealogy; Christ, the seed of Abraham, is both the fulfillment of the genealogical promise to Abraham and the end of genealogy as a privileged locus of access to God; faith in Christ replaces birth into a people. As a consequence, all peoples can have access to the one God of Abraham and Sarah on equal terms, none by right and all by grace.[50]

The point here is that God makes us all equal as we become Abraham's offspring. We don't need to take on a different national identity (no longer Jew or Greek), but are made equal by virtue of uniting with Christ. There is still difference and distinction but not in rank or privilege. There is a flattening of status as the Spirit gives gifts irrespective of differences.[51] Inclusion into the body of Christ is not like different colors of paint mixing to make a new

---

[49]While in 1 Corinthians 12 Paul calls us unified when we're in the Spirit, here Paul shows how we're unified in Christ. As we've come to understand in chap. 4, these points are not dualistically opposed but work in tandem to talk about the deeper point of being unified with God through Christ *and* the Spirit.

[50]Volf, *Exclusion and Embrace*, 37.

[51]Volf, *Exclusion and Embrace*, 40.

color. If you've ever mixed oil paint before, you know that when the vibrant primary (red, yellow, and blue) and secondary (orange, purple, and green) hues are all carelessly mixed together, the result is an unflattering, neutral, brownish-gray color. The colors lose their individual chromas and their lustrous finishes. Inclusion in the body is more like a pointillist painting where each color is applied as a small, distinct dot. While the individual dots of color are distinguishable up close, viewed from a distance they form an image that's more radiant than the sum of its parts. We do not lose our particular identity in the body of Christ, rather becoming like Christ means our individuality is incorporated into a body where Christ is the head, as we are emplotted (to borrow the term from Ricoeur) into God's grand narrative. We are vibrant dots of color in God's painting.

As the Spirit preveniently leads us, we can come to the cross as we are, but we cannot *stay* as we are when we live a cruciform existence. There is a transformation that takes place when we are in Christ. While we're made equal and our differences are celebrated, we must denounce our tribal deities. As Volf writes, "Religion must be de-ethnicized so that ethnicity can be de-sacralized. Paul deprived each culture of ultimacy in order to give them all legitimacy in the wider family of cultures."[52] In other words, while culture can demarcate the way we understand many aspects of ourselves, it cannot define us fundamentally. Matters of ultimacy belong to Christ, and while people enter the one body as discrete people, what unifies them is not cultural homogeneity, but an ultimate allegiance to God. People can remain ethnically distinct, but not insofar as their ethnicity leads to the worship of another god. As mentioned above and in chapter three, anything put forward in front of God becomes a tribal deity.

When someone takes on an identity that precedes and supersedes their identity in Christ, they are idolizing whatever it is that's taken precedence. Race, heritage, orientation, class, occupation, and so on are categorical constructs we have made to classify and understand ourselves and each other, but as we are adopted into the family of God, all of these designations come second. Taking on the image of Christ means that we are identified, first and foremost, as redeemed children of God. Each of us, as redeemed children, have other

---

[52]Volf, *Exclusion and Embrace*, 41.

categorical constructs that we fit into, and often not perfectly. We must remember that while these categories are useful, they are constructed and fallible and cannot ultimately define our identities. In Christ we allow the Spirit to desacralize any part of those constructs that have become idols. Being unified is recognizing and celebrating diversity, while understanding that our identity is in Christ and the Spirit is at work discretely conforming us to his image.

As we've already stated, worship that is in the Spirit unifies us. But the sort of unity found in worship is a "differentiated unity" that celebrates diversity. As Macchia writes, "In a global context, it is important to note that Spirit baptism leads to a differentiated unity that opposes all uniformity."[53] Taking on the image of Christ is a matter of the heart; it does not conform us to the image of a first century Jew. This is part of what Paul was talking about when he referred to true circumcision as being a matter of the heart: "For a person is not a Jew who is one outwardly, nor is true circumcision something external and physical. Rather, a person is a Jew who is one inwardly, and real circumcision is a matter of the heart—it is spiritual and not literal. Such a person receives praise not from others but from God" (Rom 2:28-29). Paul was arguing that Gentiles did not have to become Jews first in order to become Christians, which implies that in Christ people are able to keep their ethnic uniqueness. As Colossians 2:11-12 indicates, the new covenant in Christ is no longer marked by a nationalizing symbol (circumcision) but by a confessional symbol (baptism). Renewal worship should, therefore, promote diversity as a differentiated unity. For David Taylor, church should engage in and adopt worship practices that allow constituents to be fully themselves in their diversity.[54] The Spirit works to enliven and enrich the uniqueness of diverse people as worshipers open themselves up to the image of Christ *in others*.[55] As Taylor writes, "The Spirit *deepens* the particularity of liturgical identity; the Spirit *opens up* liturgical identity to the possibility of genuine newness; the Spirit *opens out* liturgical identity to others (to God, to each other, to cultural context, and to the physical world)."[56] An important

---

[53]Macchia, *Baptized in the Spirit*, 212.

[54]W. David O. Taylor, "Mother Tongues and Adjectival Tongues: Liturgical Identity and the Liturgical Arts in a Pneumatological Key," *Worship Journal* 92 (2018): 55.

[55]Taylor, "Mother Tongues," 63.

[56]Taylor, "Mother Tongues," 63.

aspect of Christian unity is recognizing God's work and image in the life of others. As a relational response to the reconciling Spirit, renewal worship catalyzes such unity with God and others.

While these sentiments are fitting and aspirational, how do they work out practically in worship as churches aim to diversify without disenfranchising their current constituents that have grown accustomed to particular styles of worship? Sandra Van Opstal's book *The Next Worship* engages these issues head-on with astute observations and prescriptions. She puts the issue bluntly: "God invites us to come to his table in unity. That has always and will continue to cause tension, given the diverse nature of his people. This is particularly pronounced in worship, where people desire authentic spaces to express themselves."[57] Contextual worship practices authentically express a community's culture. Included in this, and significant for renewal worship, is musical style. In the West, for instance, there are distinct musical styles in renewal worship that are popular and influential. Pentecostal worship from the African diaspora carries an entire musical syntax in gospel music. For instance, vocal techniques like runs, commands, and call and responses; lyrical structures; instrumentation; chord voicings; and progressions all carry their own particular meanings that are culturally and historically bound. The same can be said about the musical syntax of contemporary worship collectives like Bethel, Hillsong, and Elevation, or of worship from Latino/a communities, or any other culturally identifiable worshiping community. Multicultural worship is an act of solidarity that invites communion between cultures—it's when distinct cultural and musical syntaxes join in conversation.[58]

Van Opstal discusses several approaches for including multiethnic expressions in worship,[59] but at the root of all of them is a respect and celebration of the histories, cultural roots, and legacies of the various cultures. Multicultural communication requires deep, genuine listening and response.[60] When this is done in worship, we see the fruit of communal reconciliation. Van Opstal writes, "Reconciliation in worship is expressed in three ways:

---

[57]Sandra Van Opstal, *The Next Worship: Glorifying God in a Diverse World* (Downers Grove, IL: InterVarsity Press, 2016), 23.

[58]Van Opstal, *Next Worship*, 22.

[59]Van Opstal, *Next Worship*, 103-10.

[60]Douglas Jacobsen, *Global Gospel: An Introduction to Christianity on Five Continents* (Grand Rapids, MI: Baker Academic, 2015), 227.

hospitality, solidarity and mutuality. This biblical reconciliation therefore calls us to welcome one another, stand with one another and depend on one another. Through congregational worship we can and should communicate: 'I welcome you.' 'I am with you.' 'I need you.'"[61] True multicultural worship allows worshipers to move from acknowledgment of each other to dependence on each other. Just as family members depend on each other, multicultural worship takes seriously the biblical metaphor that we are the "family of God" united in Christ (1 Thess 4:10; 1 Pet 2:17).

There are a number of ways that renewal worship artists in the West have engaged multicultural worship efforts. Major artists from the gospel and Christian contemporary music realms have teamed up to cowrite and perform multicultural worship fusions. For instance, in 2018 Elevation Worship collaborated with gospel superstars Tasha Cobbs Leonard, Israel Houghton, Travis Greene, Tye Tribbett, Kierra Sheard, and the Walls Group to form *Elevation Collective*, a special joint project that offered gospel-inflected renditions of popular Elevation Worship songs. Furthermore, artists such as Israel & New Breed, B. J. Putnam, Evan Craft, and Lucía Parker regularly blend contemporary, gospel, Caribbean, and Latin American worship styles and the Spanish language in their music. These crosscultural engagements typically involve cultures and subcultures from the North American context.

One of the greatest examples of multicultural renewal worship from the West comes from Maverick City Music of Atlanta, Georgia. Maverick City is a worship collective that intentionally blends gospel and contemporary music to create a new, intercultural expression of worship. The group's stated goal on their website is to form a worshiping family out of those who were pushed to the margins:

> Maverick City started with a dream to make space for folk that would otherwise live in their own separate worlds. To break the unspoken rules that exist in the CCM and Gospel World! But I think more importantly to be a megaphone for a community of creatives that have been pushed to the margins of the industry of Church Music. What brings us together, and that sound that is vivaciously smacking you in the face the first time you hit play on a Maverick track. Isn't the sound of a community that centered around their

---

[61]Van Opstal, *Next Worship*, 62.

deprivation, it's the audacious sound of true belonging: The beautiful harmony of long lost family.[62]

Specifically, Maverick City has blended the expressive musical syntax of gospel
with the extemporaneous musical syntax of contemporary spontaneous worship. The result is a sort of ambient, soulful, prophetic worship that successfully
merges popular musical expressions from predominantly White and predominantly Black contexts of worship to form something truly interurban and
multicultural. While these examples demonstrate efforts in the West toward
multicultural worship, we will now look at renewal worship's various approaches
to global engagement.

Various approaches to global engagement. As the church is increasingly
taking on a global identity, its worship trends reflect an intertwining of local,
transnational, and global engagements. According to Duck, the emergence of
the global church is the greatest change to Christianity in the twenty-first century, and Christians all over the world are "seeking to relate worship more closely
to the contexts in which they live and seeking to learn from the liturgical practices of churches of Christians in other places."[63] To begin to grasp how renewal
worship has advanced globally, we must briefly survey the growth trends of
global Pentecostalism. While Pentecostalism has grown steadily since Azusa
Street, it has grown exponentially around the world since the 1980s.[64] As they
reflect on the history of Pentecostal scholarship, Nimi Wariboko and Bill Oliverio state that Pentecostalism initially grew through missionary efforts, but
since the twenty-first century an increasing amount of growth is happening
due to birth rate.[65] This has to do with Pentecostalism's popularity in the Majority World as it has become a truly global expression of Christianity. As of 2010
there were more Pentecostals in China and Brazil than the United States, and
out of the ten countries with the most Pentecostals, all except the United States
were from Africa, Asia, and Latin America.[66] It is estimated that by 2050 there

---

[62]"About Maverick City," www.maverickcitymusic.com/about (accessed December 19, 2020).

[63]Duck, *Worship for the Whole People of God,* 271.

[64]Bryant Myers, *Engaging Globalization: The Poor, Christian Mission, and Our Hyperconnected World* (Grand Rapids, MI: Baker Academic, 2017), 199.

[65]Nimi Wariboko and L. William Oliverio, "The Society for Pentecostal Studies at 50 Years: Ways Forward for Global Pentecostalism," *Pneuma* 42 (2020): 329.

[66]Todd Johnson, "The Global Demographics of the Pentecostal and Charismatic Renewal," *Society* 46, no. 6 (2009): 80. In his article, Johnson terms all those that come from Pentecostal and charismatic backgrounds as "Renewalists."

will be over one billion Pentecostals in the world, and Pentecostalism will be the only Christian tradition to reach that number outside of Catholicism.[67]

Due to early Western missionary efforts, global renewal worship has strong Western roots, but as Pentecostal expansion has localized in recent decades, so has its expressions of worship. In the book *Making Congregational Music Local in Christian Communities Worldwide*, editors Ingalls, Swijghuisen Reigersberg, and Sherinian explore the formation of music-making practices throughout the global church. They employ the term "musical localization" as an umbrella classification to refer to the way global communities "adapt, adopt, create, perform, and share congregational music."[68] They contend that communities around the world "localize" their musical worship by actively negotiating their own cultural, ideological, and political concerns with whatever musical form they are in dialogue with.[69] Localization basically entails a global worshiping community's efforts in making their own authentic expressions of worship while being conversant with transnational and global musical forms. There are a number of methods worshiping communities have used to localize musical worship, but we'll consider three that I've designated the reproduction model, the contextualization model, and the indigenization model. We will look at these three models descriptively, explaining what's being done and how, rather than prescriptively, stating which way is superior for global engagement. Christianity is multifaceted, and each of these models has found success in spreading the gospel through renewal worship. It would be a mistake to categorically prefer one method over another, because different contexts require different approaches for global engagement. Instead of adopting a single model for every occasion of global engagement, we must evaluate which approach is more fitting for the given context. All these approaches are, after all, working toward the same goal of making disciples of all nations. Let's look at each of these models in turn.

---

[67]Aaron Earls, "10 Key Trends in Global Christianity for 2017," Facts & Trends (2016), https://factsandtrends.net/2016/12/12/10-key-trends-in-global-christianity-for-2017/ (accessed December 23, 2020).

[68]Monique Ingalls, Muriel Swijghuisen Reigersberg, and Zoe Sherinian, "Introduction: Music as Local and Global Positioning: How Congregational Music-Making Produces the Local in Christian Communities Worldwide," in *Making Congregational Music Local in Christian Communities Worldwide*, ed. Monique Ingalls, Muriel Swijghuisen Reigersberg, and Zoe Sherinian (London: Routledge, 2018), 3.

[69]Ingalls, Swijghuisen Reigersberg, and Sherinian, "Introduction," 4.

REPRODUCTION

The reproduction model sees Western renewal worship music being repro-
duced into global cultures around the world. Perhaps the greatest exponent
of this model is Hillsong Church, which extends the Australian megachurch's
style and culture into new regions around the world. Because of Hillsong
Worship's popularity, one might initially envisage the "Hillsong style" of
contemporary worship when referencing Hillsong. Wen Reagan points out
that before the emergence of major Hillsong churches in US cities like New
York, Los Angeles, and Phoenix, Americans knew Hillsong primarily as a
"sound" or style of contemporary worship that was "easily abstracted from its
context of production."[70] Since the 1990s the Hillsong sound has been adopted
and adapted by churches all over the world. Not only have Hillsong songs
been translated into other languages,[71] but songwriters from other cultures
actually learned, implicitly, "*how* to speak/sing worship music from an established theo-affective dialect before ever attempting to contribute to the canon
from their localized context."[72] Because of Hillsong Worship, Hillsong
UNITED, and Young & Free's influence, the pervasive Hillsong sound has
entered the ethos of contemporary worship around the world through efforts
of reproduction. Hillsong's reproducibility goes beyond the music, however.
As Gerardo Martí points out, "Hillsong is more than just a church, a collection
of music, a style of worship, an approach to ministry, and a set of corporate
entities—it is an impressive ecclesial force, a global phenomenon that builds
on a set of historical developments, a wave of understandings and practices
zooming into our religious future."[73] The sense that Hillsong's influence is a
"wave of understandings and practices" is essential to the reproduction model
of global engagement.

---

[70]Wen Reagan, "'The Music That Just About Everyone Sings': Hillsong in American Evangelical
Media," in *The Hillsong Movement Examined: You Call Me Out upon the Waters*, ed. Tanya Riches
and Tom Wagner (New York: Palgrave Macmillan, 2018), 157.

[71]As an example, Hillsong Music launched "The Hillsong Global Project," a project where Hillsong
Music worked with various Hillsong Church campuses around the world, along with international
worship ministries. The project created nine albums in nine different languages (Spanish, Portu-
guese, Korean, Mandarin, Indonesian, German, French, Swedish, and Russian) that all feature
translations of popular Hillsong songs. See https://archive.is/20130125133625/http://hillsongglo
balproject.com/ (accessed December 24, 2020).

[72]Reagan, "'Music That Just About Everyone Sings,'" 158.

[73]Gerardo Martí, foreword to Riches and Wagner, *Hillsong Movement Examined*, vi.

Hillsong's ecclesial structure does not function like a traditional denomination of churches that are united by theological and ecclesial distinctions.
Instead, the many Hillsong churches around the world are viewed as part of
the same church that is headquartered in Sydney, Australia.[74] The husband
and wife founders of Hillsong, Brian and Bobbie Houston, serve as the global
senior pastors of Hillsong Church,[75] and the numerous churches in more
than thirty countries around the world are led by local lead and campus pastors that serve under the purview of the Houstons. Brian Houston consistently
refers to Hillsong Church as "one house, many rooms." Houston writes, "As
a now far-reaching, diverse, and beautiful global church, Hillsong remains
united. We are one house, one heart, one vision, serving a world in need
through countless 'rooms' and congregations around the world but all under
the banner of Jesus Christ."[76] To establish and maintain a unified Hillsong
culture, every year Hillsong participates in "Vision Sunday"—a weekend of
presentations where the Houstons cast a vision for the upcoming year. Here
the church rolls out a unifying vision that is broadcasted to every Hillsong
Church around the world.[77] The vision is typically uplifting and prophetic
and guides the global Hillsong Church toward a unified heart and mission.
This sense of connection helps Hillsong churches unite, not merely by pro-
grams or through church materials, but by inhabiting and carrying an inter-
nalized, embodied history.[78]

Another way Hillsong fosters a unified culture is through the church's
mission and vision statements. The mission statement of the church is simple
and missional but demonstrates a commitment to reproducibility through
global influence. The mission of Hillsong is "to reach and influence the world
by building a large Christ-centered, Bible-based church, changing mindsets

[74]Although Hillsong became an autonomous denomination in 2018, in order to ordain pastors and
conduct weddings as marriage celebrants, they still consider their ecclesial structure as that of a local
church with a global footprint. See Brian Houston, "Has Hillsong Really Become Its Own Denomination?," *Hillsong Collected* blog, October 4, 2018, https://hillsong.com/collected/blog/2018/10/has
-hillsong-really-become-its-own-denomination/#.X_ovHS2ZOL8 (accessed January 9, 2020).
[75]"Hillsong Church Fact Sheet," https://hillsong.com/fact-sheet/ (accessed December 24, 2020).
[76]Brian Houston, *There Is More: When the World Says You Can't, God Says You Can* (New York:
Waterbrook, 2018), 222.
[77]Houston, *There Is More*, 221.
[78]Tanya Riches, "'The Work of the Spirit': Hillsong Church and a Spiritual Formation for the Marketplace," in *Australian Pentecostal and Charismatic Movements: Arguments from the Margins*, ed.
Christina Rocha, Kathleen Openshaw, and Mark Hutchinson (Leiden: Brill Academic, 2020), 176.

and empowering people to lead and impact in every sphere of life."[79] This statement shows that their global influence is to spread the gospel through the transnational network of a unified church.[80] The *vision* of the church is captured through a longer prophetic statement that is mounted on a wall at every Hillsong campus. In 1993 Brian Houston put out a guiding church vision statement titled "The Church I See," which highlighted the church's aspirations for influence, growth, worship, and above all, dutifully carrying out the Great Commission by the power of the Spirit. In 2014 Houston modified the statement to reflect the church's efforts in global engagement. The newer statement is titled "The Church I Now See," and addresses the nature of Hillsong's global ministry in the opening paragraph:

> The church that I see is a global church. I see a global family: One house with many rooms, outworking a unified vision. I see a church apostolic in calling, and visionary in nature; committed to boldly impacting millions for Christ in significant cities and nations throughout the earth with the greatest of all causes—the Cause of our Lord Jesus Christ.[81]

Hillsong has not only adapted to globalization in the twenty-first century, but one might argue that it helped perpetuate globalization on a cultural level through its reproduction model of global engagement. One thing is certain, through effective leadership and a dynamic worship ministry, Hillsong has productively aided the spread of renewal worship and the message of Spirit empowerment throughout the globe.

Nevertheless, despite Hillsong's seemingly genuine concern for the global expansion of the gospel, some have argued that Hillsong's reproduction model is only a new form of colonization.[82] Does the reproduction model disallow locals "space to be themselves"? Does Hillsong force uniformity? For Hillsong, each church is a local expression of the Hillsong culture and ethos. It's less about contextualization and more about finding partners that already align

---

[79]"The Vision," Hillsong Church, https://hillsong.com/vision/ (accessed December 24, 2020).

[80]Martí, foreword to *Hillsong Movement*, ix.

[81]"The Vision."

[82]Nate Lee, "Hillsong Church: Do Not Colonize San Francisco" (2016), https://natejlee.com/hillsong -church-do-not-colonize-san-francisco/ (accessed December 24, 2020). This blog post was retweeted by notable church leaders and educators, including Soong Chan Rah, David Fitch, Derek Radney, and Michael Frost.

with the Hillsong vision and culture. So while the reproduction model does not make explicit efforts toward contextualization or indigenization, naming the model a form of colonization is excessive. The church does not look to coerce or force the Westernization of non-Western cultures, but intentionally seeks out partners that mesh with their vision and culture. As Yip, Ainsworth, and Hoon point out, "Hillsong has traditionally focused on 'Western' markets in growing its brand (its first overseas expansion was the UK) and tightly manages its brand expansion strategy which assures consistency, coherence and amplification of its church brand in both global and local settings."[83] If a cultural fit is not possible, Hillsong does not expand to those regions. Because of this, Hillsong has only expanded into areas that are technologically equipped to carry the Hillsong brand and culturally able to authentically embody the Hillsong ethos.[84] It would be a mistake, then, to *categorically* regard the reproduction model as a colonizing endeavor. The reproduction model is a good and appropriate form of global engagement *if and only if* the global expansion evinces a cultural and relational fit. If there isn't a cultural and relational fit, then the gospel should be contextualized in order to be understood and adopted.

CONTEXTUALIZATION

The contextualization model sees worship music locally pronounced, but in dialogue with Western renewal worship music. Contextualization translates and integrates Western worship songs and rituals into local traditions. It involves "the capacity to respond meaningfully to the gospel within the framework of one's own situation."[85] Contextualization, and the more Catholic variant of "inculturation," seeks to find commonalities between cultures.

---

[83]Jeaney Yip, Susan Ainsworth, and Chang Yau Hoon, "JPCC: A Megachurch Brand Story in Indonesia," in *Routledge International Handbook of Religion in Global Society*, ed. Jayeel Cornelio, François Gauthier, Tuomas Martikainen, and Linda Woodhead (Oxon, UK: Routledge, 2021), 46. It should be noted that "Hillsong Family" churches are a bit more diverse but still align with the Hillsong Vision and culture. These are churches that maintain their own name and autonomy while entering into a familial relationship.

[84]This is also why there are only 150,000 weekly attendees globally at Hillsong churches. This number may seem high, but when compared to denominational global attendees, the number is quite low.

[85]Bruce Nichols, *Contextualization: A Theology of Gospel and Culture* (Vancouver: Regent College Publishing, 2003), 21.

Inroads to sharing the gospel are made when a Christian belief resonates with a local cultural practice.[86] The difference between contextualization and inculturation is that the former seeks to primarily find commonalities between Scripture and a cultural practice, whereas the latter looks for commonalities between a cultural practice and the ecclesial institution, hence inculturation is the preferred term of the Roman Catholic Church.[87] But both cases presume Christian authority in cultural engagement. The key for contextualization is to find out what values and traditions are compatible and incompatible with the gospel.

Finding what's compatible with the gospel is tricky, however, when certain cultural attributes are deemed sinful not because there is any explicit biblical claim to the practice being sinful, but because it was deemed such by the West. Which ceremonial chants and dances, fashion and aesthetic styles, culinary traditions, and so on, are explicitly affirmed or repudiated in Scripture in their localized forms? Scripture always renounces idolatry, but the issue here is knowing when something is merely a cultural expression or whether it's become a tribal deity. Ethnomusicologist Roberta King recognizes these challenges and thus advocates for a "critical contextualization." She writes, "Critical contextualization encompasses a process that addresses old beliefs, rituals, stories, songs, customs, proverbs, art, and music—the stuff of expressive culture."[88] The "expressive culture" of a society entails the various modes of communication that are used to express a culture's ideas, feelings, and values both cognitively and affectively.[89] The critical, selective acceptance of expressive culture is important for contextualization to avoid two extremes: for a particular version of the Christian faith to be entirely domineering, or for the Christian faith to be entirely subsumed into another culture.[90] In other words, a hermeneutical approach to contextualization is needed to adequately navigate a social context's expressive culture.

King's critical contextualization is analogous to the "dynamic equivalence" method of contextualization that involves "re-expressing components of

---

[86]Ingalls, Swijghuisen Reigersberg, and Sherinian, "Introduction," 6-7.

[87]Ingalls, Swijghuisen Reigersberg, and Sherinian, "Introduction," 7.

[88]Roberta King, *Global Arts and Christian Witness: Exegeting Culture, Translating the Message, and Communicating Christ* (Grand Rapids, MI: Baker Academic, 2019), 39.

[89]King, *Global Arts*, 31.

[90]King, *Global Arts*, 39-40.

Christian worship with something from a local culture that has an equal meaning, value, and function."[91] Here the worship practices are not merely translated, but a deep understanding of both the worship practice and the local cultural practice are disclosed so the worship practice can be encoded and "re-expressed in the language of local culture."[92] Worship and the arts are, according to King, essential for offering this sort of contextualization because the arts, as expressive culture, provide the "social arenas, languages, processes, and products necessary for doing contextualization."[93] In other words, worship and the arts are communicators of the gospel par excellence because they have the ability to communicate multifaceted meaning in both verbal and nonverbal ways. The arts help us understand deep cultural meaning in ways beyond mere translation, and worship enacts the arts to ritualize religious meaning. Renewal worship contextualizes well around the globe because Pentecostalism focuses on experiential spirituality, which translates easily across cultural lines. As theologian Allan Anderson writes,

> In the holistic worldview of most societies, all existing things are seen as a present material-spiritual or holistic unity in a pervading spiritual world. In Pentecostalism worldwide, the all-encompassing Spirit is involved in every aspect of both individual and community life, the context. Prophetic or charismatic leaders are seen as men or women of the Spirit. Rather than being theorized about, a contextual theology is acted out in the rituals, liturgies and daily experiences of these Pentecostals.[94]

Since many cultures around the world already have a sense of holistic unity in a porous spiritual reality, Pentecostalism's narrative of the universal outpour of the Spirit clearly conveys congruent affections. In other words, renewal worship songs may not share the same system of words for communication, but they often speak the same spiritual language.

A significant way contextualization is expressed in renewal worship music is through hybridity, which comingles Western and local Majority World

[91]Maxwell Johnson, *Sacraments and Worship: The Sources of Christian Theology* (Louisville, KY: Westminster John Knox, 2012), 78.
[92]Johnson, *Sacraments and Worship*, 78-79.
[93]King, *Global Arts*, 38.
[94]Allan Anderson, "Contextualization in Pentecostalism: A Multicultural Perspective," *International Bulletin of Mission Research* 41, no. 1 (2017): 34.

idioms.[95] Lim Swee Hong sees this happening most prominently in Asian worship music, which is beginning to embrace local cultural expressions adapted and adopted from Western musical traditions.[96] As an example, Swee Hong cites "Ibadat Karo,"[97] a popular worship song written by South Asian songwriter Anil Kant. This song fuses a South Asian singing style that incorporates melisma and glides with Western harmonies and instrumentation. The result is a worship song that "offers a rendition that is neither idiomatically strictly South Asian nor Western."[98] This sort of hybridity is common among the contextualization of renewal worship.

We are also seeing contextual notions of hybridity return to the West from the Majority World. This concept is known in sociology as "reflexivity" where "what happens 'out there somewhere' has an impact on what happens here . . . what happens here reflects back on what happens there."[99] If we have truly entered a global pluralistic age, then global engagements will not be one-sided where only the West influences the Majority World. The Majority World will inevitably influence the West as well. Perhaps the best example of global reflexivity is the massive global popularity of "Way Maker,"[100] a renewal worship song written by Nigerian Pentecostal worship leader SINACH. When viewing the song's original music video (now with over 160,000,000 views), one can clearly hear a mixture of Western and Nigerian musical sensibilities as African sounding beats accompany a common Western 4-1-5-6 progression. Although "Way Maker" was licensed by Integrity Music in 2016, the song grew to massive appeal in 2019 and 2020 when it was covered by many Western worship leaders including Leeland, Michael W. Smith, Steffany Gretzinger, Darlene Zschech, and William McDowell. The song became a sort of protest anthem in the United States after the death of George Floyd in 2020

[95]Lim Swee Hong, "'Where Is Our Song Going?' vis a vis 'Where Should Our Song Be Going?': The Trajectory of Global Song in North America," The Hymn Society (2018), https://thehymnsociety.org/resources/lim-article-summer-2018/ (accessed May 5, 2019).
[96]Swee Hong, "Where Is Our Song Going?"
[97]"Ibadat Karo," words and music by Anil Kant © Rebeat Digital GmbH (administrated by Trinity Sounds PVT LTD and 5 Music Rights Societies).
[98]Swee Hong, "Where Is Our Song Going?"
[99]Roberta King, "The Impact of Global Christian Music in Worship," Brehm Center (2017), www.fuller.edu/posts/the-impact-of-global-christian-music-in-worship/ (accessed May 5, 2019).
[100]"Way Maker," words and music by Osinachi Kalu Okoro Egbu, CCLI 7115744 © 2016 Integrity Music Europe (administrated by Capitol CMG Publishing, Integrity Music, David C Cook).

and a source of hope during the Covid pandemic.[101] To date the song has been translated in over fifty languages, and it truly marks the emergence of contextual reflexivity in renewal worship. Through efforts of hybridity and reflexivity, the contextualization model is the commonly adopted model for global engagement, and likewise, the most common mode of renewal worship's global proliferation. Like the reproduction model, the contextualization model also effectively extends the message of renewal through worship, but unlike the reproduction model, it focuses critically on investigating, translating, and communicating the gospel message globally through cultural hermeneutics.

INDIGENIZATION

The final model we'll discuss in this chapter is the indigenization model, which is closely related to the contextualization model. The indigenization model sees churches empower people from *within* the indigenous culture to worship in ways that more authentically form that group. Like the contextualization model, the indigenization model has a missional goal to make the gospel comprehensible to uninitiated cultures, but it does so by training and empowering local leaders to lead their own churches and groups. This helps prevent the unwarranted westernization of other cultures, while maintaining the proliferation of the gospel. As biblical scholar Pedrito Maynard-Reid writes,

> Much of the discussion regarding diversity and contextualization has to do with indigenization on a more global scale. For centuries conversion to Christian faith required an African or Asian to discard indigenous ways as inferior and superstitious and adopt the "superior" Western European culture.... A relatively new movement rejects such ethnocentric understanding and behavior. Missionaries are now attempting to restrain themselves from imposing Western customs and practices on converts who are non-Western.[102]

In the indigenization model, local worshiping communities reject general forms of westernization in music. Instead, they create songs from their own

---

[101]Megan Fowler, "How 'Way Maker' Topped the US Worship Charts from Nigeria," *Christianity Today* (2020), www.christianitytoday.com/ct/2020/june-web-only/way-maker-worship-song-sinach-leeland-michael-w-smith.html (accessed December 28, 2020).
[102]Pedrito Maynard-Reid, *Diverse Worship: African-American, Caribbean & Hispanic Perspectives* (Downers Grove, IL: InterVarsity Press, 2000), 47.

heritage in ways that retain and engage the historical conditions and social circumstances of the worshipers.[103] In fact, ethnodoxologist Jacob Joseph believes that indigenization is perfectly circulated through worship. The church can initiate radical change in a culture by focusing first on the worship of the community rather than missions. By taking this route, "indigenized missions will flow naturally from the indigenized worshiping church."[104] Worship practices help a church focus on the central gospel event, and when worship orients a community's narrative, the whole ethos will be reoriented centripetally.[105]

This method utilizes music that is typically sung in the indigenous culture's language and is faithful to its native musical traditions.[106] Non-Western musical traditions often use different tuning systems, scales, and approaches to melody and harmony. Some of these traditions are modal and don't even use musical scales. For instance, Indian *ragas* function modally by utilizing "interval patterns between 'scale' notes, have different expectations for how each note of the *raga* is to be used, and may use slightly different tunings."[107] The *raga* dictates how notes will be used, how they'll be emphasized, and in what sort of ornamentations they'll be used. Unlike Western music notation which uses a single uniform system, each *raga* follows its own particular rules.[108] An example of this sort of indigenization can be seen when fusion and experimental sitar performer Sanjeeb Sircar performed the worship song "Jai Jai Yeshu" in a style based on the *Raga Bhuopali*.[109] Here Sircar performs a distinctly Hindi expression of the gospel in a totally non-Western style. Some have argued, however, that these traditional styles should not be appropriated

---

[103]Maynard-Reid, *Diverse Worship*, 48-49.

[104]Jacob Joseph, "Indigenized Christian Worship in India: Some Considerations," Mission Frontiers (2014), www.missionfrontiers.org/issue/article/indigenized-christian-worship-in-india (accessed December 28, 2020).

[105]B. A. Müller, "The Role of Worship and Ethics on the Road Towards Reconciliation," *Verbum Et Ecclesia JRG* 27, no. 2 (2006): 658-59.

[106]King, "Impact of Global Christian Music."

[107]Catherine Schmidt-Jones, "Modes and Ragas," Understanding Basic Music Theory, https://cnx.org/contents/KtdLe6cv@3.70:Fxmh7wKe@16/Modes-and-Ragas (accessed December 28, 2020).

[108]Schmidt-Jones, "Modes and Ragas."

[109]"Hindi Christian Song 'Jai Jai Yeshu' Based on the Raga Bhupali. Sitar and Vocal—Sanjeeb Sircar," www.youtube.com/watch?v=YztJddJEQCM (accessed December 28, 2020). It should be noted that churches around the world follow the indigenization model even if they don't regularly publish or distribute songs globally. Consequently, examples of indigenized worship often come through field research carried out by ethnomusicologists or ethnodoxologists.

because their non-Christian religious identities are wrapped up in their musi-cal styles.[110] To Christianize this traditional music would be to fundamentally skew its connection to tradition, which is essential to the music. This is a strong point, showing that in some instances compromise may not be possible. Any form of Christian worship must exclusively be aimed at, and in conversa-tion with, the triune God, or it will give ear to tribal deities. Of all these models, the indigenization model respects a community's cultural expression the most, but if the worship is not desacralized, then the global engagement of Christian renewal becomes mere religious syncretism. In this case of Christian engage-ment, one will either have to choose a different contextual style of worship to pursue or will have to be okay with possibly offending traditionalists.

Nevertheless, indigenous expressions of faith are another way renewal worship is proliferated throughout the globe. In fact, as Anderson credits the rapid growth of Pentecostalism to its ability to adapt to different cultures and contexts, he notes that early missionary efforts resembled the indigenization model of global engagement. Anderson writes,

> To their credit, pentecostal missionaries, themselves largely untrained and uneducated, practiced "indigenous church" principles. They quickly found and trained thousands of local leaders who took the "full gospel" much further than the foreign missionaries had done. This swift transfer to local leadership was unprecedented in the history of Christianity, and Pentecostal churches became indigenous and "three-self" (self-governing, self-supporting, and self-propa-gating) before the older missions had even begun the process.[111]

Pentecostals have utilized several methods for proliferating the message of renewal around the world, but in each case, worship was at the center of these efforts. Each context for global engagement is different and should utilize whatever model, or combination of models, works best for that particular culture. Some cultures might prefer the reproduction model because they are already culturally aligned and want to adopt the Western style of worship outright. Others might want to learn the songs, styles, and

---

[110]Swami Venkataraman, "Christian Appropriation of Carnatic Music: Why Musicians Can't Hide Behind the 'Secular' Hypothesis," *Swarajya*, October 3, 2018, https://swarajyamag.com/politics /christian-appropriation-of-carnatic-music-why-musicians-cant-hide-behind-the-secular -hypothesis (accessed December 28, 2020).

[111]Anderson, *To the Ends of the Earth*, 250.

music theory of the West because they want to incorporate those elements into their own expressions. If so, the contextualization model fits best. Finally, some cultures might be very vigilant about protecting their own cultural identities and thus want to avoid any semblance of westernization. If that's the case, the indigenization model works best. Regardless which model of global engagement was used, renewal worship has helped foster a sense of global unity, and, as mentioned above, it has also helped bring about reconciliation between people and culture.

CONCLUSION

This chapter answered the question "Who are the renewal worshipers?" by recognizing the types of people that involve themselves with the global ministry of reconciliation from a renewal perspective. We saw that the ministry of reconciliation is foundational for renewal worship, and reconciling efforts were present at both Pentecost and the Azusa Street Revival. The universal outpour states that the Spirit will be poured out on *all* flesh, which gives biblical precedence for renewal worship's pursuit of a reconciled, multicultural worship. Finally, this chapter looked at the various methods of global engagement pursued by Pentecostals, and we saw that renewal worship was at the center of each method. Thus, renewal worship powerfully proliferates the Pentecostal message of renewal throughout the world. In so doing, renewal worship helps foster a global, charismatic community that's united by the Spirit.

The second half of this book sought to approach worship practices hermeneutically to see what the practices mean to Pentecostal communities and how those practices reinforce the guiding biblical motif of the universal outpour. The chapters in part two mirror those from part one: Chapter one ties our theological method to the *universal outpour*, and chapter four shows how renewal worship *flows*; chapter two shows how renewal worship is a *relational dialogue* with the abundantly giving God, and chapter five shows how worshipers *communicate* prophetically through worship; chapter three shows how renewal worship works to *form communities*, and chapter six demonstrates how *communities around the world* practice reconciliation through renewal worship. While part one lays the theological groundwork for our theology of renewal worship, part two demonstrates how the theological commitments are embodied in renewal worship. As we conclude the main content of this book and move onto some concluding remarks, let's first pause and reflect on the content of this chapter with one last doxology:

> *Praise God who makes us whole*
> *Healed bodies, quickened souls*
> *Praise God who calls all people to renewal.*

CONCLUSION

WHERE DO WE GO FROM HERE?

After this I looked, and there was a great multitude that no one could
count, from every nation, from all tribes and peoples and languages,
standing before the throne and before the Lamb, robed in white, with
palm branches in their hands. They cried out in a loud voice, saying,
"Salvation belongs to our God who is seated on the throne, and to the Lamb!"
And all the angels stood around the throne and around the
elders and the four living creatures, and they fell on their
faces before the throne and worshiped God, singing,
"Amen! Blessing and glory and wisdom
and thanksgiving and honor
and power and might
be to our God forever and ever! Amen."

REVELATION 7:9-12

IN THE PASSAGE above, John the revelator has a vision of heavenly worship that is universal in scope—people from all tribes and languages, and representatives from all of creation, are gathered to worship God on the throne. This isn't a scene of the consummation of the kingdom of God, but of heavenly worship during the tribulations of Revelation. The white robes likely indicate the great multitude was made up of martyrs that were washed in the Lamb's blood (Rev 7:14), but their attire is now one that demonstrates victory as they rest in the glory of the Lord.[1] Thus, they share in Christ's resurrected victory as they've already shared in his sacrifice.[2] But the best is yet to come, and Christ will still return to set all things right.

The notion of shared sacrifice and shared glory brings us back to some key ideas that developed throughout this book: Victory comes through cruciformity (chap. 4), as a life of sacrifice is generously given from what God has abundantly bestowed (chap. 2). The image of heavenly worship visualizes a foretaste of the kingdom (chap. 1) as it becomes reality. This scene also demonstrates an atmosphere of reconciliation (chap. 6). This is all pressingly important for the persecuted Christians to whom Revelation was addressed. As the early Christians looked forward to the day they would stand before the Lord and worship, this heavenly scene became conventional for Christian worship. Melissa Archer writes, "The worship of heaven is thereby paradigmatic and pedagogical, for worship is the primary purpose of the people of God and forms a crucial component of the witness of the church in the world."[3] The passage above reveals the substance of our hope: worshiping the one true king. It's the Bible's vision of renewal, but its looming completeness makes it a fitting passage to end with.

This conclusion is our *postlude*—the closing music at the end of a church service. It brings our study of renewal worship to a close, but we won't stick around to hear how this postlude resolves! We don't want this dialogue to cut off prematurely. Instead, the music will accompany our footpath out of the sanctuary and into the streets. We won't hear it resolve but will listen to it merge from one sound to another, from a musical mode to the sounds of life. Rather than cutting the dialogue off, we're setting it off. This conclusion follows a similar progression: first it looks at the song we've been singing, pulling together the various movements of our Pentecostal doxology, and then it surveys the streets we're stepping into as we consider renewal worship's contributions to world Christianity.

---

[1]Craig Keener, *The NIV Application Commentary: Revelation* (Grand Rapids, MI: Zondervan, 2009), 243.

[2]Keener, *NIV Application Commentary*, 243.

[3]Melissa Archer, *"I Was in the Spirit on the Lord's Day": A Pentecostal Engagement with Worship in the Apocalypse* (Cleveland, TN: CPT Press, 2015), 304-5.

TOWARD A PENTECOSTAL DOXOLOGY

If worship is the primary way Pentecostals do theology,[4] then we must never stray from the idea that loving God with our mind is fundamentally an act of worship. Our theology doesn't just study God in relation to the church, but confesses our love of God as the church. So in true Pentecostal fashion, the theological ideas presented in this book were summarized and expressed as doxologies, hymns of praise to God. The English word *doxology*, deriving from the Greek word *doxologia*, combines the prefix *doxa*, which means "common belief," and the suffix *logia*, which means "a spoken account of." Put together, *doxology* means an "oral expression of praise or glorification." This term fixes theological belief to its devotional expression. Not only does a doxology communicate faith, but it reveals the substance of the Christian faith through a common experience. God is praised through a communal resounding of echoed refrains, as the doxology both ascribes worth to God while unifying and shaping the worshiping community. Thus, our theology is less a treatise and more a doxology.

With that in mind, let's consider the song we've been singing. Chapter one ended with the following lines:

> *Praise God who fills our breath*
> *Renewing us afresh*
> *Praise God whose Spirit pours out on all flesh.*

These words are pivotal for understanding renewal worship. Worship starts with God's revelation, and the universal outpour marks the continuous revealing of God to humanity. Christ is the perfect revelation of God—God made flesh. The Spirit universalizes God's revelation for us. As Spirit, God indwells us and makes Christ continuously knowable. Karl Barth shows us that the Spirit connects us to God's revelation in Christ:

> The Spirit guarantees man what he cannot guarantee himself, his personal participation in revelation. The act of the Holy Ghost in revelation is the Yes to God's Word which is spoken by God Himself for us, yet not just to us, but also in us. This Yes spoken by God is the basis of the

---

[4]Kenneth Archer, *The Gospel Revisited: Towards a Pentecostal Theology of Worship and Witness* (Eugene, OR: Pickwick, 2011), 11.

confidence with which a man may regard the revelation as applying to him.[5]

Christ is God entering the created order as one of us to redeem us. Christ's death and resurrection opened us up to redemption, and as the incarnated Christ gave of himself on the cross, the resurrected Christ gives of himself by pouring out the Spirit. Only Christ was able to become the Spirit baptizer, and as Frank Macchia reminds us, Christ the baptizer affirms Christ as God.[6] Only God can give God! So if redemption is made possible by the cross, renewal is made possible by the universal outpour. This is the crux of Pentecostal spirituality: the same God who spoke all things into existence, redeems and renews us through Christ and the Spirit. As redeemed people living in the time between times, we receive continual renewal when we worship. This is a present foretaste of the imminent kingdom, which has already come but is yet to be fulfilled.

Chapter two affirmed the object of renewal worship as the relational God, which reveals what the universal outpour means to us theologically on a personal level. The contents of that chapter were summed up with the following lines:

Praise God who loves us so
Abundantly bestowed
Praise God from whom all blessings overflow.

When Christ poured the Spirit out on all flesh, God the *Giver* gave of Godself, the *Gift*. This notion has significant ramifications for our theology of renewal worship. Worship is not a distant adoration of God, but an intimate, relational partaking *of* God who is love. If gift-giving is a reciprocal action, what is being reciprocated when the Gift of the Spirit is poured out on us? Love. As we love God, we accept God's invitation to the divine dance. We join God relationally—the God who is ontologically relational as a mutually indwelling and interpenetrating Trinity. And this is no meager gift of love either. God's love is abundant and flows over us like a warm bath. God gives us

---

[5]Karl Barth, *Church Dogmatics: The Doctrine of the Word of God*, vol. 1, pt. 1, trans. G. W. Bromiley, ed. G. W. Bromiley and T. F. Torrance, 2nd ed. (London: T&T Clark, 2008), 453.

[6]Frank Macchia, *Jesus the Spirit Baptizer: Christology in Light of Pentecost* (Grand Rapids, MI: Eerdmans, 2018), 64.

more than we need, and out of that overflow we extend the love of God out laterally to others. We give out of our sacrifice. We give out of our health, wealth, wisdom, and spiritual gifts. As we give of ourselves we emulate Christ who gave of himself sacrificially on the cross, and abundantly through the universal outpour. We are blessed to be a blessing.

While chapter two showed us how the universal outpour affects us individually, chapter three fleshed out what the motif means to us theologically on a communal level. The chapter's contents were summed up with these lines:

> Praise God who shows us grace
> Who's present in this place
> Praise God who is enthroned upon our praise.

We can infer a lot from David when he says, "Yet you are holy, enthroned on the praises of Israel" (Ps 22:3). Our worship *enthrones* God—it recognizes God's kingship and confesses God's primacy as Lord over all. The Hebrew word for "enthroned" is *yashab*, which also means to sit, remain, or dwell. So God dwells in the midst of our praises. God resides wherever there is the confession of God as God. It should be noted, however, that our worship doesn't *make* God God. As mentioned, God is co-indwelling and relational by nature, so creation is not necessary for God to be fully Godself. But the church gathers to confess God's lordship. Worship, therefore, simultaneously enthrones God and names the people of God. Beyond marking the people of God, worship also has a socially formative role, aligning people to one accord. It does so by continually reinforcing a narrative through ritual acts and congregational song. For Pentecostals, the reinforced narrative is the Acts 2 account of renewal through Pentecost. The universal outpour motif is poured into us every time we reinforce the story in worship.

Chapter four sought to build on the abstract theological notions of part one and show how the concept of the universal outpour plays out in renewal worship. The contents of this chapter were summed up with the following lines:

> Praise God who sanctifies
> Who burns away our lies
> Praise God who sees us when we're glorified.

Renewal worship not only is pneumatological but sees both the Word and Spirit at work in the lives of believers. There are times when we need to be spiritually built up, and other times when we need to be broken down. God builds us up through the Word, a structured, formational power that creatively orders things, and breaks us down by the Spirit, the spontaneous, deconstructing power that sanctifies us and strips away our iniquities. Sometimes our life circumstances require creative formation and other times they require creative deconstruction. The problems arise when formation is uncritically seen as triumphalist victory. Yes, theologies of abundance situate worshipers in victory, but even the notion of triumph implies that something needed to be overcome. Triumphalism arises when dire circumstances are either not fully addressed or willfully disregarded. To avoid this, renewal worship must fully engage in lament. When victory *is* proclaimed, it should not be an escapist mirage, but a cry of hopeful defiance in the face of despair.

Chapter five advanced the idea of a "hopeful defiance" by evaluating the role of prophecy in renewal worship. The contents of that chapter were summed up with these lines:

Praise God who makes us see
Inspires us to speak
Praise God who gives us words of prophecy.

If renewal hope is situated in the eschaton, the gift of prophecy is like a compass that either lets us know we're headed the right way or that we've strayed off path. The Spirit opens our eyes and gives us a glimpse of the way things are and the way they should be. If things are wrong, as they often are, the prophet is emboldened by the Spirit to speak out and bring awareness so the church can grieve and energize a new hopeful vision of an attainable future. The Spirit of prophecy is at work on all levels—individually, communally, societally, and globally—and renewal worship creates the space for us to prophetically hear God's voice.

Finally, chapter six disclosed the context of renewal worship by profiling who renewal worshipers are, and how they participate in the global ministry of reconciliation. That chapter was summarized with the following lines:

Praise God who makes us whole
Healed bodies, quickened souls
Praise God who calls all people to renewal.

Instead of counting renewal worshipers as simply those who come from Pentecostal and charismatic backgrounds, perhaps it's best to think of them as those who follow the precepts and implications of the universal outpour motif. The Spirit who was poured out on all flesh is a reconciling Spirit—the same Spirit who empowers and commissions us with the ministry of reconciliation. We see diverse expressions of the reconciling Spirit all over the globe, and we're all united because we've been baptized by the one Spirit (1 Cor 12:13). As we look at the worship practices of Pentecostals and charismatics globally, we can see if they practice what they preach, if their actions and attitudes line up with their confessions of Christ and the Holy Spirit. Taking the themes of the last three chapters together we see that the Spirit, the abundant Gift of God, is a sanctifying, prophetic, and reconciling Spirit. This is the Spirit's ministry, and if we really are renewal worshipers, then we'll carry out the ministry God has entrusted to us.

RENEWAL WORSHIP'S CONTRIBUTIONS TO WORLD CHRISTIANITY

This book set out with a twofold agenda: to communicate a theology of worship that helps Pentecostal insiders better articulate their own worship practices and spirituality, and to enrich readers from every corner of the universal church by offering a nuanced account of renewal worship. As mentioned in the book's introduction, world Christianity is growing increasingly Pentecostal, so our study concerning renewal worship can also help profile the state of world Christianity. Concerning the current state of our global faith, Kwabena Asamoah-Gyadu states, "The current growth and significance of the global Pentecostal movement as an important player in world Christianity cannot be explained apart from the mainstreaming of the experience of the Spirit in Christian life, thought, and practice."[7] As was discussed last chapter, the Pentecostal experience and narrative of Spirit empowerment has been proliferated

---

[7]J. Kwabena Asamoah-Gyadu, "'I Will Not Leave You Orphaned': Select Impactful Contributions of Global Pentecostalism to World Christianity," *Pneuma* 42 (2020): 371.

through various missional efforts. Many of these efforts rely prominently on renewal worship to express the encoded and operant theological commitments of Pentecostalism. Asamoah-Gyadu sees global Pentecostalism as normalizing the experiences of the Spirit and in particular the extravagant manifestations of the Spirit often experienced in worship.[8] Embodied worship and spiritual gifts like tongues, prophecy, and healing were once viewed as nonstandard in Christian spirituality, but are receiving more and more acceptance around the world. Asamoah-Gyadu writes, "In Pentecostalism the experiences of the Spirit that were considered abnormal or an aberration by historic Christianity is what defines spirituality and the same manifestations excluded from the church are now included as biblical and real."[9] One of the major contributions renewal worship has made to global Christianity was the proliferation of a pneumato-centric message of renewal.

But is the pentecostalization of world Christianity really what's best for the global church? Think about it this way: without Pentecostalism world Christianity would be shrinking, not growing.[10] The message of renewal is resonating with people around the world in ways that other approaches have not been able to. Missiologist Scott Sunquist argues that the message of Spirit empowerment is attractive to marginalized people, and fitting for evangelistic purposes, because of its commitment to abundance: "Pentecostalism is most notable in how it has attracted the least, the lost, and the lonely with nothing but a message and a promise of spiritual power. . . . Since its very nature was evangelistic, it spread very rapidly, and, because of the varied contexts where it soon found a home, its evangelistic nature soon became much more broadly missionary."[11] If we remember that we are all one body, it should be less about the form Christianity is taking around the world, and more about celebrating the fact that the gospel is still being spread, and rapidly.

Another contribution to global Christianity is renewal worship's communal focus. The post-Enlightenment theology of the West was markedly personal.

---

[8]Asamoah-Gyadu, "'I Will Not Leave You Orphaned,'" 376.

[9]Asamoah-Gyadu, "'I Will Not Leave You Orphaned,'" 376.

[10]Ed Stetzer, "Why Do These Pentecostals Keep Growing?," *Christianity Today*, 2014 (accessed January 3, 2021).

[11]Scott Sunquist, *The Unexpected Christian Century: The Reversal and Transformation of Global Christianity, 1900–2000* (Grand Rapids, MI: Baker Academic, 2015), 127.

This has certainly to do with the Western attraction to a buffered individualism,[12] but theologically it may also evince the West's proclivity toward christocentrism, especially considering the Pietist directive of developing a personal connection with the Savior.[13] Much of the Global South, however, never modernized like the West, and always maintained a communal sense of life and faith. Considering that, perhaps Pentecostalism's communal focus on the Spirit resonated well with the communally focused people of the Global South. Unlike the revelation of God in Christ, which was particular, special, and individual, the revelation of God through the Spirit is universal, general, and communal. That's not to say global Pentecostalism avoids Christ, but, as discussed in chapter four, it holds both Christ and the Spirit together as a christo-pneumatocentric expression of the Christian faith.[14] In worship the espoused and operant theological message of renewal is both/and, indicating the Spirit of Christ's work in both the individual and the community. When we worship together in a darkened room with hands raised, we are both separate *and* together. Worshipers experience personal encounters with God but fully recognize that the Spirit is at work all around the room and beyond. The Spirit leads us to pray for each other, to intercede for each other, and to embrace each other regardless of the singular or plural pronouns we use in song. If you recall in chapter two we discussed the three layers of response to God's relational invitation in worship. It starts with the up-down relationship where the Spirit is poured out on all flesh as the abundant Gift of love, it then proceeds with the down-up relationship where believers respond to God by turning their hearts toward God. As these layers of response continually repeat, they create a third lateral relationship where the community reconciles and unites in a shared solidarity and with God. These three layers of response demonstrate the both/and of renewal worship, which bridges the gap between the individual and the community.

---

[12]Charles Taylor, *A Secular Age* (Cambridge, MA: Harvard University Press, 2007), 37-38.

[13]Peter Vogt, "Nicholas Ludwig von Zinzendorf (1700–1760)," in *The Pietist Theologians: An Introduction to Theology in the Seventeenth and Eighteenth Centuries*, ed. Carter Lindberg (Malden, MA: Blackwell, 2008), 213.

[14]Amos Yong also makes this argument in Yong, *Beyond the Impasse: Toward a Pneumatological Theology of Religions* (Eugene, OR: Wipf & Stock, 2014). He makes the claim that the Spirit's universality creates a strong theological pathway for global missions and a theology of religions. He does not say we should discard Christ, but that the Spirit's universality gets us past the impasse exclusivism has created.

As we consider some of the contributions renewal worship has made for world Christianity, one thing becomes clear: evaluating the worship practices of global Pentecostalism is key for understanding the movement in general, and global Christianity broadly. And although I set out to speak of Pentecostalism and renewal worship broadly, I am fully aware that my perspective is not neutral or without presuppositions. What's put forward is a Pentecostal doxology. Considering the fact that no one is properly suited to speak on behalf of an entire global movement, there are a number of ways I may have fallen short along the way. Perhaps my whole-exegetical endeavors are wrong. Why should anyone articulate a whole theology of worship through a single Acts 2 passage anyway? Have I defined concepts broadly enough to encompass what's happening in renewal worship around the world, and narrowly enough to distinguish it from other traditions? These fine lines demand a lot of care. It's certainly the case that because my scope is limited, at times my observations are too anecdotal. Also, because I'm a Pentecostal insider, at times my readings of renewal worship are likely too generous, aspirational even. But through it all, my hope is that I've offered a faithful account of renewal worship, not necessarily a definitive one. My hope is that this study strengthens the body of Christ, those within and outside the renewal tradition. My hope is that all of us are continually renewed as we invite the Spirit to break into our present circumstances and guide us toward God's abundant love. To close I'll offer one last lyric that sums up the contents of this book:

I see water in a barren land
Your age to come is right here at hand
Cause I feel You breaking through unplanned,
My life, renewed, like flowers in the desert.[15]

---

[15]See and hear the Pentecostal doxology put to music here: "Flowers in the Desert (Official Music Video) The LIFE Collective feat. Social Architects," YouTube video, Life Pacific University Worship Arts & Media, November 23, 2020, https://youtu.be/rBJdXf-s3_Q.

BIBLIOGRAPHY

"About Maverick City." Accessed December 19, 2020. www.maverickcitymusic.com/about.

Adeleye, Femi. "The Prosperity Gospel and Poverty: An Overview and Assessment." In *Prosperity Theology and the Gospel: Good News or Bad News for the Poor*, edited by J. Daniel Salinas, 5-22. Peabody, MA: Hendrickson, 2017.

Albrecht, Daniel. *Rites in the Spirit: A Ritual Approach to Pentecostal/Charismatic Spirituality*. Sheffield: Sheffield Academic Press, 1999.

———. "Worshiping and the Spirit: Transmuting Liturgy Pentecostally." In *The Spirit in Worship—Worship in the Spirit*, edited by Teresa Berger and Bryan Spinks. Collegeville, MN: Liturgical Press, 2009.

Althouse, Peter. "Ascension—Pentecost—Eschaton: A Theological Framework for Pentecostal Ecclesiology." In *Toward a Pentecostal Ecclesiology: The Church and the Fivefold Gospel*, edited by John Christopher Thomas. Cleveland, TN: CPT Press, 2010.

———. "Betwixt and Between the Cross and the Eschaton: Pentecostal Worship in the Context of Ritual Play." In *Toward a Pentecostal Theology of Worship*, edited by Lee Roy Martin, 265-80. Cleveland, TN: CPT Press, 2016.

Altizer, Jim. *The Making of a Worship Leader*. Thousand Oaks, CA: Sound & Light Publishing, 2013.

Alvarado, Johnathan. "Pentecostal Worship and the Creation of Meaning." In *Toward a Pentecostal Theology of Worship*, edited by Lee Roy Martin, 221-34. Cleveland, TN: CPT Press, 2016.

Anderson, Allan. *An Introduction to Pentecostalism: Global Charismatic Christianity*. Cambridge: Cambridge University Press, 2004.

———. "Contextualization in Pentecostalism: A Multicultural Perspective." *International Bulletin of Mission Research* 41, no. 1 (2017): 29-40.

———. *To the Ends of the Earth: Pentecostalism and the Transformation of World Christianity*. Oxford: Oxford University Press, 2013.

Archer, Kenneth. *The Gospel Revisited: Towards a Pentecostal Theology of Worship and Witness*. Eugene, OR: Pickwick, 2011.

———. "The Fivefold Gospel and the Mission of the Church: Ecclesiastical Implications and Opportunities." In *Toward a Pentecostal Ecclesiology: The Church and the Fivefold Gospel*, edited by John Christopher Thomas. Cleveland, TN: CPT Press, 2010.

———. *A Pentecostal Hermeneutic for the Twenty-First Century: Spirit, Scripture and Community*. London: Bloomsbury, 2004.

Archer, Melissa. *"I Was in the Spirit on the Lord's Day": A Pentecostal Engagement with Worship in the Apocalypse*. Cleveland, TN: CPT Press, 2015.

Arjmand, Hussain-Abdulah, Jesper Hohagen, Bryan Paton, and Nikki Rickard. "Emotional Responses to Music: Shifts in Frontal Brain Asymmetry Mark Periods of Musical Change." *Frontiers in Psychology* 4 (2017). Accessed January 22, 2020. www.frontiersin.org/articles/10.3389/fpsyg.2017.02044/full.

Arthurs, Jeffrey. "John 3:16 in the Key of C." In *The Art & Craft of Biblical Preaching: A Comprehensive Resource for Today's Communicators*, edited by Haddon Robinson and Craig Brian Larson, 8-9. Grand Rapids, MI: Zondervan, 2005.

Asamoah-Gyadu, J. Kwabena. "'I Will Not Leave You Orphaned': Select Impactful Contributions of Global Pentecostalism to World Christianity." *Pneuma* 42 (2020): 370-94.

Asbury, Cory. "The Power of Love—God's Reckless Love." Good News Fellowship. Accessed November 21, 2020. https://gnf.ca/blog/2019/04/17/the-power-of-love-gods-reckless-love-liturgy-service/.

Athanasius and Didymus. *Works on the Spirit: Athanasius's Letters to Serapion on the Holy Spirit, and Didymus's on the Holy Spirit.* Translated by Mark DelCogliano, Andrew Radde-Gallwitz, and Lewis Ayres. Crestwood, NY: St. Vladimir's Seminary Press, 2011.

Attanasi, Katherine. "Introduction: The Plurality of Prosperity Theologies and Pentecostalisms." In *Pentecostalism and Prosperity: The Socio-Economics of the Global Charismatic Movement,* edited by Katherine Attanasi and Amos Yong, 1-14. New York: Palgrave Macmillan, 2012.

Augustine. *On the Holy Trinity; Doctrinal Treatises; Moral Treatises.* Edited by Philip Schaff and Anthony Uyl. Woodstock, VA: Devoted, 2017.

Augustine, Daniela. "Liturgy, *Theosis,* and the Renewal of the World." In *Toward a Pentecostal Theology of Worship,* edited by Lee Roy Martin, 165-86. Cleveland, TN: CPT Press, 2016.

———. *The Spirit and the Common Good: Shared Flourishing in the Image of God.* Grand Rapids, MI: Eerdmans, 2019.

Banjo, Omotayo, and Kesha Morant Williams. "A House Divided? Christian Music in Black and White." *Journal of Media and Religion* 10 (2011): 115-37.

Barnes, Zachary. "How Flow Became the Thing." In *Flow: The Ancient Way to Do Contemporary Worship,* edited by Lester Ruth, 13-26. Nashville: Abingdon, 2020.

Barth, Karl. *Church Dogmatics: The Doctrine of the Word of God,* Vol. 1, pt. 1. Translated by G. W. Bromiley. Edited by G. W. Bromiley and T. F. Torrance. 2nd ed. London: T&T Clark, 2008.

———. *The Göttingen Dogmatics: Instruction in the Christian Religion.* Vol. 1. Translated by Geoffrey Bromiley. Grand Rapids, MI: Eerdmans, 1991.

Bartleman, Frank. *Azusa Street.* New Kensington, PA: Whitaker House, 1982.

Bass, Dorothy, and Craig Dykstra. "Introduction." In *For Life Abundant: Practical Theology, Theological Education, and Christian Ministry,* edited by Dorothy Bass and Craig Dykstra, 1-20. Grand Rapids, MI: Eerdmans, 2008.

Beale, G. K. *We Become What We Worship: A Biblical Theology of Idolatry.* Downers Grove, IL: IVP Academic, 2008.

Beatty, Christopher. "Holy Ground." CCLI 19526 © 1982 Universal Music—Brentwood Benson Publishing, Birdwing Music. Administrated by Brentwood Benson Music Publishing, Inc., Capitol CMG Publishing.

Begbie, Jeremy. "Faithful Feelings: Music and Emotion in Worship." In *Resonant Witness: Conversations Between Music and Theology,* edited by Jeremy Begbie and Stephen Guthrie, 323-54. Grand Rapids, MI: Eerdmans, 2011.

Best, Harold. *Unceasing Worship: Biblical Perspectives on Worship and the Arts.* Downers Grove, IL: InterVarsity Press, 2003.

Bethel TV. "What a Beautiful Name + Spontaneous Worship—Amanda Cook and Jeremy Riddle." Accessed January 11, 2020.

Boer, Ken. "The Worship Leader and the Gospel." In *Doxology & Theology: How the Gospel Forms the Worship Leader,* edited by Matt Boswell, 207-24. Nashville: B&H, 2013.

Boswell, Matt. "Doxology, Theology, and the Mission of God." In *Doxology & Theology: How the Gospel Forms the Worship Leader,* edited by Matt Boswell, 5-23. Nashville: B&H, 2013.

Bowler, Kate. *Blessed: A History of the American Prosperity Gospel.* Oxford: Oxford University Press, 2013.

Brathwaite, Renea. "Tongues and Ethics: William J. Seymour and the 'Bible Evidence': A Response to Cecil M. Robeck, Jr." *Pneuma* 32 (2010): 203-22.

Briggman, Anthony. "Irenaeus: Creation & the Father's Two Hands." *Sapientia* (2017). https://henry center.tiu.edu/2017/04/irenaeus-creation-the-fathers-two-hands/.

———. *Irenaeus of Lyons and the Theology of the Holy Spirit.* Oxford: Oxford University Press, 2012.

Brooks, Steven. *Worship Quest: An Exploration of Worship Leadership.* Eugene, OR: Wipf & Stock, 2015.

Brueggemann, Walter. *A Gospel of Hope*. Compiled by Richard Floyd. Louisville, KY: Westminster John Knox, 2018.

———. *Hopeful Imagination: Prophetic Voices in Exile*. Philadelphia: Fortress, 1986.

———. "The Liturgy of Abundance, The Myth of Scarcity." *Christian Century* 116, no. 10 (1999): 342-47.

———. *The Message of the Psalms: A Theological Commentary*. Minneapolis: Augsburg, 1984.

———. *The Practice of Prophetic Imagination: Preaching an Emancipating Word*. Minneapolis: Fortress, 2012.

———. *The Prophetic Imagination*. 2nd ed. Minneapolis: Fortress, 2001.

———. *Reality, Grief, Hope: Three Urgent Prophetic Tasks*. Grand Rapids, MI: Eerdmans, 2014.

Calder, Helen. *Prophetic Worship: Develop Your Ministry of Encounter*. Melbourne, FL: Enliven Ministries, 2017.

Carr, Jekalyn. "Changing Your Story." Words and music by Jekalyn Carr © 2020 The Orchard Music. Administrated by Lunjeal Music Group.

———. "Changing Your Story: Jekalyn Carr Previews New Powerful Song!" Interview by Erica Campbell (2020). https://getuperica.com/149991/jekalyn-carr-changing-your-story/.

Cartledge, Mark. *Charismatic Glossolalia: An Empirical-Theology Study*. London: Routledge, 2016.

———. "Charismatic Prophecy: A Definition and Description." *Journal of Pentecostal Theology* 5 (1994): 79-120.

———. "Locating the Spirit in Meaningful Experience: Empirical Theology and Pentecostal Hermeneutics." In *Constructive Pneumatological Hermeneutics in Pentecostal Christianity*, edited by Kenneth Archer and L. William Oliverio Jr. New York: Palgrave Macmillan, 2016.

———. "Practical Theology: Attending to Pneumatologically-Driven Praxis." In *The Routledge Handbook of Pentecostal Theology*, edited by Wolfgang Vondey. London: Routledge, 2020.

———, ed. *Speaking in Tongues: Multi-Disciplinary Perspectives*. Eugene, OR: Wipf & Stock, 2006.

———. *Testimony in the Spirit: Rescripting Ordinary Pentecostal Theology*. London: Routledge, 2017.

Cartledge, Mark, and A. J. Swoboda, eds. *Scripting Pentecost: A Study of Pentecostals, Worship and Liturgy*. Surrey, UK: Ashgate, 2017.

Chan, Simon. "Evidential Glossolalia and the Doctrine of Subsequence." *Asian Journal of Pentecostal Studies* 2 (1999): 195-211.

Cherry, Constance. *The Worship Architect: A Blueprint for Designing Culturally Relevant and Biblically Faithful Services*. Grand Rapids, MI: Baker Academic, 2010.

Clark, Gordon. *The Atonement*. Jefferson, MD: The Trinity Foundation, 1987.

Cooper, Adam. *Holy Eros: A Liturgical Theology of the Body*. Kettering, OH: Angelico Press, 2014.

Copeland, Gloria. *God's Will Is Prosperity*. Tulsa, OK: Harrison House, 1978.

Courey, David. *What Has Wittenberg To Do With Azusa? Luther's Theology of the Cross and Pentecostal Triumphalism*. London: Bloomsbury, 2015.

Crawley, Ashon. *Blackpentecostal Breath: The Aesthetics of Possibility*. New York: Fordham University Press, 2017.

Culver, Caleb, Cory Asbury, and Ran Jackson. "Reckless Love." CCLI 7089641 © 2017 Cory Asbury Publishing, Richmond Park Publishing, Watershed Worship Publishing, Bethel Music Publishing. Administrated by Bethel Music Publishing, Essential Music Publishing LLC, Watershed Music Publishing.

Dayton, Donald. *Theological Roots of Pentecostalism*. Grand Rapids, MI: Baker Academic, 1987.

Duck, Ruth. *Worship for the Whole People of God: Vital Worship for the 21st Century*. Louisville, KY: Westminster John Knox, 2013.

Dunn, James D. G. *Baptism in the Holy Spirit*. London: SCM Press, 1970.

Earls, Aaron. "10 Key Trends in Global Christianity for 2017." Facts & Trends (2016). Accessed on December 23, 2020. https://factsandtrends.net/2016/12/12/10-key-trends-in-global-christianity-for-2017/.

Egbu, Osinachi Kalu Okoro. "Way Maker." CCLI 7115744 © 2016 Integrity Music Europe. Administrated by Capitol CMG Publishing, Integrity Music, David C Cook.

Eikelboom, Lexi. "Flow and the Christian Experience of Time." Accessed on September 12, 2020. The Rhythmic Theology Project. https://rhythmictheologyproject.com/2016/10/08/flow/.

Espinosa, Gaston. *William Seymour and the Origins of Global Pentecostalism*. Durham, NC: Duke University Press, 2014.

Félix-Jäger, Steven. *Spirit of the Arts: Towards a Pneumatological Aesthetics of Renewal*. New York: Palgrave Macmillan, 2017.

Foley, Edward, ed. *Worship Music: A Concise Dictionary*. Collegeville, MN: Liturgical Press, 2000.

Foster, Richard. *Streams of Living Water: Celebrating the Great Traditions of Christ*. San Francisco: HarperCollins, 2010.

Fowler, Megan. "How 'Way Maker' Topped the US Worship Charts from Nigeria." *Christianity Today* (2020). www.christianitytoday.com/ct/2020/june-web-only/way-maker-worship-song-sinach-leeland-michael-w-smith.html.

Frye, Jordan, Kim Walker-Smith, and Skyler Smith. "Just One Touch." CCLI 7084175 © 2017 Capitol CMG Genesis, Jesus Culture Music. Administrated by Capitol CMG Publishing.

Gabriel, Andrew. "God's Love Is Not Reckless, Contrary to What You Might Sing: An Evaluation of 'Reckless Love' from Bethel Music." Accessed November 21, 2020. www.andrewkgabriel.com/2018/02/06/gods-love-reckless-bethel/.

Gorman, Michael. *Inhabiting the Cruciform God: Kenosis, Justification, and Theosis in Paul's Narrative Soteriology*. Grand Rapids, MI: Eerdmans, 2009.

Green, Chris. "Saving Liturgy: (Re)imagining Pentecostal Liturgical Theology and Practice." In *Scripting Pentecost: A Study of Pentecostals, Worship and Liturgy*, edited by Mark Cartledge and A. J. Swoboda. London: Routledge, 2017.

———. *Toward a Pentecostal Theology of the Lord's Supper: Foretasting the Kingdom*. Cleveland, TN: CPT Press, 2012.

Greene, Travis. "Travis Greene—Intentional Live." Accessed on January 12, 2020. www.youtube.com/watch?v=IDv0ZCnqJME.

Gregory of Nyssa. On *"Not Three Gods."* In *Readings in the History of Christian Theology*, edited by William Placher and Derek Nelson, rev. ed, vol. 1. Louisville, KY: Westminster John Knox, 2015.

Guthrie, Steven. *Creator Spirit: The Holy Spirit and the Art of Becoming Human*. Grand Rapids, MI: Baker Academic, 2011.

———. "Singing, in the Body and in the Spirit." *Journal of the Evangelical Theological Society* 46, no. 4 (2003): 633-41.

Hayford, Jack. *Worship His Majesty: How Praising the King of Kings Will Change Your Life, Revised and Expanded*. Ventura, CA: Regal, 2000.

Hibbert, Vivien. *Prophetic Worship*. Texarkana, AR: Judah Books, 2020.

Hicks, Zac. *The Worship Pastor: A Call to Ministry for Worship Leaders and Teams*. Grand Rapids, MI: Zondervan, 2016.

"Hillsong Church Fact Sheet." Accessed on December 24, 2020. https://hillsong.com/fact-sheet/.

Hillsong Music. "The Hillsong Global Project." Accessed December 24, 2020. https://archive.is/20130125133625/http://hillsongglobalproject.com/

"Hindi Christian Song 'Jai Jai Yeshu' Based on the Raga Bhupali. Sitar and Vocal—Sanjeeb Sircar." Accessed on December 28, 2020. www.youtube.com/watch?v=YztJddJEQCM.

Hinn, Costi. *God, Greed, and the (Prosperity) Gospel: How Truth Overwhelms a Life Built on Lies*. Grand Rapids, MI: Zondervan, 2019.

Houston, Brian. "Has Hillsong Really Become Its Own Denomination?" *Hillsong Collected* blog. October 4, 2018. Accessed January 9, 2020. https://hillsong.com/collected/blog/2018/10/has-hillsong-really-become-its-own-denomination/#.X_ovHS2ZOL8.

———. *There Is More: When the World Says You Can't, God Says You Can*. New York: Waterbrook, 2018.

Houston, Joel, Benjamin Hastings, and Michael Fatkin. "So Will I (100 Billion X)." CCLI 7084123 © 2017 Hillsong Music Publishing Australia. Administrated by Hillsong Music Publishing, Capitol CMG Publishing.

Houston, Joel, Matt Crocker, and Salomon Ligthelm. "Oceans (Where Feet May Fail)." CCLI 6428767 © 2012 Hillsong Music Publishing Australia. Administrated by Capitol CMG Publishing.

Ingalls, Monique. "Introduction: Interconnection, Interface, and Identification in Pentecostal-Charismatic Music and Worship." In *The Spirit of Praise: Music and Worship in Global Pentecostal-Charismatic Christianity*, edited by Monique Ingalls and Amos Yong, 1-28. University Park: Pennsylvania State University Press, 2015.

———. *Singing the Congregation: How Contemporary Worship Music Forms Evangelical Community*. Oxford: Oxford University Press, 2018.

Ingalls, Monique, and Amos Yong, eds. *The Spirit of Praise: Music and Worship in Global Pentecostal-Charismatic Christianity*. University Park: Pennsylvania State University Press, 2015.

Ingalls, Monique, Muriel Swijghuisen Reigersberg, and Zoe Sherinian. "Introduction: Music as Local and Global Positioning: How Congregational Music-Making Produces the Local in Christian Communities Worldwide." In *Making Congregational Music Local in Christian Communities Worldwide*, edited by Monique Ingalls, Muriel Swijghuisen Reigersberg, and Zoe Sherinian, 1-32. London: Routledge, 2018.

Irenaeus of Lyons. *Against Heresies*, 4.20.1. In *The Cambridge Edition of Early Christian Writing*, Vol. 1, *God*, edited by Andrew Raddee-Gallwitz. Cambridge: Cambridge University Press, 2017.

Jacobsen, Douglas. *Global Gospel: An Introduction to Christianity on Five Continents*. Grand Rapids, MI: Baker Academic, 2015.

Jenkins, Philip. *The Next Christendom: The Coming Global Christianity*. New York: Oxford University Press, 2011.

Jennings, Mark. *Exaltation: Ecstatic Experience in Pentecostalism and Popular Music*. Bern: Peter Lang, 2014.

Jesus Culture. "Jesus Culture—Freedom (feat. Kim Walker-Smith) (Live)." Accessed on January 12, 2020. www.youtube.com/watch?v=dKxeZsZvp7E.

Johnson, Luke Timothy. *Prophetic Jesus, Prophetic Church: The Challenge of Luke-Acts to Contemporary Christians*. Grand Rapids, MI: Eerdmans, 2011.

Johnson, Maxwell. *Sacraments and Worship: The Sources of Christian Theology*. Louisville, KY: Westminster John Knox, 2012.

Johnson, Todd. "The Global Demographics of the Pentecostal and Charismatic Renewal." *Society* 46, no. 6 (2009): 479-83.

Johnston, Robert. *God's Wider Presence: Reconsidering General Revelation*. Grand Rapids, MI: Baker Academic, 2014.

Jones, David, and Russell Woodridge. *Health, Wealth, and Happiness: How Prosperity Gospel Overshadows the Gospel of Christ*. Grand Rapids, MI: Kregel, 2017.

Joseph, Jacob. "Indigenized Christian Worship in India: Some Considerations." Mission Frontiers (2014). www.missionfrontiers.org/issue/article/indigenized-christian-worship-in-india.

Justin. *The First Apology of Justin Martyr*, chap. 5. In Philip Schaff, *Ante-Nicene Fathers*, vol. 1. Christian Classics Ethereal Library.

Kant, Anil. "Ibadat Karo." Rebeat Digital GmbH. Administrated by Trinity Sounds PVT LTD and 5 Music Rights Societies.

Kay, William K. *Pentecostalism*. London: SCM Press, 2009.

Keener, Craig. *Gift Giver: The Holy Spirit for Today*. Grand Rapids, MI: Baker Academic, 2001.

———. *The NIV Application Commentary: Revelation*. Grand Rapids, MI: Zondervan, 2009.

King, Aodhan, and Hannah Hobbs. "Pursue." CCLI 7032394 © 2014 Hillsong Music Publishing Australia. Administrated by Hillsong Music Publishing, Capitol CMG Publishing.

King, Roberta. *Global Arts and Christian Witness: Exegeting Culture, Translating the Message, and Communicating Christ*. Grand Rapids, MI: Baker Academic, 2019.

———. "The Impact of Global Christian Music in Worship." Brehm Center (2017). Accessed on May 5, 2019. www.fuller.edu/posts/the-impact-of-global-christian-music-in-worship/.

Knight, Henry, III, ed. *From Aldersgate to Azusa Street: Wesleyan, Holiness and Pentecostal Visions of the New Creation*. Eugene, OR: Pickwick, 2010.

Kraeuter, Tom. *Times of Refreshing: A Worship Ministry Devotional*. Lynnwood, WA: Emerald Books, 2002.

Labberton, Mark. *The Dangerous Act of Worship: Living God's Call to Justice*. Downers Grove, IL: InterVarsity Press, 2007.

Lake, Brandon, Nate Moore, Tasha Cobbs Leonard, and Tony Brown. "This Is a Move." CCLI 7123068 © 2018 Bethel Worship Publishing, Brandon Lake Music, Mouth Of The River Music, Tony Brown Music Designee, Meadowgreen Music Company, Tasha Cobbs Music Group. Administrated by Bethel Music Publishing, Capitol CMG Publishing.

Land, Steven. *Pentecostal Spirituality: A Passion for the Kingdom*. London: Sheffield Academic Press, 1993.

———. "William Seymour: The Father of the Holiness-Pentecostal Movement." In *From Aldersgate to Azusa Street: Wesleyan, Holiness, and Pentecostal Visions of the New Creation*, edited by Henry Knight III. Eugene, OR: Pickwick, 2010.

Larson, Craig Brian. "A Weekly Dose of Compressed Dignity." In *The Art & Craft of Biblical Preaching: A Comprehensive Resource for Today's Communicators*, edited by Haddon Robinson and Craig Brian Larson. Grand Rapids, MI: Zondervan, 2005.

Law, Terry, and Jim Gilbert. *The Power of Praise & Worship*. Shippensburg, PA: Destiny Image, 2008.

Lee, John Alan. *Colours of Love: An Exploration of the Ways of Loving*. New York: New Press, 1973.

Lee, Nate. "Hillsong Church: Do Not Colonize San Francisco" (2016). Accessed on December 24, 2020. http://natejlee.com/hillsong-church-do-not-colonize-san-francisco/.

"Left Hand, Right Hand." In *A Dictionary of Biblical Tradition in English Literature*, edited by David Lyle Jeffrey. Grand Rapids, MI: Eerdmans, 1992.

Leonard, Tasha Cobbs, and Todd Galberth. "I'm Getting Ready (Ready for Overflow)." CCLI 7099373 © 2017 Meadowgreen Music Company, Tasha Cobbs Music Group, Integrity First Music Publishing. Administrated by Capitol CMG Publishing, Kobalt Music Publishing America, Inc.

Levitin, Daniel. *This Is Your Brain on Music: The Science of a Human Obsession*. New York: Plume, 2006.

Lewis, C. S. *The Four Loves*. New York: HarperCollins, 1960.

Ligertwood, Brooke, Cody Carnes, Kari Jobe, and Scott Ligertwood. "Heal Our Land." CCLI 7070516 © 2016 Kari Jobe Carnes Music, SHOUT! Music Publishing Australia, Worship Together Music, Writer's Roof Publishing. Administrated by Capitol CMG Publishing, Hillsong Music Publishing.

Lim, Swee Hong, and Lester Ruth. *Lovin' on Jesus: A Concise History of Contemporary Worship*. Nashville: Abingdon, 2017.

Lindbeck, George. *The Nature of Doctrine: Religion and Theology in a Postliberal Age*. Louisville, KY: Westminster John Knox, 1984.

Lindsey, Aaron, Israel Houghton, and Martha Munizzi. "More Than Enough." CCLI 5174816 © 2008 Integrity's Praise! Music, Sound Of The New Breed, Martha Munizzi Music. Administrated by Capitol CMG Publishing, Integrity Music, David C Cook, Say The Name Publishing.

Lord, Andy. "A Theology of Sung Worship." In *Scripting Pentecost: A Study of Pentecostals, Worship and Liturgy*, edited by Mark Cartledge and A. J. Swoboda, 84-93. London: Routledge, 2017.

Lyon, David. *Jesus in Disneyland: Religion in Postmodern Times*. Cambridge, UK: Polity, 2000.

MacArthur, John. *Charismatic Chaos*. Grand Rapids, MI: Zondervan, 1992.

Macchia, Frank. "A Call for Careful Discernment: A Theological Response to Prosperity Preaching." In *Pentecostalism and Prosperity: The Socio-Economics of the Global Charismatic Movement*, edited by Katherine Attanasi and Amos Yong, 225-39. New York: Palgrave Macmillan, 2012.

———. "Babel and the Tongues of Pentecost: Reversal or Fulfilment?" In *Speaking in Tongues: Multi-Disciplinary Perspectives*, edited by Mark Cartledge, 34-51. Eugene, OR: Wipf & Stock, 2006.

———. *Baptized in the Spirit: A Global Pentecostal Theology*. Grand Rapids, MI: Zondervan, 2006.

———. *Jesus the Spirit Baptizer: Christology in Light of Pentecost*. Grand Rapids, MI: Eerdmans, 2018.

———. *Justified in the Spirit: Creation, Redemption, and the Triune God*. Grand Rapids, MI: Eerdmans, 2010.

———. "Signs of Grace: Towards a Charismatic Theology of Worship." In *Toward a Pentecostal Theology of Worship*, edited by Lee Roy Martin, 153-64. Cleveland, TN: CPT Press, 2016.

Martí, Gerardo. Foreword in *The Hillsong Movement Examined: You Call Me Out Upon the Waters*, edited by Tanya Riches and Tom Wagner. New York: Palgrave Macmillan, 2018.

———. "Maranatha (O Lord, Come): The Power-Surrender Dynamic of Pentecostal Worship." *Liturgy* 33, no. 3 (2018): 20-28.

Martin, Lee Roy, ed. *Toward a Pentecostal Theology of Preaching*. Cleveland, TN: CPT Press, 2015.

Mason, Matt. "The Worship Leader and Singing." In *Doxology & Theology: How the Gospel Forms the Worship Leader*, edited by Matt Boswell, 191-206. Nashville: B&H, 2013.

Mauss, Marcel. *The Gift: The Form and Reason for Exchange in Archaic Societies*. London: Routledge, 2010.

Maynard-Reid, Pedrito. *Diverse Worship: African-American, Caribbean & Hispanic Perspectives*. Downers Grove, IL: InterVarsity Press, 2000.

McFague, Sallie. *Life Abundant: Rethinking Theology and Economy for a Planet in Peril*. Minneapolis: Fortress, 2001.

Menzies, Robert. *Speaking in Tongues: Jesus and the Apostolic Church as Models for the Church Today*. Cleveland, TN: CPT Press, 2016.

Meyer, Birgit. "Aesthetics of Persuasion: Global Christianity and Pentecostalism's Sensational Forms." *South Atlantic Quarterly* 109, no. 4 (2010): 741-63.

Mittelstadt, Martin. *Reading Luke-Acts in the Pentecostal Tradition*. Cleveland, TN: CPT Press, 2010.

Moltmann, Jürgen. *The Source of Life: The Holy Spirit and the Theology of Life*. Minneapolis: Fortress, 1997.

———. *The Spirit of Life: A Universal Affirmation*. Minneapolis: Fortress, 2001.

Muindi, Samuel. *Pentecostal-Charismatic Prophecy: Empirical-Theological Analysis*. Oxford: Peter Lang, 2017.

Müller, B. A. "The Role of Worship and Ethics on the Road Towards Reconciliation." *Verbum Et Ecclesia JRG* 27, no. 2 (2006): 641-63.

Myers, Bryant. *Engaging Globalization: The Poor, Christian Mission, and Our Hyperconnected World*. Grand Rapids, MI: Baker Academic, 2017.

News, Hallels. "Hillsong United's 'Oceans (Where Feet May Fail)' is the #1 Song on Billboard Hot Christian Songs for the 2010s." JubileeCast (2019). Accessed on November 11, 2020. https://jubileecast.com/articles/22607/20191120/hillsong-uniteds-oceans-where-feet-may-fail-is-the-1-song-on-billboard-hot-christian-songs-for-the-2010s.htm.

Nichols, Bruce. *Contextualization: A Theology of Gospel and Culture*. Vancouver: Regent College Publishing, 2003.

Nydam, Ronald. "The Relational Theology of Generation Y." *Calvin Theological Journal* 41 (2006): 321-30.

Nygren, Anders. *Agape & Eros*. Translated by Philip Watson. 1953. Reprint, Chicago: University of Chicago Press, 1982.

Packiam, Glenn. *Worship and the World to Come: Exploring Christian Hope in Contemporary Worship*. Downers Grove, IL: IVP Academic, 2020.

Pannenberg, Wolfhart. *Jesus—God and Man*. Philadelphia: Westminster, 1978.

Papa, Matt. "The Worship Leader and Mission." In *Doxology & Theology: How the Gospel Forms the Worship Leader*, edited by Matt Boswell, 75-92. Nashville: B&H, 2013.

Pattinson, Pat. *Writing Better Lyrics: The Essential Guide to Powerful Songwriting*. 2nd ed. Cincinnati: Writer's Digest Books, 2009.

Payne, Leah. "'New Voices': Pentecostal Preachers in North America, 1890-1930." In *Scripting Pentecost: A Study of Pentecostals, Worship and Liturgy*, edited by Mark Cartledge and A. J. Swoboda. London: Routledge, 2017.

Perez, Adam. "Sounding God's Enthronement in Worship: The Early History and Theology of Integrity's Hosanna! Music." In *Essays on the History of Contemporary Praise and Worship*, edited by Lester Ruth, 15-31. Eugene, OR: Pickwick, 2020.

Pew Research Center. *Spirit and Power—A 10-Country Survey of Pentecostals*. October 5, 2006. www.pewforum.org/2006/10/05/spirit-and-power.

Piper, John. "Should We Sing of God's 'Reckless Love'?" Desiring God (2018). Accessed on November 21, 2020. www.desiringgod.org/interviews/should-we-sing-of-gods-reckless-love.

Plantinga, Cornelius, Jr., and Sue Rozeboom. *Discerning the Spirits: A Guide to Thinking About Christian Worship Today*. Grand Rapids, MI: Eerdmans, 2003.

Poloma, Margaret, and Ralph Hood, eds. *Blood and Fire: Godly Love in a Pentecostal Emerging Church*. New York: New York University Press, 2008.

Portmann, John. *A History of Sin*. Lanham, MD: Rowman & Littlefield, 2007.

Price, Deborah Evans. "Tori Kelly Teams Up with Cory Asbury on 'Reckless Love': Exclusive." Billboard (2020). Accessed on November 21, 2020. www.billboard.com/articles/columns/pop/8547607/tori-kelly-cory-asbury-reckless-love-exclusive.

Rah, Soong-Chan. *Prophetic Lament: A Call for Justice in Troubled Times*. Downers Grove, IL: InterVarsity Press, 2015.

Reagan, Wen. "Blessed to Be a Blessing: The Prosperity Gospel of Worship Music Superstar Israel Houghton." In *The Spirit of Praise: Music and Worship in Global Pentecostal-Charismatic Christianity*, edited by Monique Ingalls and Amos Yong, 215-29. University Park: Pennsylvania State University Press, 2015.

———. "Forerunning Contemporary Worship Music: The Afro-Pentecostal Roots of Black Gospel." In *Essays on the History of Contemporary Praise and Worship*, edited by Lester Ruth, 116-45. Eugene, OR: Pickwick, 2020.

———. "'The Music that Just About Everyone Sings': Hillsong in American Evangelical Media." In *The Hillsong Movement Examined: You Call Me Out Upon the Waters*, edited by Tanya Riches and Tom Wagner, 145-62. New York: Palgrave Macmillan, 2018.

Rempel, John. *Recapturing an Enchanted World: Ritual and Sacrament in the Free Church Tradition*. Downers Grove, IL: IVP Academic, 2020.

Riches, Tanya. "'The Work of the Spirit': Hillsong Church and a Spiritual Formation for the Marketplace." In *Australian Pentecostal and Charismatic Movements: Arguments from the Margins*, edited by Christina Rocha, Kathleen Openshaw, and Mark Hutchinson. Leiden: Brill Academic, 2020.

Richie, Tony. "Translating Pentecostal Testimony into Interreligious Dialogue." *Journal of Pentecostal Theology* 20 (2011): 155-83.

Ricoeur, Paul. *From Text to Action: Essays in Hermeneutics, II*. Translated by Kathleen Blamey and John Thompson. Evanston, IL: Northwestern University Press, 2007.

———. *Hermeneutics & the Human Sciences*. Translated and edited by John Thompson. Cambridge: Cambridge University Press, 1981.

———. *Interpretation Theory: Discourse and the Surplus of Meaning*. Fort Worth: Texas Christian University Press, 1976.

Robeck, Cecil, Jr. *The Azusa Street Mission and Revival: The Birth of the Global Pentecostal Movement*. Nashville: Thomas Nelson, 2006.

———. "William J. Seymour and the 'Biblical Evidence.'" In *Initial Evidence: Historical and Biblical Perspectives on the Pentecostal Doctrine of Spirit Baptism*, edited by Gary McGee. Peabody, MA: Hendrickson, 1991.

Ruth, Lester. "An Ancient Way to Do Contemporary Worship." In *Flow: The Ancient Way to Do Contemporary Worship*, edited by Lester Ruth, 3-12. Nashville: Abingdon, 2020.

———. "Introduction: The Importance and History of Contemporary Praise & Worship." In *Essays on the History of Contemporary Praise and Worship*, edited by Lester Ruth, 1-12. Eugene, OR: Pickwick, 2020.

Ruth, Lester, and Swee Hong Lim. *A History of Contemporary Praise & Worship: Understanding the Ideas That Reshaped the Protestant Church*. Grand Rapids, MI: Baker Academic, 2021.

Saliers, Don. *Worship as Theology: Foretaste of Glory Divine*. Nashville: Abingdon, 1994.

———. *Worship Come to Its Senses*. Nashville: Abingdon, 1996.

Salmeier, Michael. *Restoring the Kingdom: The Role of God as the "Ordainer of Times and Seasons" in the Acts of the Apostles*. Eugene, OR: Pickwick, 2011.

Samuel, Josh P. S. *The Holy Spirit in Worship Music, Preaching, and the Altar: Renewing Pentecostal Corporate Worship*. Cleveland, TN: CPT Press, 2018.

Sánchez, Leopoldo. *Sculptor Spirit: Models of Sanctification from Spirit Christology*. Downers Grove, IL: IVP Academic, 2019.

Schaefer, Hans-Eckhardt. "Music-Evoked Emotions—Current Studies." *Frontiers in Neuroscience* 11 (2017). Accessed January 22, 2020. www.ncbi.nlm.nih.gov/pmc/articles/PMC5705548/.

Schmidt-Jones, Catherine. "Modes and Ragas." Understanding Basic Music Theory. Accessed on December 28, 2020. https://cnx.org/contents/KtdLe6cv@3.70:Fxmh7wKe@16/Modes-and-Ragas.

Seamone, Donna Lynne. "Pentecostalism: Rejecting Ritual Formalism and Ritualizing Every Encounter." *Journal of Ritual Studies* 27, no. 1 (2013): 73-84.

Seymour, William. "Questions Answered." *Apostolic Faith* 1, no. 9 (June-September 1907): 2.

Smith, James K. A. *Desiring the Kingdom: Worship, Worldview, and Cultural Formation*. Grand Rapids, MI: Baker Academic, 2009.

———. *Thinking in Tongues: Pentecostal Contributions to Christian Philosophy*. Grand Rapids, MI: Eerdmans, 2010.

Smith, Gordon. *Evangelical, Sacramental & Pentecostal: Why the Church Should Be All Three*. Downers Grove, IL: IVP Academic, 2017.

Sorge, Bob. *Exploring Worship: A Practical Guide to Praise & Worship*. 3rd ed. Grandview, MO: Oasis House, 2018.

Sproul, R. C. *How Then Shall We Worship: Biblical Principles to Guide Us Today*. Colorado Springs, CO: David C Cook, 2013.

Stetzer, Ed. "Why Do These Pentecostals Keep Growing?" *Christianity Today*, 2014. Accessed on January 3, 2021.

Stewart, Adam. "Azusa Street Mission and Revival." In *Handbook of Pentecostal Christianity*, edited by Adam Stewart, 43-38. DeKalb, IL: NIU Press, 2012.

Studebaker, Steven, ed. *Pentecostal Preaching and Ministry in Multicultural and Post-Christian Canada*. Eugene, OR: Pickwick, 2019.

Suh, Edward. *The Empowering God: Redeeming the Prosperity Movement and Overcoming Victim Trauma in the Poor*. Eugene, OR: Pickwick, 2018.

Sullivan, Francis. *Charisms and Charismatic Renewal: A Biblical and Theological Study*. Eugene, OR: Wipf & Stock, 1982.

Sunquist, Scott. *The Unexpected Christian Century: The Reversal and Transformation of Global Christianity, 1900–2000*. Grand Rapids, MI: Baker Academic, 2015.

Swee Hong, Lim. "'Where Is Our Song Going?' vis a vis 'Where Should Our Song Be Going?': The Trajectory of Global Song in North America." The Hymn Society (2018). Accessed on May 5, 2019. thehymnsociety.org/resources/lim-article-summer-2018/.

Swee Hong, Lim, and Lester Ruth. *Lovin' on Jesus: A Concise History of Contemporary Worship*. Nashville: Abingdon, 2017.

Swoboda, A. J. "God is Doing Something New: A North American Liturgical Experience." In *Scripting Pentecost: A Study of Pentecostals, Worship and Liturgy*, edited by Mark Cartledge and A. J. Swoboda, 121-36. London: Routledge, 2017.

———. *Subversive Sabbath: The Surprising Power of Rest in a Nonstop World*. Grand Rapids, MI: Brazos, 2018.

Synan, Vincent. *The Holiness-Pentecostal Tradition: Charismatic Movements in the Twentieth Century*. Grand Rapids, MI: Eerdmans, 1997.

Tan-Chow, May Lin. *Pentecostal Theology for the Twenty-First Century*. Burlington, UK: Ashgate, 2007.

Taylor, Charles. *A Secular Age*. Cambridge, MA: Harvard University Press, 2007.

Taylor, W. David O. *Glimpses of the New Creation: Worship and the Formative Power of the Arts*. Grand Rapids, MI: Eerdmans, 2019.

———. "Mother Tongues and Adjectival Tongues: Liturgical Identity and the Liturgical Arts in a Pneumatological Key." *Worship Journal* 92, 2018.

———. "What Makes Hillsong's 'Oceans (Where Feet May Fail)' So Popular?" *Diary of an Arts Pastor*. June 10, 2015. Accessed on November 21, 2020. https://artspastor.blogspot.com/2015/06/what-makes-hillsongs-ocean-where-feet.html.

"This I Believe (The Creed) Song Story." *Hillsong Collected* blog. July 3, 2014. Accessed on February 29, 2020. https://hillsong.com/collected/blog/2014/07/this-i-believe-the-creed-song-story/#.Xlrxay2ZPBI.

Thomas, Derick, and Israel Houghton. "New Season." CCLI 2927262 © 1997 Need New Music, Integrity's Praise! Music, Sound Of The New Breed. Administrated by Capitol CMG Publishing, Integrity Music, David C Cook.

Thomasos, Christine. "Israel Houghton Returns to Joel Osteen's Lakewood Church After Engagement to Adrienne Bailon." CP Entertainment. August 19, 2016. Accessed August 9, 2020. www.christianpost.com/news/israel-houghton-returns-to-joel-osteens-lakewood-church-after-engagement-to-adrienne-bailon.html.

Torr, Stephen. *A Dramatic Pentecostal/Charismatic Anti-Theodicy: Improvising on a Divine Performance of Lament*. Eugene, OR: Pickwick, 2013.

Townend, Stuart, and Keith Getty. "In Christ Alone." CCLI 3350395 © 2001 Thankyou Music. Administrated by Capitol CMG Publishing.

Tracy, David. *The Analogical Imagination: Christian Theology and the Culture of Pluralism*. New York: Crossroad, 1981.

Treier, Daniel. *Introducing Theological Interpretation of Scripture: Recovering a Christian Practice*. Grand Rapids, MI: Baker Academic, 2008.

Tubbs Tisdale, Leonora. *Prophetic Preaching: A Pastoral Approach*. Louisville, KY: Westminster John Knox, 2010.

Unger, Merrill. *New Testament Teaching on Tongues*. Grand Rapids, MI: Kregel, 1973.

Van Gelder, Craig. *The Ministry of the Missional Church: A Community Led by the Spirit*. Grand Rapids, MI: Baker Books, 2007.

Van Opstal, Sandra. *The Next Worship: Glorifying God in a Diverse World*. Downers Grove, IL: InterVarsity Press, 2016.

Venkataraman, Swami. "Christian Appropriation of Carnatic Music: Why Musicians Can't Hide Behind the 'Secular' Hypothesis." *Swarajya*, October 3, 2018. Accessed on December 28, 2020. https://swarajyamag.com/politics/christian-appropriation-of-carnatic-music-why-musicians-cant-hide-behind-the-secular-hypothesis.

"The Vision." Hillsong Church Accessed on December 24, 2020. https://hillsong.com/vision/.

Vogt, Peter. "Nicholas Ludwig von Zinzendorf (1700–1760)." In *The Pietist Theologians: An Introduction to Theology in the Seventeenth and Eighteenth Centuries,* edited by Carter Lindberg, 207-33. Malden, MA: Blackwell, 2008.

Volf, Miroslav. *Exclusion and Embrace, Revised and Updated: A Theological Exploration of Identity, Otherness, and Reconciliation*. Nashville: Abingdon, 2019.

———. "Exclusion and Embrace: Theological Reflections in the Wake of 'Ethnic Cleansing.'" *Communio Viatorum* 35, no. 3 (1993): 263-87.

Vondey, Wolfgang. "Pentecostal Sacramentality and the Theology of the Altar." In *Scripting Pentecost: A Study of Pentecostals, Worship and Liturgy*, edited by Mark Cartledge and A. J. Swoboda, 94-107. London: Routledge, 2017.

———. *Pentecostal Theology: Living the Full Gospel*. London: Bloomsbury, 2017.

Wacker, Grant. *Heaven Below: Early Pentecostals and American Culture*. Cambridge, MA: Harvard University Press, 2001.

Waddell, Robby. "Prophecy Then and Now: The Role of Prophecy in the Pentecostal Church." In *Transformational Leadership: A Tribute to Dr. Mark Rutland*, 129-44. Lakeland, FL: Small Dogma Publishing, 2008.

Wariboko, Nimi. *The Pentecostal Principle: Ethical Methodology in New Spirit*. Grand Rapids, MI: Eerdmans, 2012.

Wariboko, Nimi, and L. William Oliverio. "The Society for Pentecostal Studies at 50 Years: Ways Forward for Global Pentecostalism." *Pneuma* 42 (2020): 327-33.

Warrington, Keith. *Pentecostal Theology: A Theology of Encounter*. London: T&T Clark, 2008.

Webber, Robert. *Worship Old and New*. Rev. ed. Grand Rapids, MI: Zondervan, 1994.

"What is Spontaneous Worship." Worship U, 2019. Accessed on September 26, 2020.

Wilkinson, Michael, and Peter Althouse, eds. *Annual Review of the Sociology of Religion*. Vol. 8, *Pentecostals and the Body*. Leiden: Brill, 2017.

Wilkinson, Michael, and Peter Althouse. *Catch the Fire: Soaking Prayer and Charismatic Renewal*. DeKalb, IL: NIU Press, 2014.

Williams, Andrew Ray. *Washed in the Spirit: Toward a Pentecostal Theology of Water Baptism*. Cleveland, TN: CPT Press, 2021.

Williams, J. Rodman. *Renewal Theology: Systematic Theology from a Charismatic Perspective*. Grand Rapids, MI: Zondervan, 1996.

Wilson, Andrew. *Spirit and Sacrament: An Invitation to Eucharismatic Worship*. Grand Rapids, MI: Zondervan, 2019.

Wolterstorff, Nicholas. *Art in Action: Toward a Christian Aesthetic*. Grand Rapids, MI: Eerdmans, 1980.

Yan, Holly, Cheri Mossburg, Artemis Moshtaghian, and Paul Vercammen. "California Sets New Record for Land Torched by Wildfires as 224 People Escape by Air From a 'Hellish' Inferno." CNN. Accessed on September 6, 2020. www.cnn.com/2020/09/05/us/california-mammoth-pool-reservoir-camp -fire/index.html.

Yip, Jeaney, Susan Ainsworth, and Chang Yau Hoon. "JPCC: A Megachurch Brand Story in Indonesia." In *Routledge International Handbook of Religion in Global Society*, edited by Jayeel Cornelio, François Gauthier, Tuomas Martikainen, and Linda Woodhead, 42-51. Oxon, UK: Routledge, 2021.

Yong, Amos. *Beyond the Impasse: Toward a Pneumatological Theology of Religions*. Eugene, OR: Wipf & Stock, 2014.

———. "Disability and the Gifts of the Spirit: Pentecost and the Renewal of the Church." *Journal of Pentecostal Theology* 19 (2010): 76-93.

———. *The Spirit Poured Out on All Flesh: Pentecostalism and the Possibility of Global Theology*. Grand Rapids, MI: Baker Academic, 2005.

———. "A Typology of Prosperity Theology: A Religious Economy of Global Renewal or a Renewal Economics?" In *Pentecostalism and Prosperity: The Socio-Economics of the Global Charismatic Movement*, edited by Katherine Attanasi and Amos Yong, 15-34. New York: Palgrave Macmillan, 2012.

Zschech, Darlene. "Cry of the Broken." CCLI 5894220 © 2010 Wondrous Worship. Administrated by Music Services, Inc.

GENERAL INDEX

SCRIPTURE INDEX

DYNAMICS OF CHRISTIAN WORSHIP

Worship of the triune God stands at the heart of the Christian life, so understanding the many dynamics of Christian worship—including prayer, reading the Bible, preaching, baptism, the Lord's Supper, music, visual art, architecture, and more—is both a perennial and crucial issue for the church. With that in mind, the Dynamics of Christian Worship (DCW) series seeks to enable Christians to grow in their understanding of the many aspects of Christian worship. By harvesting the fruits of biblical, theological, historical, practical, and liturgical scholarship and by drawing from a wide range of worshiping contexts and denominational backgrounds, the DCW series seeks to deepen both the theology and practice of Christian worship for the life of the church.

TITLES INCLUDE

+ John Rempel, *Recapturing an Enchanted World: Ritual and Sacrament in the Free Church Tradition*

+ Glenn Packiam, *Worship and the World to Come: Exploring Christian Hope in Contemporary Worship*

+ Noel A. Snyder, *Sermons That Sing: Music and the Practice of Preaching*

ADVISORY BOARD

Constance Cherry, Indiana Wesleyan University
Carlos Colón, Baylor University
James Hart, Robert E. Webber Institute for Worship Studies
Todd Johnson, Fuller Theological Seminary
Trygve Johnson, Hope College
Glenn Packiam, New Life Downtown Church, Colorado Springs, CO
Melanie Ross, Yale Institute of Sacred Music
Lester Ruth, Duke Divinity School
John Witvliet, Calvin Institute of Christian Worship